MW01506230

How To Seek God

Swami Yatiswarananda

Sri Ramakrishna Math
Mylapore, Chennai - 600 004

Published by
Adhyaksha
Sri Ramakrishna Math
Mylapore, Chennai - 600 004

First Edition, February 2009
Third Print,   May 2017
1M2C

ISBN 978-81-7823-537-0

Total number of copies
printed till now: 5,600

Printed in India at
Sri Ramakrishna Math Printing Press
Mylapore, Chennai-4

Publisher's Note

Swami Yatiswarananda (1889-1966) was Vice-President of the Ramakrishna Order, and an illustrious disciple of Swami Brahmanandaji Maharaj, who was held as the spiritual son of Sri Ramakrishna. He contributed much to spiritual life by his talks and writings and personal counsels. He was a well-known spiritual figure in the Neo-Vedanta movement and did 17 years of pioneering work (1933-1950) in spreading Vedanta in Europe and U.S.A. He guided a large number of sincere aspirants on the spiritual path in India as well in other countries. His books such as *Adventures in Religious Life, The Divine Life* and *Universal Prayers* are justly famous. *Meditation and Spiritual Life,* the book containing his teachings, has been acclaimed as a spiritual classic.

He was the President of Sri Ramakrishna Ashrama [now Ramakrishna Math] located at Bull Temple Road in Bangalore for 16 years (1950-1966). Brief notes of the weekly lectures he gave at the Ashrama were recorded by one of the listeners during the period 1954-55 and 1958-59. Later, from October 1979 to September 1985, these were published in *The Vedanta Kesari,* the spiritual and cultural monthly brought out from this Math. In all, these notes were published in 30 installments under the title *How to Seek God.* We are glad to present these notes in the present form.

These have been rearranged under different themes. This forms the main body of the book. To this we have added four articles—*Continence, Unreality of the World, How to Sublimate our Tendencies,* and *Preparing for Divine Company.* The first two are based on the notes of his class-talks on *Vedanta-Sara* of Sadananda, taken at Wiesbaden (Germany) during January-February 1934. The other two are based on his talks on *Narada Bhakti Sutras.* The notes on *Drig Drishya* iv

Viveka are from his talks at Camfer (Germany) delivered in 1935.

The section on *Spiritual Teachings* is based on the *Reminiscences of Swami Yatiswarananda* by late Pravrajika Saradaprana of the Sarada Math, Dakshineswar, Kolkata. They were rearranged and were published in *The Vedanta Kesari* with her kind permission. *Questions and Answers* [published in The Vedanta Kesari in 1999] are also from Saradaprana's collections.

We are indebted to Sri S. V. Unnikrishnan, former Senior Deputy Accountant General, Jaipur, for the manuscript of *How to Seek God;* to Mr. Kurt Friedrichs of Hamburg, Germany and Mr. John Manetta of Athens, Greece for notes on the *Vedanta-Sara, Uddhava Gita* and *Narada Bhakti Sutras* and to the late Pravrajika Saradaprana for her notes. Swami Brahmeshananda, former editor of *The Vedanta Kesari,* and the present head of Ramakrishna Mission Ashrama, Chandigarh, organized the contents and gave present shape to the book. Sri S. Sudarshan of Bangalore and the volunteers at *The Vedanta Kesari* Office have helped in the preparation of book in various ways. Our thanks to them for their labour of love.

We are grateful to Advaita Ashrama for their permission to include the article *Preparing for Divine Company* published in the August 2008 issue of *Prabuddha Bharata.*

Although we have tried to arrange these notes under different themes, they are not necessarily sequential. There is also repetition of ideas which is unavoidable in a work like this. Though in some places, there was need for deleting some parts to make the text free from repetitions, we have desisted from doing it.

We hope the present book will help all spiritual seekers and they will find it of immediate and practical value.

Bhagavan Sri Ramakrishna Jayanti
27.02.2009

Contents

viii

PART II

Part - I

① On the Threshold

Beginning of Religion

What man wants is eternal bliss, only he does not know where and how to get it. He mistakes sense-pleasures for pure bliss. Hence he desires to have the attractive things of this world and the next. Wealth, progeny, fame and hundreds of other things of this world attract him and he runs after them. He seizes some and is happy for a while; some elude his grasp and he feels miserable, while some others remain in his clutches for a time and then suddenly disappear. Such losses hurt him. Then again, as soon as he gains some coveted things, fresh desires crop up and make him restless. He finds to his dismay that the senses cannot be appeased by enjoyment. Rather, their craving is increased by the process. Thus his life becomes a non-stop race after these fleeting pleasures. On this path he never attains contentment. Misery, born of unfulfilled desires and forced parting with coveted things, follows him at every step. And this goes on from life to life. Even the higher and finer world where he gets un-alloyed pleasures does not give him eternal bliss. A man of meritorious deeds may go there after death and enjoy intense pleasure. But this is only for a time. After that, he has to come down and be born again on this earth. Really, so long as man is driven by desires, neither this world nor the next can bring him eternal Bliss. Desire is verily the chain that binds him to the wheel of birth and death.

Yet man is reluctant to part with desires. The craving for sense objects dominates him. The camel likes to browse on prickly shrubs though they make his mouth bleed. Similarly man repeatedly wants to enjoy sense pleasures though they bring him untold miseries through repeated

1

cycles of birth and death. The majority of people belong to this category. For such men, the first step is to take to the Karma-marga that is the path of works. They are not to give up all desires. Only they have to regulate these by faithfully following the injunctions and prohibitions of the Sastras. Those who do this enjoy the good things of this world and of the next. And their minds become purified to some extent. After enjoying the intense pleasures of the higher world, they come back to this earth and again lead a life of works with more devotion. Again their meritorious deeds lead them to the intense pleasures of the higher world after death. This process goes on over and over again till their minds become very pure. At this stage they realise the vanity of desires. By their repeated experience they grasp the truth that desires are never quenched by enjoyment, just as fire can never be quenched by butter and that unfulfilled desires make one unhappy. Moreover, even in the higher worlds, the period of enjoyment is limited. By their own observation they become convinced that the path of desireful works cannot lead them to eternal bliss. And it is this eternal bliss that they have been seeking all the time. Realizing the futility of desires, they go out in quest of the path that may lead them to eternal bliss, eternal life and infinite knowledge. This quest is the very starting point of real religion. The pravritti marga is no more than a preliminary discipline. It serves its purpose by making our minds pure enough to realise the futility of running after sense objects. This precisely is its scope. It takes us no farther than that on the road to perfection and eternal bliss, eternal life and infinite knowledge. Our desire for sense-objects is therefore the only hurdle on the road to perfection. It makes us world-bound. We have to cross the hurdle. Real religion begins and ends with this crossing. The moment we are free from desires we become divine.

Some people ask: 'If there be God, why should He give us misery in this world?' This question is the result of a wrong concept of Godhead. It is the question of low minds intent on pleasure. There is no such thing as exclusive pleasure in the world. Creation, preservation and destruction are all

His Lila. There cannot be creation or sustenance without dissolution. But people are frightened of death. Yet if there were no death at all in the world, it would be terrible. Dissolution does not mean completely destroying something that exists and creation does not mean producing something out of nothing. But this is not generally understood.

In youth, the mind is plastic like fresh clay and can be molded into any shape. It has not become hard like burnt bricks, - not yet baked in the fire of worldliness. Therefore in youth one should mould the mind into the shape of the divine. It is very hard to collect one's thoughts. The real nature of the mind is known only when one attempts meditation. Like scattered mustard seeds, mental energy is spent in worldly thoughts. It is very hard to concentrate and direct it towards God.

We have forgotten our real nature. The teacher has to repeat the same lesson many times to brush up the student's memory. We are deluded by the sense-perceptions. We should doubt our very existence—with that our spiritual life begins. Buddha was brought up in a palace, and was not shown what old age; disease, death and want were like. But when he actually saw them, he began to doubt the very existence of this world, the very purpose of life. He renounced his luxurious life and discovered the Truth. Age is not a factor in this undertaking. Do not hesitate to undertake this journey thinking that you are old and that you have to start as a spiritual baby.

The law of nature is the survival of the fittest. We can verify this if we observe the vegetable and animal kingdoms. But man is equipped with a discriminating intellect and is expected to use it. The rule of the survival of the fittest must be applied with regard to the lower and higher natures in man. The discriminating intellect must be used to subdue the lower nature and to bring out the higher tendencies. Thus one is able to fulfill the purpose of having taken a human birth.

In the world you try to build a huge structure on a foundation of sand. Then comes a terrible crash and you think: 'Everyone is failing me. What am I depending on?' That is a spiritual crisis. You think: 'What I call real appears to be unreal.' You have been depending on others for security. They themselves are insecure. How can they become a security for others? If you have not known your own Self, you have known nothing. Not knowing this Reality, there is no foundation for your life at all.

The little happiness that is derived from this world is finite and short-lived. If we want Infinite Bliss, we have to attain the Infinite. For this, we should expand from the individual to the Cosmic. Narrow-mindedness should be discarded. If only we think for a while, it is evident that the individual is a small whirlpool in the ocean of the Infinite. Individual body, mind and soul are parts of the Universal Body, Universal Mind and the Paramatman. The individual body which is derived from the Cosmic Body (elements) takes its nourishment from the Cosmic Body and gives back matter to the Cosmic Body. So also with the mind. The jivatman is a reflection of the Paramatman and when it knows its oneness with the latter, it ceases to be affected by dualities.

Set the Goal and Struggle

As long as one lives in his home his desire to become a monk is intense. When he joins the Order or becomes a sannysin, he thinks his life's goal is achieved and thereafter he keeps quiet. But if one remains at home, many obstructions may come in the shape of care of parents, arranging marriages etc. Then one struggles hard to overcome those difficulties and develops character and strength. There is the manifestation of power in him. We must struggle and thereby our power is increased. Some restricting factors are necessary to develop and channelize power. A river can be useful only as long as the waters are contained by the banks on either side. Once the embankment breaks, the waters are lost. The concentrated force is lost. So, having our goal clear before us, we must struggle to overcome obstacles. Life does not have to be easy. There should be obstacles which we must overcome in the right spirit. As in work, so in sadhana—the right attitude should be maintained.

God is the soul of your soul. Father of the father, Mother of the mother and so on, and is the only Reality. But owing to ignorance we think the body to be real, and live a life of worldly pleasures and get misery. The little happiness obtained thereby is only a reflection of the infinite happiness. Do you get satisfaction by eating a reflected mango? Seek the real mango, the source of Infinite Peace. This does not mean you should give up the world. Attend to the duties of life in detachment, in a spirit of dedication. Always find time to worship and meditate. Fill up all your idle moments with the thoughts of God. We can always be sure of Him. What is permanent in this impermanent world? We want to cling to somebody who may change his attitude towards us any day, or may die. Is there anything in this world that does not change? If so, where is it? Thinking in this strain is the beginning of spiritual life. Real religion begins only after getting a glimpse of the Reality.

There are moments, at least for some, during meditation when the mind is lifted up from the lower plane to a higher plane and a glimpse of the Infinite is obtained. Try to obtain this glimpse more frequently and to make it an integral part of your life. Try to think of the Soul of your soul at least for a few moments in the course of the day. That refreshes more than anything else, even more than deep sleep. We have no inclination for spiritual food. Even if it is available, we do not want to take it; there is no spiritual hunger. If you are sincere, you move towards that spiritual food in the shape of japa and meditation, prayer etc. This is the food for the soul. If you cannot understand, learn from somebody advanced in that line, who can show you the path. And then follow the path. That will give you understanding, so that you may in your own humble way discover the path of truth.

Some people are born with good samskaras and are spiritually minded at a very tender age. They show signs of a bright spiritual future, but we cannot be sure that they would grow into spiritual men and women. Suddenly they turn a somersault and turn out to be quite worldly in due course. Many come here seeking spirituality. Equal facilities are given to all. Some benefit by it while others do not. Some who do not achieve spiritual progress, altogether give up spiritual practice. It is not the right attitude—we should go on struggling. Swami Brahmananda used to say that the newborn calf tries to stand up, but its limbs are not strong and it falls. Again and again it struggles to get up and again and again it falls, till at last its limbs are strengthened through its efforts and it is able to stand up. As soon as its mouth touches the mother-cow's teats, the milk flows and as the calf sucks, the yield of milk is increased. So too, we should not give up hope when we fail at the first attempt at spiritual practice, but should go on struggling. Once we contact divine grace, it flows towards us without hindrance.

Four Types of Worshippers

Arta, artharthi, jijnasu and *jnani* are the four types of worshippers.

One may be a jijnasu, who wants to know the truth of his own individuality. He discards the various components of his individuality, such as, body senses and mind, by the process of 'not this, not this.' Then he comes to know that he is pure consciousness. This realization requires very great struggle. The jijnasu is dissatisfied with everything in the world. He finds everything unreal and unreliable. So he wants to find out one who is real and reliable. Until he finds that out, his mental agitation will be great. The doubts in the path of sadhana would be cleared by practice only. One should follow sincerely the Guru's instructions.

Another might be calling on God to have his sufferings removed. It does not mean that man reverts to his childish mentality when he calls on God. It is the innate nature of the soul to wish to contact the Over-soul. It is tired of its limitations and bondages, and it wants to unite with the Unlimited. This is the basis of all spiritual quest. People call on God for various reasons—he lavishes His kindness equally on all. Whatever be the cause for calling on Him, it is essential that there should be intense yearning. Pray to the Lord to reveal His grace and for guidance.

Out of these, the *jnani* constantly experiences the presence of God. Hence he is also a true bhakta. Any stage below that is wavering, unsteady. God and devotee are like magnet and the needle—there is a natural attraction between them.

Many say that they want peace of mind. They do not want God for His own sake. They want to make use of Him. They find no security in the world and therefore want to use God to further their ends. There was an Insurance Company advertisement as follows: 'Buddha renounced everything to gain peace of mind and security. Now you need not give up everything. You need only to insure with our Company.' But no amount of monetary security can give us real peace of mind. Children think that their all in all is their mother or father, but when they grow older, they find that their parents are in the same plight depending on somebody else. There was a deer, the leader of a herd, who boasted that it was never afraid of tigers. But when the tiger roared, it began to tremble, its whole body shaking.

Why do we want God? Is it because He gives us boons and removes miseries, or do we want Him for His own sake? We should seek an honest answer to this question. There is really no end to our ideas of boons, removal of misery etc. The egoism in us would ever create desires, and our spiritual pursuit would get mixed up with them. Instead of dwelling on the physical and mental plane always, we should think of the atman in us. There is an inseparable connection between the individual soul and the Supreme Spirit. Our task in spiritual life is to recognize and experience this. Religion is the manifestation of this eternal union, as Swami Vivekananda puts it.

H 2

②
Mind and Its Control

The Nature of Mind

Why is it hard to meditate? Meditation is possible only when the thought waves in the mind subside to a great extent. But there is no end to thought waves arising in the mind. We complain that the noise outside disturbs our meditation. But the noise inside is far more disturbing. The outside stimuli play only a small part. If we closely watch our mind, we can see a continuous stream of thoughts arising in the mind. What is the mind? The Gita compares it to wind. It is also compared to a lake. All these are analogies meant to show its extremely mobile and vacillating nature.

The mind may be dull with tamas or restless with rajas, it is full of vrittis all the time. Yoga is the process of controlling and sublimating these modifications and finally eliminating them altogether. The dull or restless mind should be elevated into the harmony of sattva and for this, introspection is necessary. We have to discover the nature of our mind. Just as we analyse the gross body, made up of flesh, blood, etc., recognise its nature and become aware that we are not the gross body, likewise we should analyse the nature of the mind and try to go beyond it to the underlying Consciousness.

Harmonising the mind is not an easy task. Having made our home in the cellar, we now want to shift to the first-floor. We must therefore dismantle all the fixtures and arrangements made in the cellar and carry them to the first floor, where we have to rearrange them in proper order, until we feel satisfied. And for all this, we must struggle. Without struggle, there is no life at all. The mind should not be dull, like a wall or a tree. It should first become active and dynamic. Some tension is necessary to attain progress. The mind should be elevated by means of prayer and meditation. Then it would start enjoying peace. Sometimes, it is full of inner disturbances and does not settle down at all. At such times we must pray more than ever, praying to be able to think and meditate on His noble qualities.

How to Overcome Mental Distractions

How to subdue the lower nature? We find that while meditating, the mind is at times quite calm and peaceful, while at other times it is quite disturbed and uncontrollable. There should be sincerity of purpose. The mind can be calmed to a great extent through japa. Purification of the mind is necessary before it could be calmed down. For this purpose, thoughts, words and actions should always be made to correspond to one another. This is the essence of Truth. Truth is quite essential for mental peace and spiritual advancement.

Evil thoughts may arise in the mind. They can be eliminated by constant practice and renunciation—there is no other way. Surrender yourself to the Lord, make Him your own, and evil thoughts will go away. He is *Sat-Chit-Ananda, Parama-prema-ananda-svarupa*. As you fill your mind with His Infinite Love and His Infinite Bliss, evil thoughts would be replaced by noble ones and the mind would become purified.

Sometimes the mind is elevated to spiritual heights and is filled with divine joy, whereas at other times it dwells on lower thoughts. Why is it so? Here one should remember the fact about the different chakras. The condition of the mind corresponds to its position in the chakras. Always try to raise your mind to the higher chakras. Enter the temple of your body through your heart. Here, it is not the physical heart that is meant; the centre from which our emotions rise is the heart.

The great task in spiritual life is to quiten the mind. If there are too many disturbances inside and if we try to calm the mind at one stretch, the result would be that either we may fall asleep or that the disturbances may increase and there would be greater inner turmoil. One is a tamasic reaction and the other rajasic. Both are not desirable. Sometimes we feel sleepy during meditation. The remedy is to keep the eyes half open and repeat the mantra, dwelling on its meaning.

Many silly thoughts and pictures arise in our minds while we sit for meditation. These are long cherished thoughts. Their frequent appearance in mind shows that we have more interest in them than in God. This is quite logical, though we are not willing to acknowledge the fact. There is a technique to get rid of these unwanted thoughts— throw mercilessly into the burning flame of divine light all those pictures that arise in your mind other than divine pictures; merge all the divine images into your Ishtam and by an effort of the will, try to concentrate on the Ishtam. Memories of the past life, past years, or even of the immediate past come to the mind and disturb one's calmness. But by regular practice we can bring the mind under control and this is conducive to the establishment of a constant spiritual mood, giving one a taste of inner joy.

A devotee complains about the constant unrest of his mind. He asks, should we wait for the proper time and mood to practice spiritual disciplines? It would be like waiting for the waves to subside so that one could bathe in the sea. We need more solace when the mind is not at rest. We need God more when we have to face the difficulties and troubles of mind. Hence the instruction—the more you feel anxious, the more you should think of God. Connect all your miseries with the name of the Lord. What will happen then? We would gain strength to bear our troubles. We rise to a different plane of consciousness, when we become the witness of our thoughts and troubles. Don't come down and get involved in the lower planes—that is the secret.

Another secret is: fill up all your spare moments with the name and thought of the Lord. When we do not have worries, we create them. We brood over imaginary problems and create real problems. It is like a monkey which scratches and makes a small wound and then goes on scratching, making the wound wider. Is it not true in our case also? We increase our troubles beyond all proportion by brooding over them. Instead of that, why not brood over the Lord? Make this experiment. Think that He dwells in me and I in Him. Mantra has a great power. You must repeat it. It gives you a new understanding.

Be Watchful

You must always watch and find out your mistakes and try to correct them. Be an impartial judge of your own mind. Be severe and do not give in when the mind projects lame excuses to justify its faults. Often it would plead that circumstances are not conducive to meditation. It is no use waiting for better circumstances to begin spiritual practice. While we are in the world, there will be problems at every moment. One would not be foolish like the man who waited for the waves to subside in order to bathe in the sea. Waves would never subside and he would never have a chance of bathing. On the other hand, he should square up his shoulders to the surging waves and stand firmly and then bathe. Similarly, one should face any problem that might crop up in life and continue one's spiritual practice regularly. Then success is certain.

How can one control the mind? By practice and dispassion, as stated by Sri Krishna in the Gita. Practice should be done in the right way and with the right attitude. Any amount of practice will be fruitless if 'the anchor is not removed'. Always be watchful. The mind ever wanders. Evil thoughts that arise in the mind should be curbed. Practice of japa will bring mental peace and the body too will become healthy thereby. It will elevate the mind and widen the vision. No outer agency can help us to concentrate the mind. The task lies entirely in our hands. Meditation is the continuous flow of thought towards God. This is very difficult to acquire. The mind is sometimes passive and still, at other times it wavers and wanders, making concentration impossible. For a while it finds peace in God, and again, the next moment it goes after some other object. It wants to roam about. By untiring, constant practice, the mind finds peace in God for ever. After many failures, one realizes that God is our sole guide and protector. Complete self-surrender is very difficult to attain.

Observe your mind always. Beware of the vrittis, the thought waves that you are raising throughout the day. The same thoughts will come up during our meditation. Hence, be ever careful not to strengthen the ego and the related thought waves. Work with the idea of self-surrender. Swami Turiyananda would always repeat *'Bhagavaccharanam'*, meaning that he was surrendering himself to the Lord, who alone was Real. Self-control and elimination of certain unhealthy thoughts are essential. But they don't go easily. They have very deep roots in the subconscious mind. Concentrated japa and deep meditation will eliminate them.

There are obstacles on the way to meditation like doubt, jealousy and restlessness of mind. Doubt is the greatest obstacle. It must be removed and we must have complete faith. Mental restlessness on account of worldly matters also should be removed. Restlessness for the realization of God is indeed a blessed thing. It is, however, very rare. We may mistake emotions for real feelings. We must always be alert and not mistake emotional outbursts for the real craving for God-realization.

We must always be alert, and if low thoughts come, boldly tell them that they are not wanted. We must drive them away. We should never keep the mind blank. If there is a void, the tendency is that bad thoughts will fill it up. The mind should therefore be filled with good thoughts. We can either read the scriptures or repeat holy texts. Sometimes the mind feels despondent. It has no taste for anything. This is a hindrance to spiritual progress. This state is due to the evil deeds of past and present lives. Why should we thus feel miserable or helpless?

Reading Patanjali's definition that yoga is Chitta-vritti-nirodha, some think that yoga is a state of mental void. It is not a blank state of mind that is referred to here but a state above all thoughts. It is beyond good and evil. To achieve it we should think of noble thoughts for long years. As Swami Vivekananda says: 'Dream truer dreams.' A certain person dreamt of a hare with horns. What is the use of dreaming about unreal things? We must dream true dreams, noble dreams, which will ultimately lead us to the Truth. In order to go beyond both good and evil we must lead a moral life and entertain spiritual thoughts instead of worldly thoughts. The latter will weaken the mind and the senses. They do not lead to harmony and peace. So it is necessary to proceed through good to attain Truth.

We are bound by our own thoughts and actions. We cannot help thinking, and cannot stop it even for a moment. Some are under the impression that the purpose of Yoga is to create a void by forcibly stopping the functioning of the mind. It is not wise to create a void in the mind. The mind should be elevated and filled with holy and noble thoughts. However, the Void spoken of in the scriptures is of great value. It is the Void where all names and forms are reduced to their essential nature—namely, the pure Spirit or Consciousness. Ordinarily any attempt to create a void invites sleep. You will be sitting on the asana in the proper position but fall asleep. This is not good.

The mind will run in all directions. Do not allow it to do so. We should create a mood where we are not acutely aware of the external surroundings, akin to the mood in which we fall asleep. While falling asleep, we do not care to think even of our most loved ones. In deep sleep we commune with the Eternal, but we are not in a conscious state at that time. While doing japa, one should cease to be aware of the external world and establish conscious communion with the Eternal within. The Self is beyond body and mind.

Hypocrisy

Without achieving control of mind and peace in this manner, to say that 'my mind has subsided, it is now under my control, etc.' is hypocrisy and self-deceit. We can deceive others, play the hypocrite for sometime, but we cannot deceive ourselves. Hence in solitude, we must find out the true nature of our minds.

Sri Ramakrishna has said that thoughts and words should correspond to each other. What does this mean? He meant that one should maintain complete sincerity. It may be easy to be sincere with regard to others, but it is very difficult to be sincere with oneself. In our prayers we say: 'Thou art the Master, and I am Thy servant.' but we do not act up to what we say. We have become hypocrites and boss over others around us. One who is sincere cannot find fault with others. Those who do find fault have dirty minds. If we sincerely analyse our minds we will find no dearth of hidden faults in us. All our time and energy will not be enough to remove the dirt in us and then, we would have no time to think of the faults of others. Hence no one need think that one is superior or inferior. All are sailing in the same boat.

Whatever we utter or do is known to God. If our thoughts and deeds do not correspond to each other, we are just fooling ourselves. There are people who bring tears to their eyes with great effort, and pose as great devotees, doing japa and meditation in a way that makes others take them to be great devotees. This also is hypocrisy; it greatly harms us.

We want God to fulfill our petty desires. We do not sincerely want Him for Himself. In America, snow-fall is generally a protection for the flower-beds and plants. A little girl there prayed once to God that there might be a good snowfall in the night for the plants. When she woke up next morning, to her delight she saw that everything was covered with snow. She then said to herself: 'Ah! I have fooled God! I wanted the snow for the little cottage I had built.' Was He really fooled? Far from it. In similar ways we are only fooling ourselves, harming our spiritual progress when we put on any pretension. When we do any wrong, we find many excuses to justify ourselves, which we are not really prepared to accept; thus we practice hypocrisy. In the waking state we consciously practice hypocrisy and self-deceit. We are in the same plight when we dream. In sleep, there is no self-deceit, but there is also no self-consciousness. When we wake up, old memories arise, and we are in the same old boat. Thus we are constantly the victims of hypocrisy. In this way we have created misery in this world, and then complain that we are not happy. We even blame God and religion for our misery.

The mind is our greatest enemy. At any moment it may give way. When we analyse it we find a lot of justification for our wrong actions and when we are not able to see the fault in ourselves, we blame others. We should always be very, very careful, and a great deal of sincere analysis is necessary.

There are people who put on marks of religion on their forehead, wear tulsi mala etc. These are of no use unless there is inner purification. Sri Ramakrishna could not drink the water brought by a certain person who was wearing these outward marks but whose mind was impure. There are some others who talk of religion but who lead a deceitful life. Such too are hypocrites.

Sri Ramakrishna used to sigh: 'What a delirious fever is that I suffer from! Even for Thy Holy Name I have no taste, O Mother!' A Sufi Saint said: 'If you want to see the devil, look within.' There is the devil in us. Let us be sincere and admit our faults. Most of us show with outward pride that we are saintly etc, while the devil is lurking inside. This is hypocrisy, and misery comes of it. Fortunately the deity also is there within us and once He is awakened, He will drive the devil away.

We do not want to own it, but the fact is this—it is because we are interested in them that low thoughts occupy our mind. Half of the mind is interested in noble thoughts and the other half in base thoughts.

Some devotees complain that they cannot do spiritual practice regularly for various reasons, such as lack of time, restlessness of mind, etc. Often they do not reveal the real sources of their mental disturbance. It is of no use to hide anything; hidden factors are a burden to the mind and they act as impurities; then the mind will not be calm. Do not harbour secrets in your heart. Open your heart to God. If we have weaknesses, let us not publish them to the whole world. Let us analyse them and identify them and then we shall find ways and means to remove them. Some devotees who come to us want us to solve their problems, but they hide the real trouble. It is then very difficult to instruct them. That is why so much stress is laid on a moral life as a pre-requisite to spiritual life. Lead your life in such a way that you need not hide anything from anybody. For this you have to prepare your mind and regulate your living habits.

We may derive satisfaction from repeating the Lord's Name a thousand times—but how many times has he heard it? May be, not even once, because of our want of sincerity. When taking His Name we should think of Him, not allowing the mind to wander about. Doing japa in this manner is really yoga, for yoga is controlling the modifications of the mind.

You say solitude is necessary. The solitude that is wanted is mostly mental. Even in the midst of a crowd you can be at peace if the mind is trained properly. If you go into solitude and brood upon your own thoughts, it will lead you to lunacy. Again, moving with nature is not the remedy.

Sublimation of Tendencies

There are six enemies—desire, anger, greed, delusion, pride and jealousy. We have to spiritualize them. We cannot completely get rid of our passions, but we can give them a new turn. We have to give them a spiritual direction. For example, what is the cause of anger? It is caused by suppressed desires. Swami Turiyananda used to say that anger is concentrated desire. We should cultivate 'desire' for God. We should get 'angry' with things that stand in the way to spiritual realization. Be 'greedy' for spiritual experiences. Be 'infatuated' with the beauty of the divine form. Thus all emotions should be directed along spiritual channels. Turn towards that which never perishes. When you think of Nature's beauty, think of the Creator of that beauty. Once Swami Vivekananda saw the moonlit sea from the deck of a ship. It was enchanting. He looked on and on and exclaimed: 'If maya is so very beautiful, how much more so is He, the master of maya!' Keep up the sense of beauty of a poet. You have an ego—keep it; you cannot jump out of it. But cultivate a good ego, the pure ego of a devotee. Then offer it to the Lord.

People generally complain that they have not attained anything even after long years of spiritual practices. If we analyse our minds we will find that almost all the time we think on ego-centric lines, such as: 'I pray and do japa and there is no result' etc. Our thinking is mostly centered around the I. Now, instead of wasting energy in ego-centric thinking and acting, if we had concentrated on God, it would have been useful. We believe we alone are devotees! Devotees should really be very careful about such delusive thoughts. If they do not root out this I consciousness in the initial stages, it will be very difficult to do so later. Therefore, offer everything to Him and work to please Him. This is the only way to overcome the ego. We are like salt dolls which go to find out the depth of the sea. Some people complain that their minds do not plunge into sadhana even after a long period of practice. It is because the mind is still full of 'sand' i.e. ego which cannot melt in water. We have to increase the proportion of salt in us, so that we may get dissolved.

Before you try to immerse yourself in the ocean of *Satchidananda*, become a salt doll. The sand in you is to be transmuted into salt. Then it melts in the ocean. A stone doll cannot melt. The ego is to be purified. Cultivate the feeling that 'I am a child of God. a servant of God.' Then your little ego becomes merged in the Infinite Spirit. As long as we have the sense of identification with our bodies, we should keep up the concept of a divine form. When you transcend body-consciousness, when you can think of yourself as a conscious entity, then you can think that He is Infinite Consciousness and you are a part of It. This is the way. May be some day we get a glimpse of That. The progress is not from matter to spirit, but from spirit to spirit.

There are two currents of power—worldly and spiritual. An aspirant should strengthen the spiritual current. Ordinarily the mind functions at two levels—the upper and the lower, the conscious and the sub-conscious. The upper level is engaged in whatever we are doing at the moment. The lower level remains engaged in useless, vain thoughts. An aspirant has to spiritualize not only the conscious mind but also the subconscious mind. They should be in tune with each other. That would mean, first of all, living a moral life. Anger, jealousy and such feelings occupy the greater part of our mind. They have to be replaced by spiritual feelings and emotions. Try to raise a spiritual current on the conscious plane. Then it should be strengthened and extended to the lower planes. To the extent we try to develop noble virtues like Satya, Ahimsa, etc., to that extent the mind becomes clear and free from all bondages such as fear, doubt and hatred. By cleaning the subconscious mind of these impurities, we rise above pettiness.

Many complain of lust, which rears its head even during meditation and disturbs concentration. What is the remedy? The fact is that lust disturbs all aspirants. One should not mind it. Do not believe those who boast of getting good concentration. Those who can really get good concentration are very rare. Abstention from food which irritates the stomach and is hard to digest helps a great deal in controlling lust. But we take 'food' through our senses also—through our eyes and ears. Discrimination should be observed in that regard too. Avoid seeing unwholesome scenes, obscene films, etc. and hearing evil words. Thus the mind gets purified. Surrender yourself to the Lord and drive away evil tendencies.

Do Not Dwell on Past Mistakes

Some have a tendency to live in their past and dwell upon their 'sin' which really are mistakes. This is undesirable. By thinking of past mistakes, the mind gets weakened. Sin exists only in man's eyes. There is no sin in God's eyes. One glance from Him will wash away all the sins of past births. Believe yourself to be a spiritual being— Atman. Sin exists only as long as one identifies oneself with the body. Atman is ever pure. If we keep our mind always in communion with God, all the worldly tendencies of the mind will vanish. The more we think of God, the less we shall think of worldly things. The more we think of God, the more fruitful our life will become.

If bad tendencies arise in the mind we should not pay heed to them. When they crop up, we should take the help of the Holy Name. When it is repeated sincerely, bad thoughts wither away by themselves. We should not worry or feel despondent if bad thoughts come. It is good in a way that they come out instead of lurking in our bosom. We recognize them as enemies and with the help of a powerful friend we try to destroy them. It is necessary that we take the help of the mantra on such occasions because sometimes reasoning will take us nowhere as we do not have enough strength of mind to remain at the intellectual level. So it is better not to attempt a frontal attack on bad thoughts and low moods.

Our mind dwells on a thousand odd things. When someone scolds us we think of him and get angry, i.e. we imbibe his qualities. If we think of a dejected person we too begin to feel dejected. It is, therefore, most essential to have proper objects of our thoughts. We should think of the noble attributes of the Lord, so that we may acquire His compassion and Infinite Love. Our interest in objects of the world is greater than our interest in God. We have to counteract this. We should feel attracted towards God and our mental disturbances will then be lessened. This is love of God.

It is commonly said that one should eliminate worldly thoughts from one's mind. This is a negative attitude. Positive action is to think noble thoughts and do spiritual practice. Arouse the power of the soul and tread the right path. Then all weaknesses would fall away. This is what Sri Ramakrishna advised. If you want to go away from the West, you do not have to walk back with your face to the West; you have only to walk towards the East. Walk in the direction of God and all worldliness will gradually leave you. Always think you are the atman.

How are we to keep baser thoughts out of our mind? This is a problem for everyone. Baser thoughts come and go. We should not mind them. By training the mind to dwell increasingly on noble thoughts, baser thoughts can be kept away. By practice (abhyasa), the mind should be made to dwell on higher planes. Japa and meditation strengthen our will power and purify our mind more and more. Japa should be practiced with great regularity and earnestness. Even if you do not feel any taste for it, you should not give it up. When the liver is upset, the bile is not secreted properly and appetite is lost. The patient dies by gradual starvation. A little food should be administered to keep the body alive. So also in spirituality: even if we do not find any interest in repeating His Name, we should not stop the practice altogether, making place for low thoughts to take root in the mind, leading to spiritual death

There may be disturbances on account of ill-health, old age, etc. Mental disturbances are numerous. These are all to be endured. Certain disturbances can be controlled, such as illness due to indigestion. It can be taken care of by proper and regular food. Regular habits should be formed to avoid minor disturbances.

③
Values for Spiritual Life

Strength

Spirituality is not meant for weaklings. Physical and mental strength is essential for leading a spiritual life. It is not the strength of an elephant that is meant here—we should have enough physical strength to go through sustained spiritual practice. A weak, tired body does not help one to meditate. Again, by mental strength, we do not mean the type of mental strength possessed by Hitler—it is the strength required to maintain equanimity of mind under all circumstances. With the help of these two we should develop spiritual strength. Spiritual strength is gained by constant practice of japa and meditation. One in whom all the three are properly developed attains success in sadhana. As in every field, the fittest person survives. Spartans were said to throw their children over a hillock to test their strength and the child which survived was held to be the fittest citizen. Fortunately, in the spiritual field we do not test anyone in this manner. But those who persevere get the benefit and those who give up will be eliminated. Sri Krishna conveys this idea by the verse 'Manusyanam sahasreshu' etc., in the Gita. Strength is essential in all walks of life—even in worldly life, the economically weak are exploited by the economically strong, and the mentally weak are exploited by the mentally strong. If strength is necessary for success in worldly life, much more of it is necessary in spiritual life.

No one can escape difficulties in this world. We cannot correct others. But we can change our attitude towards them. Face the world and fight for the ideal. Do not allow yourselves to be swayed by circumstances. We cannot

21

forsake the world and go to the forest seeking peace. Spiritual life is not for weaklings.

Always try to think of God. By practice of japa and meditation, one gets immense strength. It is bad always to think in terms of the body and the mind. You are soul and the body and mind are means or instruments given to you for work. Understanding this, you will know what tremendous strength you get. Daily meditation is an important element in the effort to reach that source of Bliss and strength. We get a glimpse of that Bliss in meditation and that gives us peace and joy.

Weakness has no place in spiritual life. In the Gita we find Arjuna despondent in the beginning. The Lord advises him to leave all weakness and arise. 'Weakness does not become you' says the Lord, in the Gita. The Lord explains the different paths of Yoga to reach the goal. A man of realization goes beyond all weaknesses.

Go on Struggling

Feel clearly, act clearly. There are large numbers of parasites in religious life who do not want to do anything. They just depend on the Lord's grace. Should we not use the power He has given us? Use it and try to be as active as possible. Remove the dirt that covers the mirror of the mind. An impulse comes in the life of all of us sooner or later, and urges us to change this life and follow the spiritual path. The love with which we seek God is given by Him. Make the best use of this love. Purify your understanding. Buddhi must be sharpened. How? By Upasana, worship, japa and meditation. You have to struggle. In every walk of life you have got to struggle for existence and progress. Survival of the fittest is the rule. Here the struggle is not with outsiders. Our main struggle is within ourselves, between our higher and lower natures. In the Devi Mahatmya (Chandi), we read how the Divine Mother destroyed Sumbha and Nisumbha. There is a deep significance in this. Devoid of divine power, the Devas cannot conquer the Asuras. So the Mother comes and gives inspiration. The battle between the Devas and the Asuras is significant; it is always going on within us, between our lower and higher natures. How to strengthen the power of good? Through prayer and meditation. Sri Ramachandra, before fighting with the demons, worshipped the Divine Mother. He invoked Her and got Her blessings. That means that great effort is needed on our part. Then the higher nature becomes stronger and destroys the lower one. Great stress is laid upon self-effort. The divine Spirit comes in the form of the teacher and shows you the way. You must follow the path sincerely.

Yearning for God

Is Vairagya (dispassion) the result of spiritual practice? The grace of God comes in the form of yearning. Dispassion towards worldly pleasures is the negative aspect. In its positive aspect, Vairagya is yearning to realise God. This yearning is the result of past good karmas. We sometimes see spiritual yearning even in children. Suppose one is born with 60% of good karma and 40% of bad karma. A sincere aspirant should strive to increase the proportion of merit by his life's work. But the same proportion as at the beginning is maintained life after life by insincere seekers. By doing more and more selfless works and worshipping God, we acquire good samskaras and thus change the proportion. Unfortunately very few people want to change it. They do not want to get out of this phenomenal existence. We ourselves create our world of bondage by our mental processes and suffer, not willing to get out of it. It is the effect of maya or ignorance.

Just as a hungry person longs for food, you should long for God. Knowingly or unknowingly we long for peace, to go back to that Infinite state and become inactive. That is a negative attitude. People want God just to alleviate their misery. Sri Ramakrishna said that the same Supreme Spirit is inside and outside. Hence God's presence should be felt

H 3

in the world around us too. In the midst of your duties, remember Him; prepare the mind well and call on Him. This is the only way to enjoy peace in this world. Let the quality of your meditation improve. When you are hungry, do you sit at the table for half an hour to get the appetite? Certainly not. You will have no patience to wait. So also prepare the mind all through the day for meditation. Be hungry for spiritual food. Great appetite should be created for spiritual practices. Whenever you call on Him, do so whole-heartedly, even if it be only for a short time.

A taste for spiritual discipline will not come all at once. One should struggle hard for it. All the energies should be spent in spiritual discipline alone. After some time you will attain some progress, but do not be satisfied with that. A burning dissatisfaction should be created till one reaches the Supreme. Sri Ramakrishna's cry to the Mother, 'Another day is gone and I have not seen you', shows true spiritual hankering.

Austerity

Austerities have an important place in spiritual life. They are a means of controlling the mind. They are useful to some extent but should not be carried too far. Bathing daily in the Ganga is taken up by some as an austerity. But while doing so, if one does not remain conscious of the holiness of the Ganga and its power to impart purity, and engages oneself in gossip with others, then to what purpose is that austerity? There are some who bathe thrice a day. Of what use is that if one does not strive to keep the mind clean? Some observe silence but if the mind is not silenced by remembrance of God, then binding the tongue down is of harm alone. Such austerities consume our time and energy without really benefitting us. We should remember that 'Snaanam manomala-tyagah, Suchih indriya nigrahah' Bath is washing away the stains of the mind and cleanliness is control of the senses.

In order to attain divine grace, a certain amount of austerity (tapas) is needed. There are three kinds of tapas mentioned in the Gita; physical, verbal and mental (XVII, 14, 15, 16). Silence is mentioned as one of the constituents of mental tapas. What is silence? It is not merely refraining from speaking. You may not utter a word, yet your mind will be producing any number of thoughts. We experience this particularly during meditation. Thoughts are mental speech. The silence referred to by the Gita is the silence of the mind as a result of thoughts becoming fewer and fewer. As we control our speech and practice ahimsa we gain the habit of speaking the truth and truth alone, and our spiritual strength is enhanced by it. With the co-ordination of all the three kinds of tapas, mental equilibrium is attained and a person progresses rapidly in the spiritual path. Hence, be strong and struggle, struggle, struggle!

Renunciation of Attachment

Those who do not possess sincere attachment to God find it difficult to persevere in the path of spiritual practice. The mind will be restless without love for the Divine. This is the natural state of man. We should make use of this restlessness of the mind and turn it towards God, away from worldly things. It is hard to kindle any thought of God without the fire of renunciation. Sri Ramakrishna used to emphasize the need for discrimination and renunciation— discrimination between the Real and the unreal, and renunciation of attachment to the unreal. He is the embodiment of discrimination and renunciation

No spiritual progress will be made even by undergoing spiritual disciplines for years together, if the mind is not freed from attachment to sense objects. You would be familiar with the story of the drunkards who rowed their boat all through the night without removing the anchor. In the morning they were at the same old place. Spiritual practice without detachment would be a vain effort like that. Whatever role one may be assigned in the drama of life, one should play it well. The student or wife or husband or mother or father should know his or her duties and perform them well. Work and worship should go together, with detachment towards sense objects.

Any amount of spiritual practice will not take us far Godward, without His grace. What then is grace? The desire to lead a spiritual life is in itself by the grace of God. So, grace and self-effort are not contradictory. How is it that some people desiring God-realization and practicing japa and meditation do not progress spiritually? It is because they do not raise the anchor before rowing the boat, like the drunken boatmen of the story. No amount of spiritual practice will avail unless we detach our minds from worldly thoughts which are deep-seated in us. This yoga of detachment should be practiced at least during meditation. The mind which is detached and elevated during meditation will naturally continue in the same mood at least for sometime even thereafter. Reading the scriptures and holy books helps to keep up the holy mood. On the other hand, reading dirty novels and seeing cinema films drown the mind in worldliness. Though they may give momentary pleasure, they lower the mind to a great extent. The mind seeking spiritual solace will rise higher and higher through spiritual practice and the mind with a tendency towards worldly enjoyments goes lower and lower.

Regularity in Spiritual Practice

The Atman is beyond the body and the mind. To have spiritual experiences we have to go beyond mind and intellect. Egotism is the first obstacle in the spiritual path. We think too much of our body. When we advance to a higher stage we identify ourselves with the mind. Mental or intellectual understanding is not spiritual experience. To go beyond mind and body we should practice japa and meditation regularly for many years. There should be regularity in spiritual practice under all circumstances.

Some days, during spiritual practice we get peace and joy. Why can we not maintain this all the time? We need constant practice for that. Maintain inner poise in the midst of work. You would have seen how people skate on the ice without falling. You would have read how Sri Ramakrishna went to the circus and observed a lady doing wonderful feats on horseback. He saw what practice can do. So in the midst of troubles, maintain inner poise and inner balance, and be prepared not to lose it at any cost.

Desire for worldly things will never bring peace to the mind. When one desired object is attained, the mind is momentarily satisfied but immediately thereafter it wants something else. There is no end to this process. Hence always keep up His remembrance and do japa and meditation daily, at a particular place and time. No peace can be attained without worshipping God. Daily one should spend some time in singing His glories. Persistence in spiritual practice will bring in faith, devotion and knowledge. It is essential to maintain regularity in spiritual practice. To win the grace of our own mind is the great task in spiritual life. Control of the restless mind can only be achieved through constant prayer. There is no end to prayer. Always pray to God to win the grace of the mind.

Every day we should practice at fixed hours in the morning and evening. It may not be possible for some to do so in the evening after a day's tiring work. Nevertheless one should take a 'spiritual breakfast' every day—the day should begin with spiritual practices. Gradually one realises that one cannot get on without that practice. A man was mad after God. His relatives called a physician and administered medicines, thinking that he was mentally ill. At last the man himself said: 'Please do not cure me of remembering Him!' This should be our objective—ever to remember Him. If on any day, it is not possible to carry out one's practice at the fixed time owing to unavoidable circumstances, it should be done at some other time. Keeping the portrait or picture of the Ishtam before us is helpful. We should create the inclination to meditate in our mind before sitting for our practice. If the mind is disinclined, we can create the mood by following the instructions of the Guru carefully. It is very important to have devotion. If other thoughts arise, expel them by filling the mind with noble ideas, even by force if necessary.

Begin the Day with Thoughts of God

Most people find the daily routine of life monotonous and resort to reading sensational novels and detective stories for entertainment and mental stimulation. These inferior works leave undesirable impressions in the reader's minds which gradually turn into criminal tendencies. Grown-ups go to the cinema houses and shamelessly take their children along with them. Children are quickly and deeply influenced by what they see on the screen. Some people cannot do without tea or coffee early in the morning as a stimulant. None of these things can bring peace and sweetness to life. On the other hand, if we begin our day with spiritual practice, life will be sweetened. Let the first thought of the day be of God instead of about coffee or some worldly thing. Then our daily duties will not be dry. When all work is looked upon as the Lord's and offered to him, life becomes sweet and happy.

Before retiring at night, bow down before the Lord and go to sleep, mentally repeating the name. Then while getting up we will find ourselves repeating the name automatically. Keep the form of the deity before your mind's eye when retiring. Practice this daily. Before going to sleep, do meditation for some time in bed. By japa, the body and mind become pure. While repeating the mantra, we should be conscious of its meaning. Meditation and japa should go together.

Dreams arise from the sub-conscious mind. Events of one's former birth also may come in dreams. Dreams about spiritual subjects are helpful, but they are only signs on the path, not the end. One should therefore not think much of dreams. Gaining money in a dream will not buy fruits in the waking state. To have true dreams we should think of true things always in our waking state also; but most of the time we are running after delusions.

One should practice the following **six disciplines**: *sama, dama, uparati, titiksha, sradha, samadhanam* (i.e., control of the mind; having no desire for sensual objects; withdrawal of the mind from the outward world and keeping it one-pointed; forbearance; faith in the words of the Guru, in the Lord, in the scriptures; and finally samadhi—merger of the mind in the Divine.)

In spiritual practice **sincerity** is the most important factor. We sometimes deceive ourselves, believing we are very sincere. Sincerity that comes all of a sudden is short lived. We love many things and one amongst them is God. By sadhana we should make our minds pure and increase the proportion of our love for God. Our love for Him is instinctive and gradually we will come to feel the Presence of one who is dearer than father, mother and everything in the world.

Concentration

The eye, ear and other senses are mere instruments. It is really the atman that functions through all of them. The mind is said to be the divine eye. With concentration, it can perceive many things not visible to the ordinary eyes. As such, it is given a higher place. But only a mind which is trained to concentrate can aspire to this position. This concentration is something wonderful. In anger too we concentrate, but that concentration really leads to distraction because that concentration is centered on worldly matters. But, if the mind is made to concentrate on God or on some spiritual theme, then it is not distracted. This sort of concentration creates harmony, peace.

What we lack is not power of concentration. We have it but we are not accustomed to direct it in the right direction. We think of unnecessary things and thereby a little wave of a problem becomes as big as the ocean. When we want to direct the mind along spiritual lines, then comes the difficulty. Once you succeed, you will then know what a great blessing it is. You know Sri Ramakrishna's story of the angler. He was so intent on catching fish and his mind was so utterly concentrated on it that the questions put to him by a passer-by did not reach his ear at all. We should have similar concentration on God.

Purity

The way to God-realization is purity (selflessness) and concentration. The power of concentration works wonders. They even forget the needs of the body during work. Newton was working on a theory in his laboratory for some days at a stretch. Food would be kept covered on his table; he had no fixed time for eating. Once a friend played a trick on him, eating up the food and leaving the plate covered as before. When Newton removed the cover and found the plate empty, he concluded that he had already eaten. If one has similar concentration on the Lord, one succeeds in yoga. A scientist who works in a selfless spirit gains purity of mind in course of time. Suddenly a flash of intuition may bring light to him and he may realise·that there is some Power beyond the gross and subtle planes of nature.

Without striving to become pure, you cannot approach Sri Ramakrishna and the Holy Mother. Somebody complained that he could meditate on the former, but not on the latter as that frightened him. Evidently his mind was not pure. Girish Chandra Ghosh could not even look at the Mother. Many people are drawn to the spiritual ideal, but when they come closer and come to know that strict purity is needed to live this life, they, get frightened. We tell them: 'Go back to the world and enjoy life.' If you are sincere and try to make yourself purer and (purer, you would get the strength to lead a spiritual life. Sri Ramakrishna and the Holy Mother are one and the same. There is no difference between them even as between Lakshmi and Narayana, or Sita and Rama. One can meditate on either, merging one form into the other.

Enter the inner world. Be convinced that the Lord who dwells in you dwells everywhere. You cannot think of the divine in you owing to the impurity of the mind. Hence think of the divine in a holy man, an incarnation. Your Ishta dwells in your heart. When this idea becomes firmly rooted, you will be forced to maintain the sanctity of the 'temple within'— that is, the purity of body and mind. Jivanmuktas continue to live in the world even after realization. To understand these things, sadhana is to be done. One should not take up spiritual practices in the spirit of forced labour. One should practice hard and be pure.

Knowledge and dispassion are the means of attaining this purity. Complete purity comes only after Self-realization. Then the ego and mind are transformed. Higher consciousness is awakened. Then purity becomes natural and spontaneous, firm as a rock. It begins to be manifested in your mind and day-to-day life. Total dedication to Truth is the test of purity. Remember the saying of Sri Ramakrishna that he could offer everything to the Divine Mother except Truth.

Be in a Spiritual Mood

There is a form of sadhana all of us can do. Study your mind at the end of the day. How much time did you spend in studies and duties and how much on useless things? 'Somebody said something about me, and I go on thinking about it'—this is what most of us find when we look into our minds at the end of the day. Try to be in a spiritual mood. Even if anything happens, you may not feel it through divine grace. We have taken the world to be more real than the Eternal Being. If some day we come to feel that the Supreme

Being is more real than the world, then the whole view will be changed. The Lord is one who is ever the same. This understanding gives a new dimension to our lives. The whole trouble is, the unreal has become the real to us and vice versa. We have now to think of the unchanging something and feel it. Truth is always there. Some people frown, some smile. That is the way of the world. Remembrance of the Truth, of the Lord, will help us greatly. He dwells within, He dwells outside. In one aspect He is the transcendental Being beyond name and form. Still in another aspect He is the antaryami, the indwelling spirit. In another aspect, He manifests Himself as gods and goddesses, and again as the whole world. Whatever be the aspect, it is the same Being. This is the Truth we have to remember always and japa and meditation will help us to do so.

Faith in the Words of Sages

We believe in the words of a scientist who conducts experiments and gives his conclusions. Why should we not similarly believe in the words of the sages who had experienced the greater whole, the Ultimate Reality? It is left to us to try and make that experience our own. Why not try? As a basic factor one should have a certain amount of faith. Act according to the Guru's instructions and at last everything will be clear. Do not be disheartened if your meditation is not deep; go on repeating the mantra earnestly. Thus your understanding power will increase and mental vision will become clearer. Disturbing thoughts will slowly cease to appear and the spiritual ideal will become firm in the mind. Then only can we think of God. We will know more about Him as we progress further. Real meditation comes a little later.

We always feel, and think, in terms of body and mind. In fact, we are not aware of any other dimension of personality. When told that we are not the body, nor the mind, but that we are the eternal spirit, we think: 'Is this not madness?' We are told that the sun does not move but it is only the earth that does so, yet we see that the sun rises and sets. Is it not madness to say the contrary? The scientists experimented on those lines and discovered that in fact it is the earth, and not the sun, that moves. Likewise, in spiritual life too, many have discovered that the reality in us is the atman, other than the body and the mind. We have to take their word as true, have faith in them, and proceed.

But the doubt crops up: 'If we are spirit, why do we not feel its nature?' Because it is veiled by our samskaras. We have therefore to remove all impurities. Sri Ramakrishna said that pure mind and pure self are one and the same. Sadhana is the only way to remove impurities. Mere intellectualizing will not do; we must begin with practice, praying to Him for His love, bliss, and other attributes. Only a particle of that love is seen in human beings. We must pray to Him to guide our understanding and clear our consciousness. Along with prayer one should also act. Someone's house was set on fire and the whole of it was destroyed, but the man still sat in a corner, doing nothing. He explained: 'I am praying for rain!' This is not the right attitude. Self-effort should go with prayer, and we should offer everything at His feet. That is the correct attitude in understanding spiritual truth.

Contentment

Patanjali says that santosa (contentment) is one of the basic qualities of a spiritual aspirant. This contentment refers to worldly things and surroundings. One should not yearn for improvement in the external conditions as a pre-requisite for spiritual practices. Sitting for meditation and japa with the mind troubled by the immediate surroundings gives bad results. A tranquil mind is to be cultivated before sitting for prayers.

④
Continence

In Chhandogya Upanishad it is said:

Those who reach this world of Brahman by continence—to them belongs this world of Brahman; for them there is independence in all the worlds. (8.4, 3)

Sankaracharya, in his commentary on this sloka, says:

Such being the case, those who by means of 'continence' i.e. by renouncing all desire for women, reach this world of Brahman in accordance with the injunctions of the teachers of the scriptures, i.e. realise it in their consciousness, to such people as are equipped with continence, and have a knowledge of Brahman, this world of Brahman belongs; and to no others who have a longing for women, even if they know Brahman. For these people there is independence in all the worlds. Therefore, continence is the supreme means for the knower's of Brahman.

According to Chhandogya Upanishad, continence is yajna and Ishtam:

Now that which they call yajna (sacrifice) is only continence; as it is only by means of continence that the knower reaches That. And that which they call 'Ishtam' is only continence; because it is by continence that having worshipped, one reaches the Self. (8.5.1)

Need for Sublimation and Purity

Along with concentration, the process of sublimation must proceed. Otherwise you get enormous concentration, enormous onepointedness, but in the wrong direction. And the whole civilization becomes *asuric* with gun-factories and other engines of destruction.

34

The feeling of realization cannot come unless we have, to a great extent, under-mined our sex-consciousness, body-consciousness, physical-consciousness. First, your mind must be drawn away from the lower physical centres, and lifted to one of the higher centres. Then, mental purification must set in. The consciousness 'I am a man' or 'I am a woman' prevents one from having any of the higher forms of realization. Only by getting rid of our physical consciousness, even in its most subtle forms, can we attain to the highest goal.

Therefore, be always on your guard and watch the movements of your mind. The moment a tendency sets in to go to the lower centres, draw the mind away by force and fix it in one of the higher centres.

You cannot do anything without a purified mind. The purification of body and mind has to be your very first task if you want to lead a spiritual life. Proceed slowly, steadily, with great doggedness and determination, uninterruptedly day and night, day by day. Then alone you will attain the goal.

Even the house-holder, the married man or woman, must learn to lead a controlled life. This point must be stressed under all circumstances. First pay attention to this purification, above all, mental purification especially concerning sex and sex-life. First look to this cleansing process of all your thoughts and impulses. Then everything else will follow in due course, naturally and spontaneously. Get rid of your body-consciousness, and then try to transcend your mind.

First of all the bats of worldliness and worldly desires are to be driven away. In you there are nooks and corners, and bats are always fond of nooks and corners, darkness and filth. The 'eleven bats' are the ten senses and the mind. These eleven bats are making this human temple dirty and full of foul smell. Try to drive the truth of these ideas deeper and deeper into your subconscious mind by daily reading, daily pondering over them and daily steady spiritual practices and by leading a con-trolled life. A controlled life, ethical culture, and continence, are the sine qua non for all spiritual progress.

All except what contributes to the purification and restraint of mind and to knowledge of the process to be followed do not lead to real happiness. Prayers, rituals, pilgrimages etc. are useless to a man whose mind is not tranquil and purified. Therefore, one should practice purification and restraint of mind. By purification and restraint of mind one can achieve all one's aspirations.

Continence and the fulfillment of all preliminaries are necessary if you want to take up the higher forms of spiritual practice which can lead to the realization of the Absolute State. If you do not care to take up spiritual life in right earnest, then all these readings and talks have no value and become useless and a mere waste of time.

In India, we do not encourage the type of the western bachelor. Everybody ought to fulfill his duty, either by becoming a householder and maintaining his family or by becoming a monk and working for the spiritual development of his fellow-men and women. The unmarried men and the unmarried women, who lead impure lives, as you find them in the West, are not encouraged by our society. That is why the ideal of chastity and purity has never been lowered to such an extent in India. Spirituality means getting rid of one's body-consciousness, the raising of one's centre of consciousness from the lower centres to the higher centres, and self-control, physical and mental. Without perfect purification of body and mind spiritual life has no meaning, as the goal can never be reached before that has been done.

The fact that in the West women have to struggle to find their husbands themselves is bound to lower the conception of chastity and the feeling for a pure life, because they try to attract men by their physical charms and to conquer them by their beauty. In such a civilization you can-not find a very high conception of chastity and, as a consequence, very little of real spirituality in a higher sense. Not all people who feel attracted by religion and religious ideas are spiritual or fit to take up spiritual life.

Objection Against Chastity

There are many people who contend that brahmacharya is not good for health as it brings about all kinds of nervous diseases. How do they know it? How can anybody who has not led a sexually pure life know it? How many wrecks do you see among modern men and women? Do you see all these broken nerves in modern life because there has been too much of continence? Have they become wrecks by leading a moral, pure life or by leading a life of enjoyment and license? As a matter of fact, the nervous wrecks you see in modern life are not the result of repression, of too much chastity, but the result of indulging in their sexual passions and other vices. It is ludicrous to say that this extreme nervousness is brought about by a really controlled life, by a perfect and conscious control of body and mind. There is something seriously wrong in a civilization which says such things. Real brahmacharya is not bad for health. Objections to it are all nonsense. All these objections to true brahmacharya have no ground to stand upon. They are absurd. People raise these objections not out of conviction, but only because they want to find some excuse for the life they are leading. In their case it is nothing but self-justification.

The So-called Love

Beware of people who say they love everybody, that they are full of love for everybody. Ninety-nine percent of them do not love others at all, but only their being in love with somebody. They love their attachment, but they do not know what 'love' is. And this is one of the worst forms of selfishness and the sense of appropriation. They want to feel they are good, they want to cling to others with their so-called love and to appropriate them; if not their body, then at least their minds. They have never the strength to do anything, but just go on clinging and clinging to others. Their hearts bleed for others, but that only means that their hearts like bleeding, not that they love others. Tall words of love are being used by hundreds and hundreds of people, but all this is not love. Only a Christ, a Buddha, a Ramakrishna, knows what love is. Only a Vivekananda can love. We, on our plane, cannot. It is all emotional greed, and one of the worst forms of selfishness and self-consciousness. We do not want to love others, but we want to satisfy our emotional craving and thus become emotional blood-suckers. That is all. It is all sham. An unpurified body and mind cannot love. One who hasn't gone through the necessary bodily and mental disciplines cannot even know what it is to love. All falsehood! All lies! All these people are wrapping themselves up in lies. Sentimental dolls! People talk so much about 'heart' and 'love', but what they really mean is body and attachment. They are just trying to cover the festering sores with beautiful, fragrant flowers.

There must be expansion of heart, expansion of intellect. There is love in almost all human beings, but what we generally call 'love' is more or less of an animal nature, containing physical elements and mostly belonging to the realm of body-consciousness, of which, in almost all case of this so-called love, there is a higher or a lower percentage present in the lover. Love which contains these elements of desire for enjoyment on the physical or mental plane can never be 'love' in the true sense; in the sense that the term is used in spiritual life.

But love becomes free from animality, as it becomes spiritualized, as it begins to express itself in its true colour of pristine purity. We should be very careful when using the word 'love' especially in the West, and even avoid using it altogether as much as possible because of the wrong associations it calls up in the minds of others. The love that Christs, Buddhas, Ramakrishnas, etc. mean is very different from what is understood by 'love' by the average persons.

Sri Ramakrishna said: 'If somebody wants to be an obstacle on my spiritual path, am I to listen to him? No! I should rather tear such a person to pieces.'

This attitude you find in Christ too where He speaks: He that loveth father or mother more than me is not worthy of me, and he that loveth son or daughter more than me is not worthy of me. (Mat: 11, 37) 'Whosoever shall do the will of my Father which is in heaven, the same is my brother, and sister, and mother.' (Matt.12.50).

Strength and Manliness

Of the strong, I am strength devoid of desire and attachment. I am desire in beings, unopposed to spiritual life. (Bhagavad Gita VII, 11).

Tremendous will-power, tremendous energy, tremendous and unflinching steadiness are necessary if you want to attain anything on the spiritual path. Unsteady and wavering people who are not prepared to purify their minds, people who do not want to be one-pointed, cannot take to spiritual life in right earnest and have no place in spiritual life. It would be better for them not to think of it even.

'The irresolute ones who sought after children attained death, while the resolute ones who did not seek after children attained immortality.'

Manhood is worth the name to the extent it frees itself from the fetters and limitations of animal nature, and makes progress towards Divinity and real manhood. Real manhood and Divinity are not two essentially separate things. The animal impulses are obstructions in the way of real manhood and are in no way part and parcel of manhood. Most human beings live like animals or even worse than animals, but that does not mean that animal life is part of human life and belong to the human plane. This would be a wholly mistaken notion.

We do not want worms groveling in the dust, but men, real men, men expressing and living their eternal, innate

H 4

Divinity and purity. What we generally call 'men' are not men but helpless slaves to their senses, cravings and impulses. They do not deserve being called 'men'.

Don't be like weather-cocks. Don't begin to dance and to cry. We do not want either. Control all the outer impressions, so that your mind does not react, so that no wave, no ripple, no trace is left in your mind. Never become playthings in the hands of any and every stimulus and any outer events. You can be kind without becoming attached.

Always act in such a way that others don't dare to take advantage of you, don't dare to become familiar with you. Act in such a way that people who are worldly-minded, and of a different temperament, won't be able to bear your presence, and would always avoid you.

The behaviour of the aspirant must always be dignified, keeping people at a distance, without being unkind. Nobody must be allowed to take advantage of you. You must radiate such dignity and purity that worldly people won't dare to have worldly talks in your presence.

Instructions about Food

Food and sex are closely related to each other. Many people do not recognize this fully and think they can have any diet they like without endangering their spiritual development. The aspirant has to find out what kind of food helps him most and what kind of food has a bad effect on him. This means great watchfulness and merciless analysis which may sometimes become very painful to the aspirant. When we dive deep down into our mind, we find many things lying hidden in the remotest and darkest corners which we had never suspected of being there, and which make us shudder. There must be a lot of scrubbing and cleaning and merciless destruction of pet ideas and feelings and desires, before we can proceed on our path towards Reality.

There is this verse:

On the purification of the *ahara* follows the purification of the inner nature; on the purification of inner nature, the memory becomes firm; and on the strengthening of memory follows the loosening of all ties. (Chhandogya Upanishad, 7.26.2)

With reference to *ahara* (food) Sankara says, in his commentary on the above:

'*ahara* (food) is that which is taken in, viz. the experience of sound, etc. etc., which are taken in, for the experience of the agent; and when the cognition of objects becomes free from all taint of aversion, attachment, or delusion, then the 'inner nature' of one having such cognition, becomes pure, free from dirt, clean. When the inner nature has become pure, then follows a firm memory, i.e. uninterrupted remembrance of the Infinite Self. On the acquisition of such memory, comes the 'loosening', destruction, of all ties of evil due to ignorance, which might have been accumulating through the experiences of numerous births, and rebirths, and which have their residence in the heart. Because, one after the other, all this is based upon purity of *ahara* (the food that is taken in), it is this that should be attempted.'

Food is not to be taken literally as you see, but food is any and every impression that comes to you through any one of the senses; and that is why every aspirant must be very careful not to take in unclean food in the way of company, gossiping, reading, and hearing, nothing that can stimulate old tendencies in him. He must avoid all such unclean food scrupulously, making use of his power of discrimination.

It is a great point to note that we must be careful as to what kind of food we allow our senses to take in. If we scrupulously avoid all impure food by being on the alert and exerting our power of discrimination to the utmost, there will be real progress. If we do not do so, stagnation or even retrogression will set in. Only by avoiding all impure food (*ahara*) can we make our whole body and mind stronger and purer. Much more is meant by food than the physical food we take during our meals. If we lack proper discrimination as to what food we allow our senses to take in, there is great danger of slipping our foot and having a nice fall. But very often we mistake the non-essential for the essential and thus go on wasting our forces in vain. Gross minds always take things in a gross sense thus missing their real point.

⑤

Karma Yoga

Unselfish Work

Work done in a selfless spirit cleanses the mind. To the extent that the impurities of the mind are removed, the glory of the Atman in us is manifested. We all work all the time, but there is no visible manifestation of the Self in us, because we do not have the spirit of selflessness in our work. Ignorance covers the atman, and egoism is the result of ignorance. Selfish work increases this egoism and its dualistic manifestation, namely, likes and dislikes (raga-dvesa). Misery increases as they increase. Hence, the root cause of all misery is egoism and selfish work. Such work cannot bring out the glory of atman in us. On the other hand, selfless works purifies the mind, that is, reduces egoism and the desires and in the pure mind the Lord dwells.

The task in spiritual life is to lead a life of selfless activity, of love and purity. These make the mind pure. The path of spiritual progress becomes clear and one is enabled to rise higher and higher. Through spiritual practice we develop the insight to perceive our mind dwelling at different centres corresponding to different planes of consciousness.

While speaking to Vidyasagar, Sri Ramakrishna says that if one could perform work with total detachment and discarding all egoism, then one develops love and devotion to God and in the end attains God. Sincere effort lasting many years is necessary to develop complete detachment as found in the life of king Janaka.

Vidyasagar was a great worker. Seeing the misery around him, he could not say that God was merciful. Swami

Vivekananda too passed through this stage once. They are men with a spirit of enquiry (*jijnasu*). Men like Vivekananda consider that, whether God exists or not, one should work to remove the suffering of the people, Buddhists do not believe in the existence of the God, but they too cannot bear to see people suffering. They serve in a selfless spirit. Men like Swami Vivekananda want to know the nature of God. They want to see and experience God. But ordinary people are pleasure-seekers; they want to make use of God for their material welfare. Swami Vivekananda taught that one should work to alleviate people's suffering and by such selfless work, the path of liberation would be clear. But we have a beggarly mentality, always wanting to get something for nothing. We should always give, expecting nothing in return. It is then that one gets more—this is the secret. There are some who give, but grumble all the time. They curse others or themselves. Of what use is such charity?

Our ideal is not to give up service but to do it along with spiritual practice. There are many who do social service. But as they do not have the spiritual ideal, their activities become egocentric. They become self-seekers. 'Liberation of oneself and welfare of the world'—that should be the ideal.

Spiritual Practice Essential in the Path of Work

The path of work is a recognised means of Self-realisation. A doubt is expressed whether the desired object can be obtained by mere work, and japa and meditation can be absolutely given up. It can be attained provided one works in the proper spirit. But ordinarily it is not possible to maintain that high degree of perfection and selflessness in work and hence spiritual practices are essential. There are many social workers who say they are serving society, but actually they are serving themselves. Buddhists advocate selflessness as a great discipline. This is also advocated by Hinduism. We should note what is meant by working in the proper spirit. In the first place, we should be detached.

Secondly, we should offer the fruits of our work at His feet. There is a stage when the devotee works to please the Lord. If we think of Him while working we will have very good results. Three-fourths of the mind should be devoted to thoughts of the Lord; it is enough if one-fourth is given to work. No one can have full concentration in work. A great part of the energies of the mind remain distracted. Hence it is necessary to remember Him while doing one's work.

Always have an ideal to work for. Then life becomes worth living. We find joy in serving others. That is a sign of improvement. For the worldly-minded, there are various ways of breaking the monotony of life—seeing a new picture, meeting friends, gossiping and so on. Such persons develop a purely material character and acquire evil habits. Instead of this, think noble thoughts, take some time for meditation and do japa. Thus the finite comes in touch with the Infinite. Man gets a taste of real joy. Day by day a higher and higher conception of the deity is reached. One understands that the deity one worships is an aspect of the Supreme and that it is the one Self that shines in all. Play your part in life intelligently and consciously and not mechanically, keeping the Reality always in view. Meditation and spiritual practices are essential in every way. Fulfil your worldly duties, but at least once a day you must get rid of everything and be absorbed in that Infinite Spirit. Otherwise work becomes drudgery and life ceases to have any meaning

Connect All Works with God

Whatever work you do, try to offer it at His feet. This is the first stage. The second stage is: working in order to please God. Going further, you will feel you are an instrument in His hands, His power flowing through you. This body and mind should be employed in doing good works. They react only as long as there is atman in them. Atman is the Lord and the body is His temple. Instead of using it for noble purposes, we give way to its animalistic urges and degrade it. Be sincere and do not waste a moment in idleness. We must daily consider how much time we spend in meditation, prayer, service etc. and how much time in idle thoughts. We should thus train ourselves to spend all our time in noble deeds. Even charity should be practiced with proper attitude. Connect all the work you do with the Lord in some form or other. Do everything for Him. Then you can lead moral and devoted lives. Do all that is expected of you, but the central idea of your thoughts should be about God; great results will follow. There is no miracle or magic in spiritual life; it is very simple. But one must practice.

We must repeat the Holy Name of God dwelling on its meaning. We can do it silently when we are at work; others need not know it. We can think of Him, of His holy attributes. The subconscious mind will always be working. If we watch the mind we find that all our thoughts are centered in I-consciousness. 'I am reading, I am worshipping, I am doing japa, etc.' Thus the mind concentrates on the egocentric I but not on the Lord. Why not work to please the Lord? If we cook, we can think that the cooked food is for offering to the Lord in the form of father, husband, child etc. We study and pass examinations; our purpose is to earn money. That earning is to be used for Him. Thus it is possible to do anything and everything, thinking of Him. Remember the advice of the Lord in the Gita to offer everything, what one eats sacrifices, gives in charity etc. to Him. If we cultivate this habit it is easy to bring the mind under control during japa and meditation. The spirit that everything is Narayana and that we serve Him should be there.

The individual soul ever yearns for the grand union with the Divine. Always feel that you are one with the Cosmic soul. Learn to talk to God. Open your heart to Him. You have to practice the presence of God. You should feel that God is ever with you and that you are in His presence. Our thoughts should surround Him and our actions should be His worship.

Complete Self-surrender Through Karma

Two important lines from Gita mean: 'Giving up all dharma, take refuge in Me alone.' Dharma here means the various rituals and ceremonies. Though the Lord advocates Karma Yoga in the Gita, finally He advises Arjuna to relinquish all dharmas and take refuge at His feet. This is the stage when the devotee wants to be in tune with divine Consciousness and be calm and quiet. There are Karma Yogis who become more and more active when they reach this stage, but they always remain in the realm of the Lord. This is the stage in which the devotee goes beyond dharma and adharma, beyond good and evil. To reach this stage we have to follow the path of dharma. Adharma is to be conquered by dharma. Whatever work we do, the fruits thereof are to be offered to the Lord. This itself is not self-surrender. It is only the means. It lessens selfishness, and a stage comes when the devotee feels that it is the divine Energy (Prana) which is flowing through him. He becomes just an instrument. This happened in the case of Girish Chandra Ghosh. He had tremendous will power, doing whatever he wanted to, not caring for anybody's opinion. He led a fast life. But the same tendency helped him in his spiritual life later on when he followed the spiritual path, never caring for the criticism of the world. He developed a wonderful spirit of faith and self-surrender. He said: 'If I raise my hand, I feel it is not I but the Lord who is doing it.' This is the result of a great deal of practice. The best way for it is *'mamanusmarayudhyacha'*. 'Remember Me and fight.' Remember God and perform your duty. God has given us intellectual power, will power etc. We should make the best use of those powers. Again, the Lord instructs in the Gita that whatever one does, should be offered at His feet (*Yat Karosi* etc.). Each act of ours, meditation, japa, body and soul, all is to be offered to Him.

Those who remember Him while performing their duties are doing meditation. Recall the advice of the Gita:

'Remember Me and fight.' Those who feel by such constant remembrance that they are His instruments cannot do anything wrong. Whatever they undertake is done well. They prepare their mind for higher purposes—they can easily withdraw the mind during meditation.

Some devotees who come to the Ashrama blame the Lord if they fail in any of their undertakings. Is this right? Success depends on past karma and the sraddha of the worker. God should not be blamed for one's failure. On the other hand whatever work we do should be done as service to the Lord. Let this be our prayer:

'Let God, who is the Lord of all sacrifices, be pleased (with my work done as a sacrifice). If He is pleased and satisfied, the whole world would be pleased and satisfied.'

Work and Worship

Some monks raise the question as to how can one devote oneself completely to sadhana when heavy work is placed on their shoulders. If there had not been any responsible work, most of the time would be spent in idleness. This question arises when one does not understand the relation between work and worship. Work done in a right spirit is the worship of the Lord. We should think that man is a veritable symbol of the Lord. We should always try to contact the Cosmic. The divine force is within and without. He is in us and we are in Him. Every act of ours, big or small, is for Him. When we take up any work, three-fourths of the mind should be filled with divine thoughts. Then the result will be wonderful. But we think of many worldly things and the mind gets dispersed; the work also is spoilt. When work is done with full concentration, mental power is gained; our energy is stored. But instead, if we idle our time away, all our mental energy is scattered and we lose thereby. If we do not think of the Lord while we work, we will entertain all kinds of emotions and passions such as fear, jealousy, lust, anger, etc, all the time and energy will thus be wasted.

Thinking of the Lord is also an expression of energy, but thinking of Him, we contact the source of strength and energy itself, and thus we gain.

One finds time for eating, sleeping and other similar needs, but not for spiritual practices! The mind is allowed to wander all the time. Some complain that they cannot do their work properly if they think of the Lord at the same time. That is a false idea. No one uses all his mental powers during work. One part of the mind is filled with work, while another part is allowed to roam. If the mind is made to think of God while working, wonderful results will follow.

Work and worship should go hand in hand. Though one may not precisely practice meditation, one may perform work thinking of the Lord all the time. This would generate purity of mind and enable one to experience the presence of God. Some claim to practice meditation for two hours a day, but it would be worthwhile to enquire what sort of meditation is it. After a few minutes they go to sleep or sit dreaming. This is not meditation. One who works and remembers God at the same time is a better devotee.

Action and prayer should go together. We must get up early in the morning and practice regularly. Spiritual practice should become a part of our daily activities. We may be accustomed to do it at a particular time, but if this is not possible on a busy day, we should do it a little later.

Always analyse your mind—how much energy is usefully spent and how much is wasted. Egocentric activity is always harmful to spirituality for it takes us away from the Lord. Through selfless acts we serve the Lord in others. Work should be done in an organized way. A haphazard attitude is no good. Doing japa and meditation for half an hour a day and then working in a selfish spirit is no good. Through japa we contact the Lord, and through work too we should do so. During japa we must remember that we are contacting the very source of purity, strength, love and bliss and the same attitude should be kept up during work also. If anyone complains that he has no time for japa and meditation on account of heavy work, we can take it as a lie. If we cannot eat at the proper time because of any other work, we do take our food later, when the work is finished. Somehow we find time for food: hunger forces us to do so. If we have real spiritual hunger, we will never say that we have no time for spiritual practices. We gain mental poise when work and worship go hand in hand, and this is helpful for japa and meditation. An idle life is always a waste. During sleep we contact the Cosmic Source unconsciously and feel refreshed physically and mentally as well. If we contact Him consciously during meditation, we will feel the effect all the more. This does not mean that one need not sleep; it is necessary for the body.

Complaining about the environment is of no use. When we fall down, we have to take the support of the ground to rise. Similarly, we have to use our environment to lift ourselves.

Some important questions come up in the course of work. When there are too many things to be done at the same time what should one do? This is a practical question. Make a list of the things to be done, choose that which is most urgent and needs more energy, and do it first. Again, is it proper to give up the righteous path for the sake of success in work? No, never. Success achieved by foul means may be appreciated from a worldly point of view, but it has a very bad effect on our minds and on our spiritual growth. By following the right path we may fail sometimes but it does not matter. Do not condemn yourself nor think too much of yourself.

Grace and Self-effort

Some people blame karma for their misery. But what is karma? The result of your own work done in the past. If you are bound by bad karma, you can also do good karma.

Without wasting any time one should perform good karma to counteract the bad one. New impressions are created by mental and physical actions. They are all hidden in the subconscious mind. Imagine two babies looking alike and brought up together, always smiling and sweet. But when they grow up, one may become a rogue and the other a saint. It is due to the samskaras, the latent impressions in them. These impressions will not be seen outwardly. To keep the mind always steady, sadhana is the best way. Self-effort is absolutely essential. Grace is necessary, but the mind should be first prepared to make use of the Lord's grace or the Guru's grace. When the house is on fire, what is the use of praying for water? One should work and also pray sincerely.

In karma there are various factors which lead to success. Self-effort is one of them. Some may strive their utmost but yet fail; some succeed without much effort. It depends on past karma. That is the second factor. There is Sri Ramakrishna's story of an aspirant practicing 'Shava sadhana'. With great difficulty he had procured a corpse and all the necessary ingredients but the moment he sat down for worship he was killed by a tiger. Another aspirant, who came by, used the opportunity to do the worship and within a short while the Goddess appeared before him. His success, without much effort on his part, was due to his past karma. The grace of God may also be taken as one of the factors. Thus success in any work depends on many factors and since they are not under our control, we should cultivate the spirit of surrendering the fruit of our actions at His feet. The energy we put forth in thinking of the result of work can actually be utilised to immense benefit in doing the work itself. We have to do our part and let God take care of the result.

Our efforts are most important. A man's wife, who was a scholar, had gone out, asking her husband to see to the cooking. Dal was being cooked and the boiling water began to spill out; the fire was about to be extinguished. The husband, not knowing what to do, prayed to the fire-god.

Meanwhile the wife came back and put a few drops of oil into the cooking vessel and it was all right.

Work done in the right spirit purifies the mind and we feel His presence fully in our hearts. That is the state of samadhi. This purity is beyond good and evil. Sri Ramakrishna used to say: 'A master dancer need not follow the rules and regulations of the art. All his steps would be automatically correct. But the beginner has to follow the rules strictly until he attains perfection in the art.' This is the result of constant practice. Striving to one's maximum capacity is necessary. When you have done your best, God comes to your help. That is His grace, without which nothing can be achieved

Whatever you do, do it with your whole mind, consciously and intelligently. Always stress quality more than quantity.

⑥
Preparing for Divine Company

One of the chief characteristics of true bhakti or devotion is that our love for the world and worldly things keeps getting less and less. Whenever we find that in spite of following the spiritual path our attachment is not getting less, our love for the phenomenal world is not decreasing, we should know that there is something seriously wrong with our spiritual practice. Sri Ramakrishna pointed out that *vairagya*, or renunciation, means 'dispassion for the world and love for God.'

You must cultivate more and more the tendency to associate only with good people, with people who are pure-minded, for if you do not consciously avoid impure company, you will be unable to destroy the evil or impure tendencies in your own mind. All impure men and women with whom you associate awaken in you—in a very subtle way—your impure thoughts, either in the form of desire or in the form of disgust, and disgust is only desire with a negative sign. There are many people who say that one must experience all the different experiences of life oneself. But, how do you know what experience you have already had in your previous lives? If you really want to pass through all experiences yourself, then your mind will be so weak and full of ruts in the end that nothing will be possible in spiritual life. In that case you would merely want to offer your dirt and filth to God.

People often find nice theories to justify their own worldly conduct. We turn sceptics because it is comfortable for us to be sceptics, because it justifies our own conduct to some extent. As a result of your worldly conduct your body becomes diseased, your mind weakened, no energy is left for spiritual practices, and what spiritual path could be followed with such a worthless body and such a worthless mind? No, this theory of experience is out-and-out wrong, because very few find their way to spiritual life in this manner. The others become diseased in body and mind and can never regain their energies in this life. Besides, how can you pass through *all* experiences of life yourself?

When you handle a flower to smell it, you press it; then it becomes rotten. And then you dare to offer it to God. If you want to offer body and mind to God, why not do it now? Why offer them when they have become tainted and diseased?

Avoidance of Worldly Thought

The company of bad friends may be given up very easily; we may easily avoid worldly company and worldly talk. But the internal company of our former worldly friends and former impure thoughts is far more troublesome. What to do with them? *They* are the real danger in our spiritual life. First of all, energetically cut yourself away from all old associations and from the sources of the stimuli that tend to awaken your old impure ideas, thoughts, and desires; then, without accumulating fresh dirt, without making new worldly friends, try to clean all corners of your mind. Do away with the old accumulated dirt, that old dirt of ages. Without exercising great discrimination in the company we choose and in our talk and thought, this cleaning process becomes an impossibility, and without this cleaning process no spiritual path can be followed.

Even if we be very careful, we find that in the course of the day we gather at least some dirt—this may be in a very subtle form—some deep impressions that are harmful to spiritual life. Never make light of the company you are in, of the talks you are having. Stop all gossiping, all idle thinking, all random activity. All these are very harmful to the spiritual aspirant. Make it a point to use the utmost discrimination in all this. Do not go and accumulate new dirt through new worldly associations.

In the course of the day you should act in such a manner that you would be able to undo what is done. The whole account is to be altogether squared up so that the balance becomes nil. There should neither be a positive balance nor any negative account. There should be no craving for fresh worldly company and worldly talk. The whole spiritual life lies in this fearless adjustment. Today, all of you have a minus balance; and now, you must earn sufficiently to square up the account. Only then may a new account be opened.

Countering Old Mental Impressions

There are many things that are lying hidden in the corners of the mind, and when we begin stirring them up, they will arise and become very troublesome. You will be astonished to find how much dirt has accumulated in all the nooks and corners of your mind, and what a lot of cleaning is needed before you can successfully proceed on your spiritual path.

Our mind may be likened to a gramophone record with all its lines. Everything is recorded there. But see how small and insignificant the lines look! You would never think that they produce such a noise, that every single note of every single instrument is recorded in them and can be heard. It is the same with our mind. When one comes to have fewer and fewer impressions from outside, when one begins to avoid all dangerous outside stimuli, then this nice music of old impressions goes on and on. But this is an unavoidable stage and must be overcome. After having got rid of the outside stimulus, we should control the inner stimulus, lying hidden in the mind, ever ready to come up. We should stop all the wild thinking of wild thoughts. Very often, if we are not sufficiently introspective, we find that these outside stimuli leave impressions, and at some time or other these impressions which are unknown to us are going to create some serious trouble for us. All these thoughts and pictures arise especially during meditation, and then you must be able to bring very strong and definite counter-thoughts, thoughts that are clearer and stronger, pictures that are more definite than those old impressions rising in your mind. Very often this means tremendous struggle.

The semi-conscious thinking along impure, evil lines is a very dangerous thing and may create great trouble, as it makes the impressions all the more deep and lasting. One day you will realize how true all this is. You should be very very careful about what impressions you allow yourself to take in and what talks you indulge in or listen to. Never think there is no danger in them because you do not feel that any impression is being made. The impression will come up later, and then you will be at a loss what to do with it.

Never dwell on old impressions, on old associations, on old worldly company and thoughts, not even subconsciously or semi-consciously. This is one of the greatest dangers for the spiritual aspirant who really wants to go through the necessary cleaning process. There must be a definite cut, and then: thinking along new lines; new, good associations; new, good, pure thoughts and ideas.

Be as wide awake as possible so as not to take in bad impressions either through the eye, or through the ear; and if you do take them in, root them out immediately. Use your utmost discrimination as to the company you allow yourself to be in and the things you allow yourself to hear.

Our mind is very much like a photographic plate. If we could project what lies hidden in it—one picture after the other—what a nice cinema-show that would make! Everything gets recorded, mercilessly, and very often we would shudder if we could see all that lies hidden in the depths of our mind, all the impressions that are unknown to us, that we have taken in semi-consciously or subconsciously, and that are bound to rise sooner or later during our sadhana.

Purity is the *sine qua non* of all spiritual life, and real bhakti (devotion) can never be had without perfect purity in body and mind. The jnani purifies himself through tremendous self-control, the bhakta by directing all his feelings and passions towards the Lord, making the Lord the only thought of his mind.

You [the aspirants who are seriously committed to the spiritual path] must not allow yourselves to have direct relations with others. Your country and all others may only be loved through God and in God, never in any other manner; otherwise you will entangle yourselves in the meshes of God's maya.

In time you will come to realize the extraordinary usefulness of the personal ideal, the *ishta*, for your sadhana. The advantage of the personal ideal, the *ishta*, is that when the heart longs after a personal relationship, the devotee will not be allured and tempted to descend to the animal plane and to take up false human relationships. Real devotion for the *ishta* always acts as a brake. The *ishta*, as it were, says: 'Look here, you shouldn't be allowed to go down any further!'

First, the Lord watches the aspirant, seeing what he is and what he does. Later, if he finds that the aspirant is worthy of serving as an instrument for his cause, he does everything else. He gets the necessary money and all that is needed for his work. But first the aspirant has to prove his sincerity, purity, and worth. Nobody is allowed to serve Sri Ramakrishna who is not perfectly pure in body and mind, nobody who has got any personal ambition to satisfy. And if he is not pleased, nothing happens—whatever the aspirant may do, or not do.

⑦

Bhakti Yoga

How to Love God without Seeing Him?

Some entertain the doubt as to how one can love God without seeing Him? How can one love an unseen being whose very existence is doubtful? This is an interesting question and seems reasonable. We have cultivated a certain amount of faith in the unseen God, believing the words of those who have experienced His presence, and begun to love Him. Also, there are some children who love God instinctively or unintentionally. Some modern psychologists say that man wants someone to support or love him, just as a child wants its mother and father. But man's need for God is not so simple as that. The eternal soul longs to become one with the eternal God—its source.

There is always a doubt which arises in the mind: 'Since I have not known or seen God, how can I love him?' Latu Maharaj has given a fine answer to this doubt. 'If one has to apply for a job in an office one does it without knowing or seeing the officer. One gets the post if one deserves it. So also, it is not impossible to love God or pray to Him without having seen or known Him.' This doubt is removed if one gets the grace of an illumined Guru. The alternative is, one can locate a person who is proceeding along the spiritual path, progressing in it, and share one's thoughts with him. The Guru removes all the obstacles and doubts and shows the path to the Eternal. One should have intense faith in the words of the Guru and follow his precepts diligently.

Guru

We exist in Him who has become the whole universe. He Himself comes as the Guru. The outside Guru gives the

58

suggestions. To the extent you follow his instructions; you get nearer to the ideal. Sri Ramakrishna used to say: 'The teacher is a broker who arranges negotiations between God and the devotee.' The Lord is the 'Guru' of gurus. Turn to Him for strength, power, purity, knowledge, devotion and everything. Do your spiritual practice regularly. Repeat the name of the Lord—it does not matter even if it is mechanical—and think of His attributes. Think of Him in your idle moments instead of dwelling on worldly things which cause nothing but trouble. Your mind will then become pure and you will reach the goal soon. Divine grace and the Guru's grace are not different. God gives the inspiration for spiritual practice. The Supreme Being manifests in the Guru and guides our understanding. We follow the path.

Preparations

If you want to practice Bhakti Yoga you must have certain prerequisites. Try to be as detached as possible. We waste a good deal of energy in thinking of results; detachment would help us to avoid such wastage. Mind should be calm and pure. The danger in spiritual life is that easily and unknowingly we become selfish and proud. So at the beginning of your prayer salute all the human beings and pray for the welfare of all. This purifies the mind. Nothing can be achieved with a narrow, shrunken mind. People habitually grumble however much they have. Contentment is necessary. With divine Consciousness, we shall open ourselves to Truth. Let not our ego stand between the Truth and ourselves. Then only the Peace which ever flows will enter into us. Try to go deeper and deeper into the Atman. Let us regulate the energy that is flowing through us and thus achieve mental and physical harmony. Then we should meditate with a calm mind and divine joy should be absorbed during meditation. Be prepared to give spiritual dignity to everyone. To the extent the mind becomes pure, to that extent the light shines. When we get a glimpse of something higher, then we come to realise that we are achieving something by our spiritual practice.

Sri Ramakrishna once told a disciple: 'I hold a towel between my face and your eyes. You cannot see my face now, though it is there. When the towel is lowered, you can see my face.' The screen of bad samskaras which we hold in our mind prevents the vision of God. God is ever present in our hearts; His presence does not have to be created afresh. The task is to reduce the thickness of the screen and ultimately eliminate it. As it becomes thinner and thinner, God's presence and grace—the effulgence of the self—will be more and more experienced in the heart. The same Cosmic Energy which supports the universe flows through all of us, but on account of bad samskaras we do not feel it. These bad samskaras can be eliminated by broadening our view of the world, by purifying the mind through sincere spiritual practices.

Seek Holy Company

One should not speak of one's spiritual experiences to a worldly person. If one does so, it may hinder one's spiritual growth. Worldly people may discourage spiritual practice and also create doubts in one's mind. Sometimes we may be proud of our little spiritual experiences and in telling others about them. That also is a hindrance. But if we exchange our experiences with a person of like mind and temperament it may be helpful in promoting our spiritual growth. It is always good to exchange spiritual thoughts with one who has advanced in spiritual life. We can avoid the pitfalls that others have already met. If we have a guide in a strange place, we can avoid unnecessary dangers and difficulties. This is one of the benefits of keeping the company of holy men. In seeking and following their advice, our struggle will be simplified.

If we have no like-minded friends with whom to share our spiritual ideas, we need not feel despondent. Learn to speak to God. Open your mind freely to Him. Speaking to Him is far better than having any other company. Reading books on spiritual themes also is good. Death may come at any moment. Do not enter the other world without any spiritual wealth. If we have to be born again, let us take birth at least with some spiritual capital. We should always be prepared for the call to depart. In our struggle to reach reality, let us hold on to the pillar of God. One should have the self-confidence and faith in oneself to think that 'I can know God. I shall free myself from the wheel of birth and death and be His eternal companion.'

Divine Grace

At times, with a little effort, we feel elevated; at other times any amount of japa and meditation has no elevating effect. The mind itself is the cause of this contradictory experience. The breeze of divine grace is always blowing—we do not have to force it to blow. We complain that we have achieved nothing in spite of long years' struggles. But unless we unfurl the sail, i.e., turn our minds to the divine grace, we cannot get the benefit of the breeze. The mind has to be taught to immerse itself in that flow of grace by reducing the ego. Often we are not aware of the flow of grace at all. This is the biggest obstacle. One prayer taught by Swami Brahmananda was: 'Lord! I know that your grace is flowing on to me. Please bless me to become aware of it.' The sun is always shining; we do not have to force it to shine. But unless we clean the dust from the mirror, the sun's reflection will not be clear in it. Here cleaning the mirror is similar to cleaning the mind. A great deal of effort is needed in this cleaning process.

What is God's grace? There is a stage when one is immersed in worldliness thinking that attaining worldly ends is the supreme goal of life. When one does not find peace in that sort of life, doubts crop up. 'Am I a body made of flesh, bones, etc., or am I a whirlpool of thoughts and emotions? No, there is something in me which is eternal and does not undergo any change amidst all these changes pertaining to the mind and body.' One wants to know that such changelessness exists, and one becomes restless. This restlessness continues until the highest stage is reached. Some spiritual aspirants say: 'Swami, we were at peace before; all that is gone now'! This, in fact, is a good sign. Spiritual life begins with such restlessness, and that itself is God's grace. It is essential to watch whether this restlessness is leading us God wards or not.

Self-surrender

The breeze of divine grace is continuously blowing. Once we unfurl our sails and catch the breeze, our task is very much lightened. But that is not enough. The helmsman should guide the boat in the right direction; otherwise there is the risk of losing direction. Similarly, we should use our discrimination and hold on to the right path. This is quite necessary until we achieve complete self-surrender at His feet. The ego vanishes completely only in samadhi. But we can practice self-surrender in our own way, offering japa and meditation at His feet and praying: 'O Lord! guide our understanding.' That is the best prayer. Without His blessings, how much perfection can we achieve by our effort alone? But how many are willing to surrender themselves in this manner? We want to use God; we do not want Him for His own sake. We pray to Him to remove our misery. We need Him only for our selfish ends.

'Smarane na kalah.' There is no specific time for remembering the Lord. Sincerity is the only essential requirement. We should ask ourselves, 'Since the Lord dwells in me all the time, why should I not think of Him always?' With one part of our mind we want the Lord; with another part of it we don't want Him. The ego stands as a barrier between us and Him. Here comes the question of self-surrender. Swami Turiyanandaji used to tell me that complete self-surrender comes only in the end. Till then we have to act as the Lord advised Arjuna, 'Mamanusmara yudhya cha.' Fight the battle of life and at the same time think of the Divine which is the only Reality behind all names and forms. Strengthen the spiritual thought-currents.

Relation with God

We should have a clear conception of God. He is Bliss Itself. By constantly thinking of Him, we too enjoy Bliss. He is full of Love. He is the Father of the father, Mother of the mother, Friend of friends and Soul of the soul. In such circumstances where is the place for fear or despondency? Even a drop of His Love or Bliss is enough to transform our lives. We should create a loving and close relationship with Him. He is our Father, Mother, Friend and all in all. We will call on him as a child calls on its father. Does a child fear its parent? Or, if we are bold enough, we can think of ourselves as parts of Him and He as the whole. He is pure Consciousness. The Seers of the Upanishads sang: 'You are neither man nor woman nor neuter'; and again they said: 'You are man as well as woman.' His light surrounds us. The body is the temple. He is both inside and outside, all-pervading. This Light has taken the form of the deity and we too are the same Light which has put on a body. Hence we should know that God—Light and Consciousness—is our true self. If we feel that we are anything else, such thoughts should be carefully eliminated. They should be merged and dissolved in that pure Consciousness, the light of the Supreme Self.

God is our beloved Father and we should approach Him with love and trust. Sri Ramakrishna told some Sikh devotees that there was nothing extraordinary in God looking after us since we were all His children. We should have love of God rather than fear of God. The child wants its mother for her own sake; it does not test whether the mother is good or bad. One should think of God in the same way. An attitude of absolute love and trust takes us quickly to Him. The positive attitude of love and trust is better than the negative attitude of fear. Fear is the cause of all bad qualities such as jealousy, doubt, suspicion, anger, hatred etc. By meditating more and more on Him who is purity itself, these lower tendencies disappear gradually. Sometimes we call Him the remover of miseries. Instead of this negative aspect, we should think of Him as Bliss itself, i.e. in His positive aspect. The true dualist who worships the Lord as a master, father, mother or friend, is better than an Advaitist who practices nothing. Advaita is not attained through mere talk.

First of all we should have a clear conception of the God we worship. What is He doing? He is said to be the giver of boons. But though we have been praying for long, He has not heard our prayers. Is He deaf? Can't He speak? Why does He not remove our misery? The reason is: We do japa, we repeat His Name, but our mind wanders elsewhere. So we rarely come into real contact with Him. We are not praying properly. What is the use of such japa? Repeat His Name consciously dwelling on its meaning. We should feel very close to Him. He is not a stranger. He is the Soul of our souls. He is dearer than the dearest. So why fear Him? If we do sincere and regular practice, we will surely find changes taking place in us. All the joy of the world is as nothing, compared to the joy we get through japa and meditation. That is the peace we aim to attain.

Try to love God. Let your heart be filled with His presence. Do not approach Him as a beggar but as a true lover. As you practice, you will find pleasure in meditation and that will make you do it regularly. The day you do not practice you will feel dry. As the body requires food, so does the soul. Meditation is the food of the soul. Meditation awakens the consciousness that 'I am something divine.' The gap between the heart and the head is reduced and harmony develops between the two. This leaves a favourable effect in our practical lives too. When you feel depressed or disturbed, the consciousness that you are an integral part of the Divine, which, you came to sense during your meditation, would give you strength and enthusiasm. It would encourage you to meditate on God and regain that consciousness. The mind should be given proper spiritual education. Give something good and real to your imagination and you will find pleasure. God is Supreme Divinity. Think of Him and feel His presence. He is dearer than the dearest. At least for the time of meditation let your interest be more in God than in worldly things.

Tulasidas said:

Bhaktim prayaccha Raghupungava nirbharam me Kamadi dosha rahitam kuru manasamcha.

'Please give me the fullness of devotion and empty my mind of evils like lust and desires.' The mind can be made devoid of desires by filling it with devotion. It may take time, but this is the only way. No shortcut is possible. Amulets cannot work in spiritual life. Without concentration no one can exist in the world. Give that power of concentration a new channel. A spiritual mood should be maintained throughout the day. Nobody need know it; silently, quietly, we can keep up our higher mood, without any outward show.

Love for the Divine Mother

It is said that Sri Ramakrishna by His worship had awakened Mother Kali in Her image at Dakshineswar. What does it mean? Is it true that the deity sleeps and the worshipper through his worship awakens the deity? When a devotee calls, the Lord manifests Himself through the image or any symbol adopted by the devotee. Sri Ramakrishna, through His loving worship, awakened Kali the Mother, there in Dakshineswar.

We are surrounded by vibrations of the Reality. We do not have to create them. If you are pure and sincere, you can experience them. It is through the will of the deity that the devotee worships the deity. The great philosopher Spinoza said: 'The love with which we love God is given by God.' A little of that love comes to us, but we pollute it. Water may become filthy but you can purify it by distillation. This is the secret and necessity of all sadhana. It is from the Cosmic Source that we get love and faith. With that we worship Him. Once Raja Ram Mohan Roy criticised a devotee: 'You are plucking flowers from the Lord's garden and offering to Him His own flowers —how very ludicrous!' But the devotee replied that he felt an inexpressible joy in offering something to the Lord. The mind is thereby uplifted to a higher plane. The same devotion and love appear as terrible attachment on the lower plane. Behind everything is the unbelievable Lila, the sport of the Lord. He is the deity and He is the devotee. He alone knows the secret of His Lila. Sri Sankara's prayer to the Mother runs thus:

O Mother, You have, for the sake of sport, divided the One Spirit into two, namely, Siva and jiva, and then given the characteristics of a jiva to Siva; and again you convert the jiva into Siva.

This is the sport of God. The impure mind cannot know the I behind 'I am doing', 'I am saying' etc. When you progress in sadhana you will realise that the power and love flowing through the individual are a reflection, a part, of the power and love of God. When we worship God, it is God worshipping Himself.

When great ones come a tremendous energy is created. The Supreme Spirit incarnating Itself is like a dynamo. In course of time the energy is dissipated. The manifestation has lost its power. But the source remains as powerful as ever. Turn to Him, to the Power, from which the manifestation has come. He is the Cosmic Source. Let us worship that divine Power. There is the well-known prayer to the divine Power: '*Ya Devi sarva-bhuteshu,*' etc. It repeatedly emphasizes the Divine present in every being in different forms such as love, faith, strength etc. Let everybody take to the Lord and have their hearts filled with His divine presence, divine love and divine knowledge.

Who is Mother? Is she somewhere outside? She is within us. She is without also. She is all-pervading. Though inseparable from us, She seems far away on account of our mental and physical barrier. Remove the barriers through prayer, japa and meditation. This will help you to attune yourself with the Infinite. We are dirty mirrors which do not reflect light. We have only to clean our mind to get light. The relationship with Mother is very close. Recognise Her. Pray to Her. Be in tune with Her. Then She grants renunciation, love, devotion and all that you wish. By lifting ourselves to the Infinite, we get all that we want. As a result of prayer and self-surrender, joy and peace come. Why does She give us misery? She places two things in front of us and we are free to choose either one or the other. She is Vidya maya and Avidya maya. If we choose vidya, she would give us renunciation, love, devotion and knowledge. If we choose avidya, she would give us the pleasures and pains of the world. For ultimate liberation, we have to adopt vidya and then go beyond that too. She does not want us to be attached to happiness or be terrified by misery. 'When all the heart's desires are burnt, Mother Kali would dance there', as Swami Vivekananda has put it. If you are sincere, something will come out of you. If you are a pleasure-seeker, take the misery too. Do not be afraid of death. Do not cling to life. Accept whatever is given by the Mother. Swami Turiyananda during his last illness, used to sing: 'Mother, you are all auspiciousness.' In spiritual life tremendous tenacity is required. Hold on to the chain of the divine name. Why not be prepared for death and when it comes, smile at it? The Divine Mother is saguna Brahman—Reality with attributes, the power that creates, sustains and dissolves the universe. Again, Mother is the source of Infinite Love and Bliss. A particle of it is seen in earthly relatives. Have Her infinite joy and share it with others. She is there but we close our eyes. Skepticism and doubt are the obstacles in spiritual life. Our approach to the Divine should be two-sided—outer and inner. See the Divine within and also without. Bore holes on both sides. Outside approach is through japa and inside through meditation. Pray and surrender yourself to the Divine at least at that time. Your ego lessens and you will have experience of God.

Love Divine and Human

Turn to the Mother; learn to love everybody with Mother's love, with divine love, not as a beggar but as a giver. We gain much more if we do so. But man, the selfish creature, thinks only of himself; not of giving, but only of getting. Do not think of Sakti only in terms of *srsti*, *sthiti* and *laya*. Think of the Power that comes to us as divine knowledge and devotion. What does the world worship? Power—may be physical, may be economic, moral or spiritual. We want that Power manifested as spirituality: as knowledge, love and devotion. Turn to the original source for harmony and love. Just as the Mother dwells in you, She dwells in all. Think thus, otherwise the love of today will turn to hatred tomorrow. Our love is correlated with hatred. It should be love for love's sake. At least have as little bartering as possible. Then comes a stage when you want to give more than what you get. The highest stage is where one does not think of oneself at all. Sri Ramakrishna found it in Narendra. To teach him, the Master showed complete indifference towards him for a whole month, then asked him one day: 'My boy, why do you come here even though I do not speak to you?' What a tremendous remark Narendra made: 'I love to see you; so I come. I do not come to hear your words!' Ours is all bartering. 'How much can I get in return?' We believe in 'fifty-fifty'. Do you know the story of the '50-50 sausage?' In Germany, there was a hotel famous for sausages of rabbit-flesh preparation. Once a customer found the taste had changed. The Police was called in. The lady hotelkeeper said: 'Sir, what can we do? Rabbit flesh has become rare, so I added a little horsemeat.' 'In what proportion,' asked the Police. She answered: 'Fifty-fifty; one rabbit to one horse!' Our so-called love for others is of the weight of a rabbit, our self-love is of the weight of a horse—fifty-fifty indeed!

Turn to the Infinite Source of Love. We have received a drop of that true Love but it becomes adulterated with selfishness. Purify it. Self-love is in everyone. How to sublimate it? Sublimation is the process of purification. Christians call it purgation. That is our life's task. Don't give up self-love; purify it. Increase your love for God. Then love for others increases automatically. Mother connects us all. We gradually realize that we are souls, parts of the Infinite Spirit. That was the one great panacea that the Great Ones taught us. Increase this sublime love, seek it in others, treat one another with dignity. Think of the spiritual substance in each one. That is common to all of us and is the real connecting bond. Family love or friends love is all selfish. You know the story in the Gospel: A Guru taught his disciple how to test the love of his wife and mother. Taking some medicine given by the Guru the disciple became inert, as if he were dead, but could hear all that was being said around him. His mother and wife were crying. But when the Guru, in the guise of the doctor, proposed to bring the 'dead man' back to life, provided the mother or wife would give her own life, the mother said: 'There are my other sons; they will not allow me to die.' His wife said: 'My children are too young. Who will look after them? I cannot die.' That is family love. Not that it is totally false; but it is limited. Know that it is a drop of that Infinite love. Try to connect it with divine love. After your spiritual practice salute the Lord in your father, mother, relatives, friends and even in those who dislike you. Try to love everybody selflessly. Latu Maharaj (Swami Adbhutananda) said that just as love cannot be expressed in words, so also God cannot be described or explained. Only the lover and the beloved know what love is.

Two Approaches to the Divine

Approach the Infinite from two positions—as a jiva and as Atman. 'I am a soul. I have forgotten my real nature and have become identified with the body and mind and things of the world. In my helplessness I pray to the Infinite Spirit, the Soul of my soul, who has brought this world into being. The Divine Mother has kept me bound here, giving me some toys to play with. I pray that She may take back the toys and give Herself unto me.'

The soul becomes tired of playing with the toys of this world. It yearns to go back to the Lord, the Self, its source. In sleep it does go there but it does not know the fact. The effort in spiritual life is to rest consciously in the Mother's lap. Pray to Him when you are in difficulties. Open yourself to Him and pray sincerely: 'Lord, have mercy! You have been graciously saving many people. Why not me also?' Pray for purity for yourself and pray for His mercy for others too. Be broad-minded. As souls you are all parts of the Infinite Spirit. It is the ego which hides this truth and creates differences. The more you deny the ego, the more light you get. From the point of view of the Atman we are all pure. The same power is working in all of us. Impurity is from the ego, mind and body. Always think of yourself as pure.

The other way is to ever remember that you are the Self. '*Tad Brahma nishkalamaham na cha bhutasamghah*', 'I am the pure, undivided Spirit; not an aggregate of elements.' Pray to the Divine: 'I am of the same nature as You, Mother; enable me to remember this.' Complete self-surrender is a very difficult discipline. One should practice it, like a kitten which depends solely on its mother. It requires great purity of mind. Pray sincerely. Speak to Him with an open heart and pray with a pure mind.

Prayer

We are all the time in the presence of the Divine, the 'wishfulfilling tree'. What are you going to wish for? Coming to this Kalpataru, wish for that which is the highest and permanent. Sri Ramakrishna narrates the story of a man who wished for all kinds of things and at last was eaten up by a tiger. So be careful and ask for something valuable. Pray for divine grace and understanding. The higher and subtler the object of desire, the more difficult it is to get. We are tempted to ask for worldly things but we do not know whether it is good or bad for us. So, if you have to ask for worldly things, let your attitude be: 'Lord, I feel the need for such-and-such a thing. If it is good for me, please grant it; otherwise, please do not. Please guide me along right lines.' It is like the lawyer who after pleading his case leaves everything to the judge's decision. The safest course is to pray for illumination, sympathy, love, wisdom and all the noble qualities required for living a spiritual life. Repeat the Lord's Name at all times.

What is the meaning of prayer? Prayer is based on the fact that there is the cosmic source of all purity, knowledge, power etc. who can be contacted and by such contact the human limitations can be overcome. This is the effort that we make in meditation also. Create a better mood. Be at peace with yourself and with everyone. See the Divine in everyone. Be in tune with the Cosmic source when you feel limited. With an effort of the will, get over your mental obstacles and try to contact the Divine. More energy and more power will flow into you. This is the efficacy of prayer. He is the source of tremendous renunciation, purity, and so on. if the baby goes on crying for its mother, can she stay away from it? It is the same with God and His devotees. Always think of the Mother. If you call with perfect concentration, Mother would appear. She is there already.

⑧
How to Sublimate Our Tendencies

Following the Path Suited to Us

The direct and straight path of renunciation is too difficult for most people, and you should see that you give people an ideal on which they can concentrate their whole feeling and sentiments, because this draws away all energy from the lower centres, the centres of desire and animal procreation. And then their path becomes easier. The direct path without this kind of pure Bhakti is too difficult for most people, as I said; it is too difficult for them to lead a controlled life without an ideal on which to centre their love, thus transmuting their human love which generally seeks some expression on the physical plane into divine love which helps in liberating the human soul from all earthly ties and fetters and all animality. For most people the Bhakti-path is the easiest, because in it there is not so much stress on controlling the senses, only every passion has to be directed towards God. '*If I want to love, let me love God. If I want to steal, let me rob the King's treasure. If I want to hunt, let me hunt the rhinoceros*', as Swamiji used to say. This directing of all one's sentiments and desires towards the Divine is a very important point to note in Bhakti-Yoga.

Since we cannot get rid of our feelings, we must sublimate them, centre them on God, in some relationship or other, best suited to our temperament. Have the love that the worldly man has for his possessions, the love of the chaste wife for her husband, the love of a cow for her calf. Our feelings and sentiments by themselves are not bad, but

72

they must be given a proper direction. The moment they become centred on human idols, they bring misery and bondage for us and for our idol. Sublimation becomes possible because during his sadhana, the true bhakta [devotee] directs all his sentiments and feelings towards the Lord.

Somehow or other our heart must come in touch with the philosopher's stone, and then only even the base metals are converted into pure, unalloyed gold. There is no place for unsublimated feelings in the bhakta's path.

Sankara says: All our tendencies are to be given a higher direction in Bhakti Yoga. Bhakti Yoga does not suppress the tendencies, but directs them all to God.

Iron touched by the philosopher's stone is transformed into gold. The waters of the road being mixed with those of the Ganges become pure. In like manner, O Mother, being attached through devotion to Thee, will not my heart become pure, greatly soiled though it be by many sins?

Narada says: Surrendering all actions to God, lust, anger, pride etc., must be directed towards God. (*Narada Bhakti Sutras*, 65)

If you want to get angry, get angry with things that stand in the way of your spiritual life, or be angry with God. The devotee's method is to give a higher turn to all his passions, to direct all his passions and desires to God, and to the extent he succeeds in doing this, he advances in the path of devotion, he becomes the true bhakta.

The six enemies are: *Lust, anger, greed, infatuation, pride* and *jealousy*. Psychologically they are closely allied. There can never be any anger unless there be some yearning or other.

We crave for human love and union, we crave for human beings to satisfy our selfishness, but the devotee is asked to *crave* for God alone and for union with Him, and he is told that all human relationships are fleeting and turn his mind away from God Who ought to be his only love and Goal.

One embrace of the Lord removes all passion from the heart.

Get *angry* with things that stand in the way of your God-realization. Get angry with God for not removing the obstacles that stand in your way. Instead of having greed for wealth, have *greed* for Him, greed to possess the greatest thing in the world. Be *infatuated* with the glory of the Lord; thinking of the Lord's Glory let the devotee be charmed. There is a Great Enchanter. He draws away from the devotee all charm for the world, for worldly things, for 'Woman and Gold' [meaning lust and greed] in general. Says *Devi Mahatmya:*

Before the Lord's Beauty worldly beauty becomes nothing; wonderful, beautiful forms appear like dead bodies. Think of my Mother, my Mother's Beauty illumines the whole world. See It if you have the eyes to see. A fragment of Thy Beauty makes beauty beautiful. Salutations to the Mother, to Thee Who manifests Thyself as all Beauty, because of Whose Presence the beautiful appears to be beautiful. Salutations, salutations, salutations to Thee!

A little glimpse of this divine charm just brings about perfect self-control in the devotee. Let the divine beauty infatuate us and save us from the infatuation of the world.

Be *proud* of the Lord instead of being proud of anything worldly; be proud of the Lord because in Him you possess the greatest wealth.

Ramprasad [the mystic singer of Bengal] sings:

I have become the Mother's child, O Death, hereafter thou hast no hold on me.

The devotee is asked to direct all feelings of *jealousy* towards the Lord alone. Let him jealously have the Lord before him, and let nothing stand in the way. Let him do away with everything and anything that stands between him and the Lord. Let him do away with all worldly loves and desires, all worldly infatuation so that the Lord alone may live in his heart and fill his whole being. Let him jealously guard his God so that nothing can snatch him away from Him. Let him make it a point not to care for anything else but for God.

If you want to fall in love, *fall in love* with God, but not with any human being.

Ramprasad says in one of his songs:

With great tenderness keep the Mother in thy heart. O my mind, let thee alone see the Mother, Let Her not be seen by anybody else.

There must be this absolute one-pointedness of love in the devotee; every feeling of his must be centred in God, and nothing else must be allowed to attract him and draw away his mind from the Divine.

In this way, through consciously directing all his desires and passions to the Lord, the bhakta's feelings and sentiments become purified and sublimated. In *Srimad Bhagavatam* it is said:

Be it desire or fear or anger or affection or friendship or even the desire for union, when directed towards the Lord, it brings the greatest blessing to the devotee. These bring about his union with the Lord.

The fire and agony of separation burns away all the passions of the devotee, all the allurements and charms of the phenomenal plane. God appears to the devotee, but then He disappears again, as we see in Sri Ramakrishna's sadhana too, and a tremendous agonizing yearning sets in. This is the stage of separation, something like what the Western Mystics call the Dark Night of the Soul.

Divine love, real divine love is something that is all-consuming, something that burns away all baser metals, all worldly attractions, all forms of physical love. [Says Tulasi Das] *Where Rama is, there Kama cannot be; where Kama is, there Rama cannot be.* Rama is God, and Kama is all worldly desires and all forms of greed and lust.

The touch of the Divine brings about a wonderful transformation. Just as in our dreams we think of our beloved, man or woman, the devotee thinks of Him day and night. And if some day he comes to have a touch of his Beloved, all dreams and infatuations fall off from him for good.

Cultivate Purity of Mind

Nobody who clings to his sex-consciousness can attain Him. Sri Chaitanya said, *'He is neither a man, nor am I a woman.'* And in this attitude of the lover towards the beloved there is no trace of sex, so it can only be understood by men who have themselves lost all sex-consciousness. The play of the gopis at Brindavan with Sri Krishna can only be understood by a person who has become perfectly pure.

One day Mira Bai, the great Vaishnava Saint, wanted to speak to a holy man in Brindavan. He sent her the answer, 'I never see the face of a woman.' Whereupon she replied, saying, 'I believed Sri Krishna to be the only man in Brindavan, and am astonished to hear that there is another man living in this place.' Then the holy man thought, 'Who is this person that is able to talk like this?'—and begged her to come. After that they had long talks on God.

Unless all the passions have been burnt away, it is not possible for a devotee to appreciate this attitude, i.e., the idea that God is the Eternal Lover of the human soul. Even in Christian Mysticism you find this attitude in mystics like St. John of the Cross, but he does not dare to express himself clearly as this path is too dangerous for most people. Before anyone can take up and follow this ideal, even the slightest trace of sex-or-body-consciousness must have been destroyed in him. Every other person who tries to follow that path is sure to slip his foot. Sri Krishna advised Uddhava:

The foolish man who, with his vision blinded, is tempted by such illusive creations as women, gold, ornaments, apparel and the like, considering them as objects of

enjoyment, is destroyed, like the moth. (*Uddhava Gita,*
Advaita Ashrama, 3.8)

The clever man should take the essence out of all
sources, from scriptures small as well as great,—like the
bee from flowers.(*ibid,* 3.10)

The wise man should never court the company of
women as if it were death to him; for he would be killed
as is the elephant by other elephants. (*ibid,* 3.14)

Expectation is surely the greatest misery, and the giving
up of all expectations is the greatest bliss.—As Pingala slept
happily, getting rid of the hankering for lovers. (*ibid,* 3.44)

Purity is the *sine qua non* of all spiritual life, and real
Bhakti [devotion] can never be had without perfect purity
in body and mind. The jnani purifies himself through
tremendous self-control, the bhakta by directing all his
feelings and passions towards the Lord, making the Lord the
only thought of his mind.

Sankara says in one of his hymns:

Mother, no desire have I for Liberation nor any
hankering after wealth. Neither do I cherish any yearning for
knowledge, nor a desire for happiness. O Mother Divine, this
only I beg of Thee: May my life pass in reciting Thy Name
and That of Thy Consort.

(*Devyaparadhakshamapana stotra,* 8)

Boldness of Devotees and Jnanis

Prahlada sings:

O Lord, may I think of Thee with that strong love which
the ignorant cherish for the things of the world, and may
such a love never cease to abide in my heart. Lord, should
thousands of births fall to my lot, may I always possess an
unshakable, and unflinching devotion to Thee.

Sri Chaitanya says:

May He embrace me who is fondly attached to His feet, or keeping Himself beyond my vision bruise me or wound me to the core of my heart; or let the Wicked do whatever He likes, yet the beloved Lord of my soul is He alone and none else.

You very often find this disinterested and truly heroic attitude in our great bhaktas. They reject all ideas of give and take, all ideas of bartering and just love the Lord for the Lord's sake, not for the sake of that which they hope to get. The jnani tries to cultivate an attitude of indifference. Real discrimination always implies renunciation and dispassion, disgust for the world. The jnani and the bhakta, both want to avoid the worldliness of the world.

A great Vaishnava saint says:

May I be born even as a worm in the house of those who are attached to the joy of serving Thee, but let me not be born even as the four-faced Brahma in the family of those who are otherwise minded. (*Yamunacharya*)

As I said, such boldness is one of the chief characteristics of the jnanis as well as of the bhaktas, and of everybody who really wants to follow the spiritual life. If you are always in fear, you cannot achieve anything in spiritual life, whatever you may try to do.

The Five Attitudes [Bhavas] in Devotion

There are five attitudes from which the devotee can choose: Try to enter into close relationship with Him as your Father, Friend, Child, Comrade, Beloved, Play-Fellow etc. etc. Yamunacharya says in one of his hymns:

Thou art my father, mother, beloved, son, well-wisher, friend, the Guru of the world and its refuge. I am Thy servant, Thy attendant, Thou art my refuge; in such circumstances I cannot but be a burden on Thee. Thou art my father, Thou art my mother, Thou art my friend, Thou art my comrade, Thou art my knowledge, Thou art my wealth, Thou art my all in all, O God of gods.

The *placid attitude* in which there is very little play of personal attachment to the Lord. The devotee thinks that God is the author of the universe, and he His creature. This is looked upon as the lowest step.

The *attitude of a servant*. Cf. Hanuman's attitude, his infinite love for Rama. Hanuman was all his life a strict and uncompromising brahmacharin, leading a life of perfect chastity. This in itself is a source of great inspiration. Stories are stories, but then what wonderful morals they contain! Brahmacharya [continence] is necessary in spiritual life, even if it is being shown in the example of a monkey. When Rama had given him a beautiful pearl-necklace, he began to break the pearls one by one and to throw them away. Rama said: 'After all, you seem to be only a monkey, treating this beautiful necklace in such manner!' But Hanuman replied: 'No, Sir, I am only breaking every pearl to see whether it contains your picture and that of Sita. If it does not, I throw it away as useless.' Rama replies, 'Is the picture of Rama and Sita in thee, my friend?' Then Hanuman tore open his breast and showed them to their surprise that he carried the picture of Rama and Sita in his heart. You must learn to grasp the real meaning of such traditions.

Stories are stories, as I said, but you must be able to grasp their truths. It is very easy to laugh, but very difficult to understand them in the right way.

There are three more attitudes: The *attitude of a friend*, e.g., Arjuna's love for Sri Krishna; the cowherds' love for Sri Krishna at Brindavan., the *attitude of a parent* towards the Lord as Divine Child, just as Nanda and Yashoda had for Sri Krishna; and the *attitude of the lover* towards the beloved as that of the gopis' love for Sri Krishna.

A personal ideal of God has great advantage. The use of the personal ideal, the Ishtam, is that when the heart longs after a personal relationship, the devotee won't be allured and tempted to descend to the animal plane and to take up false human relationships. This always acts as a brake if there is real devotion for the Ishtam. The Ishtam, as it were, says: 'Look here, you shouldn't be allowed to go down any further!'

In time you will realize the extraordinary usefulness of the Personal Ideal, the Ishtam, during your sadhana period. Even if, for a time, some complex is formed in the aspirant the complex will be gone when his feelings have been sublimated and given the right direction. By satisfying your sensual desires you just form a complex, by not satisfying them you form a complex, so what to do? The only thing is to find out which is the more useful of the two, as a complex cannot be avoided.

9

Meditation Part 1

Four Types of Worship

Different ways of worship are suggested in the scriptures to suit different temperaments. The scriptures are records of the experiences of different sages, who have attained the Supreme, in their spiritual life. Their words therefore represent the voice of God. Thus, it is God Himself who has put before us various ways of worship through the sages and through the scriptures.

'*Prathama pratima puja japastotradi madhyama*
Uttama manasi puja dhyanam uttamottamah'

'Image worship is the primary sadhana, superior to it is recital of the Holy Name and hymns, best is mental worship and the highest is meditation.'

Image worship As we have personality consciousness, first we take the help of the outside symbol in the form of images, photos, etc. The first step is ritualistic worship. We sit before an image and worship it as a symbol of the Supreme.

There is the Kali symbol. Siva lies flat under her feet like a corpse. His power (Shakti or Kali) has come out of Him and remaining on Him performs all actions of the world. She is the cause of creation, sustenance and dissolution of the world. The Purusha, remains immovable and Prakriti, drawing power from Purusha, does everything. This world comprises three gunas: sattva, rajas and tamas; so also does maya. Peace and harmony are the characteristics of sattva. We should always attune ourselves to sattva and be calm and harmonious.

Question: 'Why should we immerse the image of Ganesha after Puja?'

Answer: In tantric worship, we raise the Prana in us. It is raised to the Sahasrara when all differentiation goes and the soul is merged in the universal soul. Differentiation starts when the mind descends to the level of the forehead and is complete at the heart centre. Hence in the heart we meditate on the deity which is an aspect of the Divine. These instructions are given to all during initiation. During Puja we impart Prana to the image or picture as the case may be. After Puja, the Prana is taken back into the heart again and the image becomes lifeless. It is, thereafter immersed in a river or a lake. So the true image is in the heart; only the form is immersed. After the Durga Puja, Mathur did not like to part with the Durga image. So Sri Ramakrishna told him: 'Devi is seated in your heart, worship Her there.' So we worship the Supreme in the form of the Ishta Devata. If we remember this we will not fight about 'our God' being the only real God and 'your God' being inferior God etc.

For us religion has come to mean some external rituals. Do you know why we put sandal paste on the forehead? The centre of the eyebrows is the seat of the jnana chakshu, the eye of divine wisdom. We do namaskara to one another. Now it has become a mechanical custom just like one doll bowing to another one. Actually we salute the Lord in the other. Remember the significance of every custom. Learn to go deeper.

Tirtha-bhranti has two meanings—wandering about the places of pilrimage and maintaining the delusion that it is the most important thing to do. Wandering in the centres of pilgrimage is an elementary sadhana. Some may need it. When people go on a pilgrimage in groups, they usually quarrel among themselves and the pilgrimage is spoiled. Then there are some really great souls who wander from place to place in a spirit of carefree detachment. They are in a class by themselves. The environment has no effect on them. Again, there are beggars who wander about as a matter of habit. When they are tired of a place, they go elsewhere. As Sri Ramakrishna said, we have to create solitude in our own hearts and do sadhana there. It is no use wandering in search of it. The Dharma Vyadha of the Mahabharata is the ideal.

Sri Ramakrishna prayed to the Divine Mother that She might manifest Her glory, not only to Himself but to all that visit Her Shrine. Hence, those who go to that divine spot have a great responsibility. They should not pollute the place with impure thoughts. They should contribute to the holy atmosphere of the temple with their own purity. If you create the right mood, you will be in tune with the atmosphere of the temple. Not only that, you will be contributing something to it. That is why we pray for physical and mental purity before sitting for worship.

Build a Holy Shrine Within

On one occasion, Swami Shivananda spoke highly of the glory of the Belur Math. Many of the direct disciples of Sri Ramakrishna had lived there. It is a holy place with a great spiritual atmosphere. But how many can visit it and how many can live there? No doubt there is a divine manifestation there. But the source is the Supreme Being. Staying at Belur Math, depending on the outer atmosphere,— will that solve our problems? Through japa and meditation you must be able to enter into the realm of spirit. Only then, outside help in the shape of a holy place will be of some use. Otherwise the place will not have any effect on us. Too much dependence on the place is of no use. No doubt, the atmosphere at such places is divine, but unless you attune yourselves properly, you will not perceive it. So, having tasted the joy of the place once, something of the atmosphere must be created within and around you, wherever you may be. We visit shrines, but what can we find there? We have to work within ourselves, create the spiritual atmosphere

within ourselves. For that you must be pure in heart. Go
deeper. Forgetting the Lord within, no amount of other help
will be of any avail. Holy places become holy by the presence
of the devotees. The illumined devotees carry the Lord in
their hearts and they impart spirituality to holy places. We
should reach the Lord within. So, the ideal is to go beyond
desa, kala and nimitta (time, space and causation). If we get
some inspiration from a place and feel too much dependent
on that, we should work ourselves out of that dependence.
For this japa and meditation are necessary. Mahapurush
Maharaj used to say: 'Merge everything into Him including
Belur Math and meditate upon Him.' All holy places are in
our heart. Why? The Lord dwells within. If one feels His
presence within, then that heart becomes a temple. We are
not separate from Him. If we cannot discover the Lord within,
we cannot see Him in temples. Outside temples awaken the
consciousness of the temple inside. Dive deep, you will
get something which you do not get elsewhere. Through
japa and meditation we reach the state of inner spiritual
atmosphere. Awaken that spiritual mood, and then you
may stay at any place. Through spiritual practice, reach that
holy Benares within you.

Japa and chanting of hymns The next step is worship
by japa, stotra and prayer. Here we worship the Lord with
a sound-symbol, i.e., mantra. At that stage we do not need
any gross symbol, a picture or an image, before us. Sound
symbol leaves an idea in the mind. We meditate on the
luminous form of our Ishtam in our hearts and repeat the
mantra. We give up the gross material symbol and take up
the subtle sound symbol, i.e., the mantra. We should always
be conscious of the meaning of the mantra. Otherwise mere
mechanical repetition will be like the work of a gramophone—
it repeats sacred songs any number of times, yet it does not
realise God! Of course, in the case of the divine name, even
mechanical repetition has some effect. One should at least
have the genuine feeling that the mantra is a symbol of the
Divine.

The third stage is **meditation**. Here we do not need either the picture before us or the sound symbol. Thoughts flow towards God all the time. One would always feel the living presence of the Divine in one's mind. Even the mantra, the sound symbol, disappears and only consciousness of the divine presence remains.

At the third stage, we think of the Lord. Think that you are sitting face to face with deity, your Ishtam, the Supreme Spirit or the Infinite Light or the Atman having a form. The various forms like Siva, Vishnu, etc. have come out of the same Spirit. So, really the Ishtam of all of us is the same. Imagine true things, as Swami Vivekananda said. Imagine that ananda and consciousness appear in the form of flashes of light. Guru Maharaj had a vision of that sort. Instead of imagining morbid things or building castles in the air or thinking of utterly non-existent things like a hare with horns, dream true dreams which will uplift you.

The highest stage is when one feels the unity of the Atman with Brahman. There is no feeling of separateness. This is the stage of realization of the Infinite. Feeling the all-pervading oneness in meditation is the highest. Thinking of the top when we are on the first rung of the ladder is not good.

These are the four stages through which an aspirant passes in his spiritual life. First we should know at what stage we stand and then proceed to the next stage. If one is qualified only for the first stage, he should not hurry up and straightway try to jump to the last stage. That would bring about very bad results. If we want to reach the roof of a house, we should climb the staircase step by step. Trying to jump to the roof in a single leap will only result in broken limbs ! For the beginner, worship of the image with flowers, perfume, sandal paste, etc., will give great joy and create a taste for japa. Japa leads to meditation, and the Divine Himself will help him further.

The Maitreyi Upanishad tells us:

'*Contemplation of the principle is the best, contemplation of scriptural truths comes next; still lower is the repetition of a mantra; and roaming about in places of pilgrimage is the lowest.*'

The highest sadhana is to feel and experience one's identity with the Supreme. Contemplating on that Reality and meditating on the Truths of the scriptures come next. Mantra-japa means choosing a particular form of God as one's Ishta, and repeating the mantra of that deity.

Just because experiencing one's identity with the Supreme is the highest state, most people cannot start with the thought: 'I am Brahman.' They may have to pass through the three earlier stages. But after undergoing all spiritual disciplines, a stage comes when one wants to feel and experience one's identity with the Supreme. There is a verse in Sri Sankara's *Kashi-panchaka:* 'The body is the city of Kasi and the discriminative knowledge flowing through it is the Ganga. Gaya is faith and devotion. Prayaga is the Yoga of meditation on the holy feet of the Guru. Why so? Because by that, the devotee, the Guru and the Ishta become one. In fact, the self of the devotee, the Guru and the Ishta are not different. Meditation on the Guru's feet reveals this truth. Hence it is Prayaga where the three holy rivers meet. The Supreme Consciousness, which is our inner Self and Witness is Visvesvara, the Lord of Kasi. This consciousness is not different in different individuals. It is the witness of the mind and Buddhi in all beings. Thus when all the holy places exist in myself, what other holy place does exist? Why should I go in search of holy places?' Of course, some do attain a sudden transformation in some holy places. It happened to Sri Chaitanya in Gaya. Recall the example given by Sri Ramakrishna: A spring is blocked by a stone. Accidentally someone removes that stone and the water gushes out. Consciousness of the Self is like a hidden spring in us. When the obstruction of the ego is removed, It manifests Itself. When the ego disappears, all names and forms too disappear.

Thus whatever you want is available in this small body. You have only to manifest it. Some aspirants wish to retire to lonely spots for sadhana. One disciple wanted to give up his work and go away in this manner, sometime ago. Now he says; 'Now there is no such hankering. I do not feel the need for any change of environment. For me longing for solitude is gone now.' He had now become established in japa and meditation.

Preparations for Meditation

The best time for japa is the early morning hours or the hours before that. Once you begin the day and start dealing with people, distraction in the form of worldly thoughts would arise in the mind. Hence before that, the mind should be led to the presence of God by japa and meditation and merged in holy thoughts and experience of His presence. Similarly, before commencing japa it is advisable to repeat a few devotional verses to create the proper mood. Regular rhythmic breathing also helps much. One should sit firm and straight in a comfortable posture. Then it would be easy to keep the mind fixed at a spot. It is harmful to attempt meditation sitting in a bent posture.

Before starting meditation, a spiritual mood should be created by reading holy books. Counting beads will help concentration. In the beginning one should meditate on the Ishtam alone. When one is established in meditation, after a spell of meditation on the Ishtam, one should meditate on the divine light in which the deity and the devotee should be merged. This latter process should, however, not be attempted by the beginners.

Before you meditate, think of Sri Ramakrishna and seek His blessings. Whoever be your chosen deity, Sri Ramakrishna would help you in your sadhana. He Himself has given this assurance. He was always immersed in that Infinite Consciousness from which all the divine forms arise.

H 7

Remembering Him, the mind gets a direct opening to enter into the realm of the Divine.

The question is asked: 'Is it necessary to give importance to external observances, such as taking a bath before meditation?' External observances are helpful for creating the mood, but should not be given too much importance. If it is possible to take one's bath before meditation, so much the better. If not, one should not worry about it. External cleanliness should help to create a feeling of internal purity. Thus, it is good to put on washed clothes before sitting down for prayers. All the instructions connected with japa and meditations are meant to create a proper mental disposition and to promote concentration by reducing distractions.

It is good to sit for a while on the seat after meditation and think about the object of meditation. Then we should recite prayers and hymns suited to our line of meditation so as to intensify and stabilize the meditative mood and inner joy. Even after leaving the seat we should not talk to anyone but rather be contemplative and remain by ourselves for some time. Such practice fosters a continuous undercurrent of meditation, helping one to keep the mind on a high level, bringing great joy to the heart. Constant repetition of the mantra results in the repetition taking place even unconsciously. Constant practice is essential, it must be done. It is no use simply hearing instructions.

These spiritual practices should be carried on step by step following the advice of the teacher or else the result will be disastrous. If someone not established in moral and ethical values suddenly takes to yoga and tries to be an adept overnight, the result would be nervous breakdown and disease. Those who preach should practice first. Charity begins at home, i.e. with oneself. Before proceeding to advise others one should carefully examine whether one's own life corresponds to the truth one wants to preach.

The centre of concentration may be either the heart or the space between the eyebrows. But it should not be changed frequently. The heart is the better place for beginners. The time for meditation should be fixed just as the time of eating is fixed. At the fixed meal time, the mind and body will be eager for food. If on any day we are late for the meals, the gastric juices would already have been secreted and indigestion follows. Similarly when we have a fixed time for meditation, body and mind would be in a receptive state during that hour. If the time of meditation is often changed, we have to struggle a little more to calm the mind. Once Swami Saradananda, after his evening meditation, said in a highly spiritual mood; 'Night is the ideal time for meditation. Meditation and japa should be performed regularly with great devotion. They purify the mind.' For some people it is not possible to meditate in the night in the beginning. Early morning is best suited for most. Evenings also are good for meditation.

Role of Pranayama and Asanas

Question: Do Pranayama and Asana help in controlling the mind?

Answer: Rhythmic breathing quitens the mind; correct posture also helps. But more important is to cultivate love for the Lord. The more you love God, the more will the mind come under control. We should have a clear conception of God. The mantra is the Lord's Name representing some aspects of His, the Creator, the Preserver or Destroyer. Never forget that the form of the Ishtam is only one aspect of the Supreme. Clinging to personality may be necessary in the beginning but remaining all the while like that is not good. We must always think of the Infinite behind it. So we proceed from the image to the mantra, then to mental worship. Here we get the idea of the Lord and think of Him. When we proceed further we cease thinking of Him but feel His Presence. In the highest stage there is no differentiation. One Consciousness will prevail. In that state Sri Ramakrishna said: 'Whom shall I meditate upon?' But that is the highest stage of realization. Even bodily sensations are lost. A doctor actually put his finger in Sri Ramakrishna's eye when he was in samadhi; but there was no reaction.

In the sitting posture we feel relaxed bodily, and that has some effect on the mind. When we lie down we feel greater relaxation, but as a result, we may fall asleep. Therefore the sitting posture is advocated. Pranayama means regulating the breath. If we observe it, we find that when our mind is disturbed our breathing becomes irregular. In deep meditation, breath becomes very thin and it actually stops in samadhi. When Sri Ramakrishna was in samadhi, his breathing would stop, but nothing happened to Him. So one does not have to strain oneself to stop the breath by exercises of Pranayama. The best means of controlling the mind is to have Love for God. Pranayama and Asanas may help in meditation but are not as essential as a peaceful mind.

The Upanishads contain the story of a dispute between the senses and the prana as to who was more important in maintaining the body. The body was only partially affected when each of the senses indulged in non-co-operation. But when prana started to depart from the body, then the entire body and all the senses were rendered helpless. The body, senses and the mind should be kept in a harmonious, efficient state. Then only one can attempt to calm down the mind and concentrate it on the spiritual ideal.

There are some yogis who practice hatha-yoga so that they might attain longevity and practice sadhana. Sri Ramakrishna practiced hatha-yoga for some time. When superconscious experiences occur during sadhana, the body nerves cannot stand the upheaval if they are not strong and harmonious. Even Swami Vivekananda, whose mind was strong, could not stand the first experience and cried 'Oh what are you doing! I have my parents at home...!' Then, what to say of us? But the Hatha-yogis in course of time become body-minded and fall from the path. There are others who leave nature to take its own course. They want to forget their personality. What personality have you got so that you have to forget it? When the body becomes weak, the mind too becomes weak. Can this weak mind forget itself or the body? The body is to be cared for. *Sariramadyam khalu dharmasadhanam.* The body is to be kept healthy so that it would not stand in the way of spiritual practices. That is the middle path. We forget our body best when it is healthy; hence the necessity to make it healthy and harmonious.

The Aadhara Chakras and Secret of Sadhana

There are pearls on the sea-bed. Some shells contain pearls, but not all of them. Be like that oyster which receives a drop of the rain falling when the star Svati is in the ascendant, dives to the depth of the ocean and produces the pearl. What does this 'diving' mean? It is to go deep within your mind, away from the body, senses and ego. Now, especially in the Tantras, as also in other paths, we are asked to meditate in the lotus of the heart. It is the easiest place to approach. The body is a remarkable thing. It contains all that is required to take us to the final goal. There is a grand meditation in the Tantra: Rise from the lowest centre and then go up through the navel, heart, throat, centre of the eyebrows, etc., and rise even above that. Now we come to the highest chakra, the centre of consciousness, the Sahasrara in the brain. There you meditate on the Supreme Being, on the Great Light. Merging yourself in your inner consciousness, you have to come to that highest state. There the union of the jivatman with the Paramatman takes place.

This is the reversal of the process by which it had come down from the sublime heights and got mixed up with matter. It had come down by the central spiritual channel, the Sushumna, and lost its way. Now, the entrance to the central channel remains closed and all the activities of consciousness are taking place through the two side channels, the Ida and the Pingala. The yogi's way is through the Sushumna channel. One cannot enter it unless one is established in purity and controls the senses. So what can the ordinary person do? If the electric lift is closed, you must use the ordinary staircase. If you can discover this electric lift, the Sushumna passage, your spiritual ascent will be very fast. Till then you have to go up the hard way. Climb along the staircase, come to the landing of the heart and there discover the electric lift. Purity and moral disciplines like truth, non-violence etc. are the means. Practice all these virtues. You will get an inner vision with the help of which you will discover this electric lift. The higher we go, the greater is the expansiveness. In the lower centers it is all darkness. There is no difference between human beings and animals in the life centered in the lower centers. Go higher and higher, and you will get more and more light.

While meditating, one is usually asked to contemplate on certain mystic centers in the body described as chakra or lotuses. Each has its distinct colour, specific number of petals etc. The Guru sometimes instructs the disciple to think of a twelve-petalled lotus in the heart and to imagine that the chosen deity is seated thereon. Similarly, it is usually said that the Supreme Guru is seated in the thousand-petalled lotus in the head. These concepts are useful in meditation. But we need not unduly concern ourselves with the colour, number of petals etc., of these lotuses. The grandest form of meditation is that on the all-pervading Light, of which our individual souls are a part. We are like small spheres of light in an ocean of light, which have put on a subtle body and a gross body. The basic cause of all movements in the universe is the Cosmic Mind. The universe is created by It and every action is controlled by It. We individuals cannot create or do anything without Its will. The aadhara chakras are different planes of consciousness. The mind is ever moving up and down among them. While engaged in worldly affairs it remains in the lower centers. It is elevated to the higher centers by spiritual practices and holy thoughts. Close observation would reveal the mind's somersaults and rapid movements among different centers. These movements control our moods. Spiritual practice consists in reducing the wayward movements of the mind, raising it gradually to the higher centers and maintaining it there. We should cultivate harmony in us and always be calm.

There are six chakras (vital centers) in our body. The animal qualities in us arise through the functioning of the three lower chakras, i.e., those at the navel and below it. The fourth chakra is in the heart. The beginner should meditate in the heart. Consciousness is aroused after regular practice of meditation in the heart for a considerable length of time and then the devotee meditates on the sixth centre, i.e., between the eyebrows. This is a higher stage in spiritual life.

Base desires arise when the mind wanders in the lower centers. Religion begins from the heart centre. If the mind is made to think or dwell on holy and elevating things, it comes to the heart and upper centers. Low thoughts should be replaced by good ones.

The mind is restless. Some days we are in a spiritual mood. At some other times we give ourselves away to the lower passions. These variations are caused by the mind's movement from one plane of consciousness (chakra) to another. This restlessness vanishes when consciousness merges into the Sahasrara, the thousand-petalled lotus in the brain. Then the mind will not wish to come back. There one realises that the outside universe is pervaded by the Cosmic Presence and that outside universe will be realised inside at this stage. The external temples are for the beginners, and are only the symbols of the greatest temple of God, that is, the body.

There is a divine eye in the centre between the eyebrows. When it is opened, the aspirant will be immersed in Bliss. This joy cannot be expressed or explained in words. It should be experienced. We should always be thinking that we are part of the Cosmic Existence. We live in Him and

He lives in our hearts. We are always blessed by His Presence in our body-temple. With this thought, we should perform our japa and meditation and do all our duties. This is the greatest advice one can give.

There are some psychological, physical and spiritual aspects about the six chakras. Sometimes our heart beats fast—this may be due to purely psychological reasons. We feel some pain in our heart or head due to purely physical reasons. We may feel inexpressible joy—a spiritual joy. A devotee in the West felt some pain in his spinal cord, and said that his Kundalini had arisen! I asked him not to mistake either physical or psychological experiences for spiritual experiences. A spiritual experience is entirely of a different order. Its bliss cannot be expressed.

Kundalini

There is a Bengali song:

'Stay by thyself, O my mind!
Why wander here and there?
Look within—in the inner chamber of the heart
There will be found whatever thou wishest.
He, the invaluable Philosopher's stone,
Can fulfil thy most cherished desires.
Thou knowest not, O mind,
What treasures lie strewn
At the entrance of the Mansion of the Lord!'

The last three lines of song contain a profound truth: 'At His door everything is available—enjoyment, liberation and even the knowledge of Brahman.' When once out of compassion He opens the gate and awakens the Kundalini— the latent spiritual power—you realize that everything is Brahman. But nothing can be achieved without the awakening of the Kundalini, through His grace. This power lies at the bottom of the spinal column, i.e. the Muladhara.

The central passage (Sushumna) is closed and the side passages (Ida and Pingala) are open. Nervous energy normally flows through them. Unless it is made to flow through Sushumna, no spiritual awakening is possible. The Tamasic and Rajasic actions are performed when the energy flows through the side channels. The flow of the energy through the central passage is related to the dominance of the Sattvic mood. It is therefore very necessary to maintain the Sattvic mood. When the energy rises to the heart centre, the devotee feels the presence of God in him but also feels the difference between himself and the deity. When it rises to the centre between the eyebrows, the devotee will have the consciousness that he and the deity have come from the same whole and with the further ascent of the energy to the crown of the head he gets the experience of non-duality.

All our energy is spent in futile ways. The mind is filled with thoughts of greed, lust, anger, fear, doubt, etc. This is all wastage of energy. Thus there is no energy left to flow upward through the Sushumna. When all the taps in the ground floor of a building are opened and water is let out, it will not ascend to the first floor. So moral practices are needed to help to store the energy in the Muladhara and then the gate of the Sushumna is to be opened by meditation or other yogic practices. Control of the mind is essential. To control the mind, some breathing exercises are usually suggested. Generally breathing takes places only through one of the nostrils. When we breathe through both nostrils our mind becomes still. It helps to create the vacuum which is to be filled with holy thoughts and holy form. The body must be kept healthy i.e. it should be harmonious in order to carry on spiritual practices. It should be strong. By this we do not mean the strength of a bull. The nervous system should be pure and strong and the body should be healthy. If we have a headache or a pain in the back, we cannot meditate. Physical ailments can sometimes be ignored, but it is the mind that creates the greatest and subtlest problems, and we must struggle constantly to bring it under control. The repetition of the Holy Name is the only way. It is infinitely powerful as it is the direct manifestation of God.

Raising the Kundalini by the power of the will needs tremendous inward discipline and, therefore, is very difficult. Japa and meditation would awaken the Kundalini in due course. So we are advised to imagine the Lord as seated in the heart, and to meditate on Him, thinking of His noble qualities. This is the easiest way and the best one. We awaken the heart-centre and then proceed to higher stages. A great deal of imagination is required in the beginning as the mind has to be encouraged to think in unfamiliar directions. It has mistaken the unreal for the real and the appearances to be true. We depend upon so many persons all through our lives and have not learnt to depend solely upon God. That is a pity! Unreal things have become real for us and the only Real Thing has become unreal! The Power by virtue of which unreal things appear as real has been forgotten and uncared for. To feel and experience the Reality is the task, and that is religion. Sri Ramakrishna used to sing the song; '*Jago Ma Kula Kundalini*' (Wake up, Mother Kundalini). Swami Vivekananda used to say that with the advent of Sri Ramakrishna, the Universal Kundalini has awakened. So we see the symptoms of a great spiritual upsurge everywhere.

A man went to a Sufi Saint, asking him for the pearl that the latter possessed: 'Let me have the pearl. Give it to me or let me pay for it any sum you would fix for it.' The saint replied: 'I cannot give it to you free, and you do not have the money to pay for it.' The value of God, of devotion, cannot be fixed—we must pay the price through sadhana. To get the pearl, the way is to dive deep in the mind.

10

Meditation Part 2

Japa

The divine name has tremendous power. How to believe this? How do we believe that such a small banyan seed contains such a big tree? Yet, it is a fact.

We take up a name as His symbol and by means of japa try to realise His presence. Patanjali says: '*tajjapah tadartha bhavanam.*' While repeating His Name, we should think of His noble attributes—infinite Love and infinite Bliss. Mere repetition is not of much use, though it has its own effect on the mind. '*Artha bhavanam*' is very essential. Counting the beads only 108 times or doing japa for 15 minutes a day is not enough for spiritual aspirants. The time devoted to it should be increased day by day. We should be able to experience the love and bliss of God during japa and meditation. And we should continue to have the same blissful mood even afterwards. If the japa became deep enough and the mind attains purity and elevation, experience of love and bliss will certainly follow. We should fill all our idle moments with His thoughts and repeat His Holy Name many times. A Dutch woman asked me why we should repeat the Holy Name so many times. I asked her: 'How many times do you think of worldly things in a day?' That, she said, she was doing all the time! So there is the need for doing japa and maintaining the stream of God-consciousness the whole day.

How many times should one repeat the Holy Name? In a way it is good to fix a number, as the mind may deceive us and try to escape from the daily exercise. We should try to remember Him as many times as possible. We keep on thinking all the time of useless things of the world; why not think of the Lord instead? If the mind is lazy, or is too disturbed during japa and meditation, it may need firm handling or a little force to continue with the practices. But one should not do this to the breaking point. Fill up idle moments with His thoughts, and visualise His attributes of love, bliss etc. The Lord's Name should be repeated as often as you can. You do not put your whole mind in the work you do. The mind wanders about in so many directions, thinking unwholesome thoughts; instead, let us think of the Lord and repeat His Name.

A mantra becomes 'alive' (conscious) when we repeat it a lakh of times a day. One should repeat it at least 108 times a day. You may repeat a mantra a thousand times, but it may hit the mark only once. The utterance of the mantra in the proper spirit even once purifies the mind. Instantly the mind becomes delighted and blissful. If we practice regularly everything will become clear. We should repeat the mantra at least 2000 times a day at first, increasing the number slowly.

In the beginning you have to draw your mind again and again towards God. These efforts are like putting dots in a line. Initially, the gap between the dots would be big. Gradually they should come nearer and nearer to one another and then become a continuous straight line. The mind, which till then was touching God at intervals, now flows to Him like a continuous stream. This is how japa leads to meditation and samadhi. As your interest increases and practice becomes perfect you can maintain this contact with God even in disturbing environment.

Control the Mind with the Help of God's Name:

The mind is always dominated by one of the three gunas—tamas, rajas and sattva. Either we are dull (tamas) or we are restless for work (rajas). Rarely we are in a peaceful and joyful mood (sattva). Our effort should be to remain in the sattvika mood as much as possible but the mind will not oblige us. It is difficult to make a frontal attack on the mind and forcibly control it; the better means is to try to pacify it and elevate it with the help of God's Name. The mantra should be repeated regularly, following instructions fully. It is no use telling beads as if it were drudgery. Japa should not be done like a day-labourer doing his labour. Whenever not watched, he will idle away his time. That is no way for doing spiritual practices. There should be an immense hunger for it.

The divine name represents the divine Personality. Think that He is everywhere and in everything. Repeat the mantra, understanding its meaning. We should be clear about certain basic facts in meditation. It is the Formless alone that assumes forms and comes to us as divine incarnations. The different methods of meditation depend upon the aptitude and stage of spiritual evolution of the aspirant. A little devotion is necessary We then will feel strength and joy through the repetition of the mantra, obstructions will be removed and a new consciousness will be awakened. Harmony is established in the mind and there by the body too will improve. A new consciousness awakens and you feel: 'I am not the body, nor thoughts, nor emotions: I am something that does not change.' The Self is blissful. As one is established in meditation, that bliss is imparted to the mind. Then, meditation, which appears dry and tedious in the beginning, becomes easy and joyful. He is infinite love and bliss unmixed.

Power of Mantra

It is commonly stated that by repeating the name of the Lord desires will be eliminated. Is it really so? Though we repeat His Name, our desires do not disappear because we do not know the proper way to repeat His Name. We do not have faith in His Name. Sri Ramakrishna said: 'If you stand under a tree and clap your hands, immediately the birds will take to wings. Similarly, japa will drive away sins.' Clapping hands is repeating the Lord's Name. If it is done frequently and with faith, the birds of desire will certainly fly away. The mantra can work miracles. Dwell on the meaning while repeating it. OM represents the all-pervading Spirit—It is Bliss Itself. If you can imagine it and experience it, then it is wonderful. But it may not be possible for all to take up this worship of the Impersonal.

Beginners have to take up the worship of a deity. The mantra, for instance, may represent the aspect of Love. The deity is thought of as the embodiment of Infinite Love. In these mantras, first there is the word OM, then words like Radhakantaya, Ramakrishnaya, Sambhave, etc. and lastly comes the word *namah*. In this process, we think of the all-pervading spirit, then the particular aspect of the deity who is the manifestation of the Infinite Spirit and then we offer ourselves at the feet of the deity. The word *namah* may sometimes come in the middle too. Whenever we pronounce it, we must feel that we offer our mind, body and soul at His feet. To use psychological terms, we must repeat His Name consciously.

The power of the sound is immense. Thoughts are subtle sounds. Personalities appear in our mind while we think of them. Sound leaves a very great impression on our minds. When people scold us we get angry. Again when others praise us we feel happy. In an uncontrolled mind, a lot of energy is wasted by all sorts of thoughts which appear and disappear. Human cats and human dogs pass through our minds. These thoughts should be replaced by holy ones 'vitarka-badhane pratipaksha bhavanam'. That is, evil thoughts should be counteracted by good thoughts. So, when you are disturbed or agitated, you may repeat the mantra or recite some holy verses of prayer. Instead of concentrating on various distracting and disturbing pictures, why not think of the blissful and conscious form of the deity?

Ishta devata should be perceived all the time. Swami Brahmananda had said 'Think of your Ishta devata as blissful and conscious. Then your very nerves will react to the sound and form.' By thinking thus, the mind becomes calm and quiet. The nerves receive new energy. We feel expanded and joyful. The deity should not be thought of as a two-dimensional picture. He is the very embodiment of consciousness and bliss and the image in the mind should be a three-dimensional one. The Ishtam is full of bliss. Look at the divine smile on Sri Ramakrishna's face or on Sri Krishna's face. Think of them as living persons and feel their bliss. When you are under the sway of passions like anger, lust, etc., or when feeling miserable, repeat the Lord's Name and watch what a tremendous change takes place. Repeating the Lord's Name means all this. Swami Yogananda told Sri Ramakrishna that now and then lustful desires cropped up in his mind. The remedy suggested was repetition of His Name. Swami Yogananda used to say later that the mantra had worked miracles.

Constant remembrance of God is necessary and japa is the best means for that. How to practice japa? Should you shout and take the life out of Him? Mental japa is the best. If you cannot concentrate without beads, use a rosary. Each time you touch a bead, the mind gets a vibration. The power of the touch brings the mind to concentration. Then comes a time when we can do without outside help. A little taste for the divine name is created. What counts is devotion. If He is 'the Ear of the ear' as declared by the Upanishads, can He not hear our mental call to Him? Call sincerely. A lukewarm spirit will not succeed. You should not have a trader's attitude towards Him. If you can call on Him sincerely even once, it has the power of awakening, creating a spiritual wave. That counteracts all worldly waves. Worldly sounds, thoughts and emotions are counteracted by divine sounds, thoughts and emotions. So a time will come when the mind will feel spiritual hunger. When it comes, we cannot but respond. A real appetite is created for the divine name and by taking spiritual food, body, mind and soul are nourished.

Repeat the mantra with great devotion. It is not the quantity of japa that counts, but the quality. It awakens a

new Consciousness. Create the mood for japa. Don't allow
the mind to dwell on useless things. Repeating the Name at
all times is the best means for that. You must stop the
wanderings of the mind as much as possible. That is the
secret of spiritual growth. The energy is being diffused and
wasted. It should be conserved and then the mind will go
up. Hold on to the 'name' and the 'form'. That helps you
to remain alert and prevents your falling into sleep. Tell your
mind: 'I refuse to let you roam about, am determined that
you are to have only one thought—that of my Ishta.'

Concentrated japa is a great strain. But don't give it up
on that account. Sit in a proper posture, relax the body and
nerves by a few deep breaths, salute all gods and goddesses,
pray for your own welfare and that of all others and then
try to rise to the level of the Divine. Thus you get the proper
mood. But don't give up japa for want of the mood. The
mind is simply deceiving you. Have a clear conception of
the deity. What is your relationship to Him? Is He a stranger,
a God of anger and revenge, ever ready to punish me? Then
I cannot have a loving relationship with Him. He is the soul
of my soul, the nearest and dearest one. He is very close
to me—He is the Eye of my eye, the Breath of my breath.
He is in my mind, in my Buddhi, in my understanding. Feel
that He is very close to you. Tell yourself: 'I am meditating
on someone who is very near and dear to me.' Meditate on
His form, think of His noble attributes and then feel His
infinite Consciousness. Identify your own consciousness with
His infinite Consciousness. This is how the bubble, attaching
itself to a big wave, can find its identity with the ocean.

There is another method: Enter the sanctuary of
the heart and feel the consciousness there. The heart
may not respond immediately, but apply all your power of
concentration and then it will. Imagine that the Infinite has
taken the form of the deity in your heart. Imagine that you
have put on a pure, luminous mental body and a physical
body. Meditate on Him for a while, repeating the mantra.
You are a part of the deity whom you worship. You are a

soul, a part of the infinite Self. Now merge your deity, the name and form, in the divine light that pervades your heart. Merge yourself, your name and form, in that Light. Now only the Light remains—all-pervading, blissful, and effulgent. You are there as a speck of light, a witness, a point of consciousness in a vast expanse of Light. With perfect purity and concentration, you may even lose awareness of your separate existence—that would be a great spiritual experience. Then come back. You are having a pure mental body and a physical body. The deity also has re-appeared from the formless Light. Recognise the deity. Offer the fruits of your meditation to Him and salute Him. Don't try to go through all this by force. By gradual and regular practice you will achieve mastery over this process which would take you from the gross to the subtlest spiritual level of consciousness.

Ishtam

The Ishtam is really the Supreme Spirit. The form which we have taken up is the form of the same Godhead. There again we should not forget the Cosmic Existence. Clinging rigidly to one aspect is fanaticism. Every form has come out of the Supreme. The Master saw the Divine Mother in everything. He saw the Spirit manifested everywhere.

There is only one Godhead: Sat-chit-ananda. We worship the one Godhead in its various aspects through different divine forms. From them, we choose one as our Ishtam—the chosen deity. This object of worship should not be changed often. If we do so, there will not be any progress in our spiritual life. When we do meditation and japa we should always feel that we are worshipping Sat-chit-ananda alone in the form of our Ishtam, as the impersonal all-pervading Reality is difficult to conceive of in the beginning. By manifesting Himself in the world as an incarnation, God makes our path easier. He Himself reveals His form to us.

God is both with form and without form. As long as we are conscious of our bodies, we must think of the body as a temple and the deity as shining in our hearts. We must enter this temple mentally and worship the Ishtam there. This whole concept has to be kept alive while doing meditation.

For success in meditation, we should also use our faculty of imagination. The Ishtam should be imagined as alive and luminous, not an inert picture or image. While meditating, we should dwell on the meaning of the mantra and the form of the particular aspect of God which we have chosen as our deity.

To have good meditation, we must make use of our natural instincts. It is natural for our senses to seek sense-enjoyment and, therefore, there is an outward movement. The attention of the senses should be withdrawn from worldly things and turned towards an object inside. The object in question is the Ishtam. One of the means or turning the senses inward is repetition of a mantra by which the inner spiritual eye is opened. Self-love is instinctive in man. That self love should be properly directed to its true object. Thinking of himself as merely body, mind and intellect, he forgets the Real Self, the greater whole. When the soul is tired of limitations, it wants to become one with the Source. Only a small spark of God's Love is seen in human beings, and the soul is not satisfied with this. Hence it wants to contact the very source and to unite with it.

The one Reality has three aspects—the Godhead (Sat-chit-ananda), the incarnation and the individual soul, which can be compared, respectively, to the ocean, a mountain-high wave and a bubble. The bubble should cling to the big wave which will at one stage merge it with the ocean. One should constantly and continuously worship the chosen Ideal. All the gods and goddesses are different aspects of the same Godhead and one should not be biased against any of them.

Meditation on Guru

Some find it easier to meditate on the Guru than on the Ishtam. After meditating on the Guru for some time, one should meditate on the Ishtam as well. We must not cling to the personality of the Guru. Think of the spirit behind him. That is the true Guru. If we cling to his personality we will only establish another worldly relationship. We should therefore think of the Lord as Guru. No doubt Guru and God are the same. We should realize the oneness of the two. The Guru also should not think of the disciples as so many possessions. He should see the Lord in his disciples too. In one aspect He is the Guru and in another aspect He is the disciple. The deity is a manifestation of the Spirit. We should not cling to the two-dimensional picture or even an image and take it for the Supreme. Sri Ramakrishna said to 'M' that He was Chinmaya i.e. the very embodiment of Consciousness, Bliss and Light. When you enter the Shrine think that He is seated there alive in full bliss. This is the type of dream or imagination that we should have. The power of imagination is great. First get intellectually convinced of the Truth, then imagine true dreams.

Disciples are instructed to meditate on the Ishtam or in some cases, on the Guru. One may not be able to concentrate one's mind on either of them, but it is of no use to say so and give up the effort. One has to go on practicing it without becoming disheartened, even though one may fail a hundred times. Swami Brahmananda has cited the example of the new-born calf which falls down again and again in its attempts to stand up, but it never gives up. With each fall it gains strength and succeeds at last. Thus, with each japa, we too strengthen our will power and concentration. Though the mechanical repetition of the Lord's Name does not do much good, it would at least keep away other foolish thoughts which keep coming up in the mind. Conscious repetition is most effective. While repeating the mantra we must meditate on the qualities of the Lord which the mantra represents.

The Form of the Deity and Other Forms

The question is often raised as to what should be done if during meditation, form of any deity other than the chosen deity, appears. Generally, no other divine form appears during

meditation. Only worldly forms and pictures arise. If any other
divine form does appear, we should think that the Ishtam
has appeared in that form. The Supreme Spirit assumes
various forms. The form which suits our feelings and our
intellect is chosen as our Ishtam. The mantra which indicates
the particular aspect of our chosen deity should be thought
over during meditation. Naturally, we cannot meditate on
more than one form. If, therefore, any other form appears,
we should think that it has come out of the same Supreme
Spirit, and we should merge that form into the Ishtam, stress
being laid on the Supreme Spirit. Some people may be
interested in a particular form for a certain period of time and
then they begin to like another form. They must choose
between the two and find out which suits their tendencies
best, and then cling to it. Again, some may have been
instructed to think of two forms, of which only one would
be the Ishtam. They must do a little mental worship and japa
for the lesser deity and then merge it in the main Ishtam and
meditate on the Ishtam. It may be asked whether this practice
of merging all the forms in the Ishtam should be adopted
in respect of any form which may appear in the mind. No.
This is to be done only when the form of a saint or an
incarnation or another deity appears. Worldly pictures come
too, and worldly sounds disturb us. Suddenly if a shoemaker's
shop appears in the mind should we meditate on that? Of
course not. We have to drive such pictures away with our
will power and reinstall the form of the Ishtam. Whatever
worldly form comes up during meditation, it should be
thrown into the Infinite Light, the divine fire from which
it has come. As we had cherished objects of the senses
previously, they now appear during meditation. All our
discrimination and will power must be used to cast away
worldly thoughts and forms from the mind.

Technique of Meditation

One should imagine that the body is the temple. The
whole atmosphere and everything else is filled with the

divine light. This light solidifies and takes the form of the chosen deity. The Ishtam is established in the heart—in the temple—and the devotee who also is a part of Divinity worships the chosen deity there. As we believe ourselves to be a body, we worship the Divine as an incarnation i.e. in the human form. Meditation should be carried on with this conception and it will gradually take us to the experience of a higher joy and understanding.

Maharaj (Swami Brahmananda) has said 'Meditate in the heart.' Pit of the stomach, the spot just above the stomach, is the heart centre. There one should think of the chosen deity as seated on a red lotus of eight petals. The body is a wonderful temple. The personality of man has three components—body, mind and spirit. The body is interpenetrated and permeated by the mind, and the mind, by the spirit. They are, respectively, parts of the Cosmic body, mind and the Infinite Spirit. We are not separate from the Cosmic Existence and this truth we have to experience through sadhana. We must proceed step by step.

Mind is the subtle body. The physical body is made up of gross matter; it is pervaded by the subtle body (mind) and that, in turn is pervaded, and interpenetrated, by the atman. The gross and the subtle bodies are not dead matter. They carry the energy of the atman which is Consciousness. To concentrate on this Consciousness as Light is the best form of meditation. As it may not be possible for all to have this conception (in the beginning, we should meditate on a form of God or a realized soul, such as, Siva, Vishnu, Krishna, Rama, Sri Ramakrishna etc. Along with meditation, one should chant a Holy Name, the mantra. The mantra has great power. While meditating we should think of Infinite Bliss, Infinite Love and Infinite Compassion of the deity. As we proceed, we feel our consciousness expanding. In later stages we see the same consciousness lying hidden in all alike.

A little devotion helps a lot. If you can feel His Presence in the picture or image in front of you and not just a lifeless object, that is good. This, however, usually happens at a later stage. The process of meditation involves a great struggle, but later on we will find the joy which is in this struggle.

At the time of japa and meditation, one should think of the deity and oneself alone. The highest and grandest type of meditation is one that is signified by the sound symbol OM, namely, Sat-Chit-Ananda. It is all-pervading Consciousness and Bliss. This conception may be difficult for the beginner. It is therefore suggested to meditate on a divine form—the all-pervading Consciousness that has taken a blissful form. That is the Ishtam, the chosen deity. He is full of Love. During meditation, the devotee should be oblivious of all other thoughts, sounds and forms except the deity. This is the technique.

You think of a form. You try to meditate on it. What is your attitude towards that form? Do you feel that it is real and living? Feel the living presence of the deity. Then you get the reaction. This is the process of spiritual practice and realization.

Meditation on Divine Attributes

Great souls are always in tune with the all-pervading Consciousness. Sri Ramakrishna gave the illustration of the water in a cup; the sun is reflected in it. Similarly God ever shines in the heart of a devotee and a jnani. Again there is the illustration of the ocean. Mountain-high waves, small waves, bubbles, all these are water. The substance is the same. The mountain-high waves represent the Deities and the small ones represent realised souls. The realized souls are always one with divine Consciousness and they are full of infinite compassion, love, kindness and bliss. They are devoid of all desires. Imagine this during meditation. Dwell more on the attributes of the deity than on the form. Clinging to mere personality is narrow-mindedness. Making much of the waves, forgetting the ocean behind, is silly, and leads to fanaticism. Sri Ramakrishna and the Holy Mother saw nothing but consciousness in all and everywhere. Countless devotees followed their instructions and achieved the goal of life. We should also achieve the same. Instead of meditating on the divine form and attributes, we think of human cats and dogs, including ourselves. If we see only the bodies, then we are no better than animals; on the other hand, animals may be better than us, for they do not tell lies and do not eat when they are not hungry. Hence we should see ourselves as well as others as embodiments of Consciousness. In order to see each other in this manner during our waking hours, we should establish our identity with the Supreme Self during the time of meditation.

If we accept Sri Ramakrishna as our ideal, what do we get? Accepting him we think of his noble qualities: his divine love, renunciation, devotion and knowledge. And the more we think of his noble qualities, the more we gain. We are all creatures of our bhava, emotion and mental attitudes. If we succeed in creating emotions of peace, we radiate peace. If we meditate on an angry, frowning person, we too become angry and become dangerous creatures. To change yourself, change your mental vibrations. Limited as we are, it is not possible for us to think of the subtle, abstract qualities and attributes of God; we cannot think of grand conceptions as they are. Hence we want a living personality who has these qualities in abundance, that is, an incarnation. The more we think of him the more we imbibe these qualities and radiate them in turn all around us.

We constantly think of worldly people, and this process creates .worldly reactions. We develop worldly emotions and attitudes. Start thinking of noble souls; then your emotions and even facial expression will change. When you are in a spiritual mood, singing devotional songs—temporarily at least you will look divine and peaceful. Vibrations of anger, dissatisfaction, etc, are temporarily replaced by those of calmness. Here is the significance of meditating on a holy personality.

Sri Ramakrishna is the embodiment of purity, love and compassion and you need all those noble qualities. There is more to it however. He is the embodiment of divine Consciousness. He used to say to his disciples: 'Think of me while meditating. When I look inside I find the Great Power there.' Hence when we think of Him, we are thinking of God Himself. Through him, we get a direct access to God-Consciousness. Or, take the example of meditation on Siva. He is lost in grand meditation. He drinks poison to save the world. Siva is completely other-worldly and divine and still He is meditating. Meditating for what purpose? For the welfare of the world. Thinking of Him, we are lost in that great ideal of an all-renouncing yogi, the Supreme Teacher, who is solely concerned with the welfare of others. This is the fruit of meditation on noble souls. By meditating on the divine attributes, we absorb those qualities in due course.

Even when you meditate on a deity or holy personality, the aim is to reach this divine Consciousness. In this process, one meditates on the luminous form which corresponds to the physical gross body; and then on the divine, noble attributes which corresponds to the mind, the subtle body. The devotee should proceed beyond these and penetrate to the divine Consciousness of the deity which is the same as his own consciousness and Universal Consciousness. The best means of achieving this ultimate stage is japa. Recall the wonderful saying of the Holy Mother (referring to the flowers dipped in sandal-wood paste offered during worship): 'Just as when you handle the flowers, the fragrance of sandal-wood paste is transferred to you, so too by thinking of the Lord the mind is uplifted.'

Meditation: from Duality to Non-duality

A meditational technique suited to one's present stage of development should be chosen. We should know our limitations. In the beginning one should not proceed to meditate upon the Supreme Consciousness which is all-pervading, like the sky.

God can be worshipped with form or without form according to one's own temperament, and here, the question of superiority or inferiority does not arise. Formless meditation has generally a great attraction for the modern mind. It is only when we are beyond body-consciousness, that we can begin formless meditation. We are fond even of our photographs. If they do not come out well, we hate them! Such is our attachment to our body! How then can we meditate on the Formless? Meditation on a form of God is essential in the beginning. But while meditating on the form of the deity, we should never forget that He is the Supreme Self and we the devotees are parts of Him. This will help us to attain meditation on the Formless gradually. In the first stage, we worship the deity with flowers, sandal paste, etc. The next stage is that of meditating on the divine form mentally, while repeating the Holy Name japa. Then will come a stage when the sound symbol wills no more be needed and the living presence of the deity will be clearly felt. The holy form and idea remain. After some time the holy form will merge into the idea, will disappear, and we will feel only a sphere of Consciousness—light within and without. These are the different stages, beginning from Dvaita and ending in Advaita. Some remain at the stage of experiencing God with form, without going to the last stage. They see Him face to face.

Meditation—on the Form and the Formless

In formless meditation we attempt to merge our individual consciousness in the all-pervading consciousness. One should start this meditation by entering the sanctum of the heart in the temple of the body and there seeing the light of the atman which is part of the Paramatman (Infinite Light). Merge yourself in it. Throw into that light all other forms and thoughts that arise in your mind. Thus gradually raise yourself from the heart to the brain centre. When you raise your consciousness from the lower to the higher centers, gross elements become absorbed in the Infinite Light. In the highest centre, our consciousness is merged in the Infinite. Consciousness and only the experience of the Infinite remain. One great use of this meditation is that we feel that there is nothing more real than our soul. In this process we undermine the reality of this world and think of ourselves at most as spheres of light, which are parts of the Infinite Light. Our minds will then become free from the limitations of the body, and outside world. When body-consciousness is strong, one cannot meditate on Formless. Even for achieving meditation on form, we have to unite heart and head. Heart is the centre for this meditation. Consider that you are a soul and that the Infinite has taken the form of the deity you worship. Meditate on that blissful form thinking of the divine attributes such as infinite love, infinite purity and kindness. Repeat the divine name and at the same time think of the divine form. As we go on thus, our minds are withdrawn from all outside impressions, at least for the time being. To the extent our interest in the object of meditation is greater than that in the objects of the world, to that extent we succeed in meditation. In either type of meditation, it is necessary to think that the body is unreal and ever-changing and that there is something in the body that does not change amidst all these changes—the Self. Hold on to it. We get real peace by this idea.

Difficulty in Meditating on a Divine Form

A devotee complains that he finds it difficult to meditate on the form of Sri Ramakrishna and asks how he should meditate. Human mind is strange. When we think of a friend, we recall the whole figure. It rises like a picture in our mind. Difficulty arises only with a divine form. The trouble is that the mind is accustomed to think of worldly things and pictures. Hence they come up clearly in the mind. The mind has to be trained to meditate on the divine form. Meditation on the gross form of a divine Personality is the first step. The Infinite Spirit who is supreme light, supreme love and supreme bliss has taken the form of your Ishta Devata. The Ishta is full of divine qualities. He is the manifestation of the Infinite Principle. We too have the Infinite as our background. But we have forgotten this. Our consciousness has become finite. So we take our refuge in a holy personality, who is a manifestation of Infinite Consciousness. If we are little bubbles, the holy personality is a mountain-high wave. He knows that he is not different from the ocean; we do not know that fact—this is the difference between us and divine incarnations. Take the instance of Arjuna and Sri Krishna. Arjuna had no clear idea about the real personality of Sri Krishna. He understood later on that He was more than a mere friend and a charioteer. He was the Supreme Spirit transcending the individual and the Universal.

In understanding the Real, we too have to pass through these various steps. Meditate on the holy personality, think of His blissful luminous form. When you think of a friend, you think with a great deal of love. Why not do the same when you think of the Ishta Devata, who is the life of your life? Think of Him as luminous and blissful. Thereby the mind will be soothed. Thinking about the various people you come across in life, feelings of hatred, jealousy, attachment etc., come up. Unhealthy vrittis are raised in the mind. On the other hand think of infinite purity, infinite love, infinite compassion of your Ishta. In spiritual life we should fill our minds with spiritual, luminous, blissful thought waves. The Ishta is a symbol of the Infinite Light, Infinite Love and Infinite Bliss. He is a link between the finite and Infinite. Our consciousness is limited, but His is infinite. The mind is to be trained to understand these truths. It has been accustomed to flow towards worldly things and persons. It is to be directed towards the holy personality. It will take time. Practice is the only way.

(11)

Light of All Lights

Shining Reality Behind All

Always maintain a clear concept of the Lord—the shining Reality behind conflicting phenomena. All things exist because of It. It is by That that we see everything. It is always shining. We say the sun is clouded over, but that is not correct. The sun is ever bright. It is our vision that is clouded. While travelling in the plane above the clouds, the sun is seen in all its glory and one sees that the earth is covered with the clouds. When we land we refuse to agree with anyone who says that the sun was clouded, because we saw the sun as it was! Similarly, discover the Light in the midst of clouds. The mind must have proper understanding to get this vision. For this, regular spiritual practice is essential. Pray for Spiritual Gifts.

He is eager to reveal Himself. On your own side do your utmost to do your part; His power will do the rest. People who are attracted by Sri Ramakrishna want light. Where is It? The one source of Light is "*Jyotishamapi tadjyotihi*'. That is 'the Light of all lights'. It is not a material light but the light of consciousness. There is a story in the Upanishads of a disciple asking the teacher: 'What is the light that shines in a mart?' The teacher wants to instruct him step by step. He says, 'The Light is the Sun'. The disciple is not satisfied. 'What happens when the Sun and the Moon are not there?' The teacher says: 'Light your lamp.' 'What happens when that lamp is put out?' 'Speech', says the teacher, 'In darkness, speech gives the direction.' The disciple asks: 'What is the light of man when speech is also hushed?' 'It is the light of Consciousness', answers the teacher. 'As long as it is there we can see.' How to perceive that light? Our body, senses, mind and ego stand in the way. The instruments by which we perceive objects, whether outside or inside, themselves become obstacles when we try to perceive the light of Consciousness in us.

From physical level, go to the mental level and be a witness of your thoughts. All the time we have been thinking that the Reality, the Light, is outside us. Now we come to know that It is inside us too. You realise that you are a witness to your thoughts, that you are distinctly different from your mind. You are aware of your I-consciousness. Proceed further and try to reach the very source of that I-consciousness, the source from which the light of consciousness proceeds. Then you discover that you are that Light and you were that Light all the time. Your identification with the body and mind was false. You think that you were proceeding toward that Light—that the needle was moving towards the magnet; but actually the movement is from the other side. The Supreme Being was reaching out and drawing you to Him all the time. If the passage is clear, if the body, senses and mind are pure, if the ego-barrier is not thick, then the Light shines very clearly and more and more brilliantly. The finite and the Infinite are ever in tune with one another but a tremendous obstacle has come in the way—the obstacle of ignorance, of body-consciousness, of impurities in the mind and senses, of ceaseless mental activity connected with worldly affairs. Once the obstacle is removed the light shines spontaneously. It had not gone anywhere and it did not have to come from anywhere outside. So it is all a re-discovery of the Truth which was ever-shining within ourselves. It is a matter of regaining the memory of our real nature. Sri Ramakrishna narrates the story of the tiger-cub which is brought up by a herd of sheep. Then it is caught by a big tiger who tells the cub about its real nature. The tiger thrusts a piece of meat into its mouth and says, 'Eat this and not grass. You are a tiger like me and not a sheep.' The Guru imparts Jnana to the disciple and tells him about his real nature. It is difficult to 'eat the meat' in the first instance as in the case of the tiger cub.

The light is in us. It is then foolish to seek it outside. You have got much more of it than you can contain. Feel it, discover it, and be blessed. You cannot achieve anything with borrowed light. Each one should find the light within himself. And the light that shines in everyone shines everywhere. The Supreme Being is in everything; He is everything. A little of His glory is manifest as what we call the soul. The whole is the soul of the universe. He is the transcendent beyond the individual and beyond the cosmic. Imagine that there is an infinite number of bubbles floating on the ocean and each is illumined with light. The entire ocean is filled with light. That infinite light manifests itself through individual forms and through the whole. Light reflected in the bubbles and the waves, and the infinite light reflected in the ocean come from one and the same source. Each one must discover the light within the light of the soul, the light of consciousness. When we discover this light, when this inner vision opens, we feel the same light manifesting everywhere. What a great joy it is to mingle one's own light in the infinite Consciousness!

This of course becomes possible only by rising above all body-consciousness, above the mind, the senses and the individual personality. Recall the Upanishadic story I related earlier. What is the light of man? It is his consciousness. That light shining, body, senses, mind and ego function. That infinite light is to be freed from the limitations of the body, mind and senses. What happens then? Sri Ramakrishna says: 'When the onion skin is removed layer after layer what remains is only akasa. That akasa of light is the basis of everything.'

Light is shining there but you are not looking towards it. You are looking outwards. It is the light of knowledge, of intelligence, the light that shines through mind and ego. When a person is in a sattvika mood he is harmonious and the light shines through him better. It shines less through rajasika nature and still less through tamasika nature. I have narrated the story of Indra and Virochana who went to

Prajapati to know the Self. What did the Guru say? 'Look at the light that shines through the eyes' etc. The man of divine nature eventually meditated on that advice and understood. But the man of asurika nature came to the conclusion that the body itself was the Self.

Clean the Mirror to Catch the Reflection

This is the process of meditation: (1) meditate on the luminous form of the Lord; (2) meditate on His noble qualities; (3) meditate on His Infinite Consciousness, not in terms of His little personality but in terms of the Infinite Principle. Sri Ramakrishna meditated on the blissful form of the Mother. She revealed to him that form is the manifestation of the Formless. He said: 'My Mother's glory fills the whole universe.' The 'Mother' to him is *'Parama Jyoti'* supreme effulgence. She is everywhere but we are not aware of Her. We come to feel Her presence when She bestows Her grace on us. By spiritual practice can you drag God to you? He is not far away. Now we do not feel His presence. With sincere spiritual practice the mind become pure and we start feeling His presence. Do you force a light to shine? The light is always there. Cleaner the mirror, more luminous the reflection. The Lord is ever eager to receive us but we don't turn to Him.

In the Bhagavad Gita, Sri Krishna speaks of four types of devotees:—Jnani, who naturally worships Him; the arta, who tries all human means to get over his misery and then turns to God; the artharthi, who wants to try God when all his desires are foiled, jijnasu, the seeker, who wants to know whether God exists and if so what He is like. They are all great and noble, says the Lord. Why? Because He is the soul of our soul; He loves us all and wants to lift us unto Him. The Philosopher's Stone is glad when it touches some metal. The Lord is gracious. His Light is ever shining. To the extent our reflector becomes clean we catch His light. This is the significance of spiritual practice.

Meditate on that light in man. When the soul leaves the body, life has gone; all the senses remain intact, but there is no functioning That light shines through the mind, body and senses. It is something alive, conscious, identifying itself with this little ego. The light of the Supreme shines through this little patch of cloud and we see the little human personality. It is through ignorance that we identify ourselves with this little ego and become small, limited beings. Consciousness and inert matter get mixed up and that is the cause of all misery and suffering. Even the mind and ego are subtle matter. We have to segregate consciousness from all else by discrimination and meditation. It is to be freed from all limitations.

The Way to the Highest

The light is within. Have no doubt about this. Think of this point of the heart—not the physical heart, but the place where you can feel the presence of your Consciousness. Imagine that this Consciousness permeates the entire body and mind. This little Consciousness is part of the Infinite Light. With the help of the little Consciousness, we have to discover that Infinite Consciousness. One who goes up and attains the higher levels gets the capacity to perceive directly the great truths of life. We possess that capacity even now to a limited degree and can readily perceive things at bodily and mental levels. What is required is the capacity to perceive the realities of the higher life. This is compared to the opening of the 'divine eye' or the 'third eye'. This path is said to be sharp as a sword's edge—*kshurasya dhara*. One should be firmly established in control and purity of the senses and mind before embarking on this journey. Otherwise, disaster may overtake the aspirant at any moment. We have to go up and then we realise that we are not the body or mind, and so we are not subject to birth and death. We are not the doers (*karta*) and therefore we have no bondage. It is not possible to attain this knowledge so easily. Till then one has to lead a noble life and do sadhana. If you have to be a worker (karta), do good, noble things. If you have to be a bhokta, one who reaps the fruits of work—a karta must necessarily be a bhokta—enjoy what is good. Change your consciousness in the spiritual direction. So, Sri Ramakrishna says: 'One cannot give up the I—let it remain as the of the child, of the disciple, or of the servant of God.' That is the way to rise.

That light of Consciousness is our ideal. 'He who sees is the Atman.' Reflect on this truth if you want peace and cessation of all sorrow. There is no other way to put an end to sorrow. The Upanishad declares; 'If the sky can be rolled up as a skin, then there can be an end to sorrow without knowing the Supreme.' Is it ever possible? All that you see is part of the cloud, maya. But the cloud itself is illuminated by the light of the sun and the sun is never really covered by the cloud. Go above the cloud and the sun is ever shining there. Dive deep; the more you go within, the higher you rise and the more you expand.

During meditation you rise very high sometimes and you feel as if you were a saint. That indicates to what heights you can rise. But there are sudden falls too. But by the grace of the Master if you follow the instructions of the Guru carefully and have your eyes fixed on the ideal, you will succeed. Pierce through the barriers of gross, subtle, and causal matter, the three bodies that cover the Self. Then the Light shines. These are all several layers upon layers of clouds—pierce through them and see the Sun, who was never clouded.

The Indirect Way

Now, since many of us cannot discover the Light through the direct way of self-analysis, place an ideal before you—a holy personality. By meditating on Him the mind becomes pure. A new consciousness, chaitanya comes. We dwell always on the plane of sense perception. As we go deeper, the movement is inward, from the physical to the mental and then to the causal. As you advance, you discover that the Light that shines in the holy personality, shines also in you, may be to a smaller degree. Evidently we have to go very much farther to discover the Light in all its glory. We find that we cannot, we fall asleep. The effort has to be re-doubled and the mind has to become more and more pure. We go from the gross to the subtle and from the subtle to the causal. From the causal you come to the spiritual. That which is subtle is vaster than the gross and permeates the gross inside and outside. That which is spiritual is infinite, all-pervading and indivisible. In that Infinite, there appears the mental universe, and in the mental universe, appears the physical universe. You have lost your way in the wilderness. If you retrace your steps carefully, eventually you will come out of the wilderness. Similarly, pure consciousness is caught in the net of maya. Identifying itself with the effects of maya, the inner light becomes dim. It becomes identified with the mind, and then with the senses, with the body. Going further outside, you will not get out of this wilderness of ignorance. So you have to retrace your steps and go back home. The mind has to become subtler and purer. During meditation one should think that the body and mind are pure and divine, and one should try to merge oneself in the divine form of the chosen deity. The Ishtam is a concrete form of the all-pervading Light, the Pure Consciousness. In deep meditation the deity and the devotee are both merged in the all-pervading consciousness, Sat-Chit-Ananda the all pervading light,

We do not see the sun because of the cloud in between, but the sun is never clouded. The Atman shines always, but we, out of ignorance, do not see It. Discriminate between the Real and the unreal. Do not waste your time in thinking about worldly things. All our faculties should be turned towards the one goal, namely, God. Have faith in Him. Let no doubts enter the mind. If doubts do come, pray to Him: 'It is only the impurities in my mind that keep me away from you. Please remove them.' Pray for purity.

(12)
Jnana Yoga

Nature of Atman

Once a devotee wanted to know Swami Sivananda's age. He said: 'Nobody can calculate the age of a person. The body alone has age; the Atman has no age. It is eternal, unborn, and imperishable.' The Atman puts on a gross body and a subtle body. They are born, they grow, and perish. But the Atman is ever there unchanged, as a witness. The subtle body is full of thoughts and emotions. As new ideas are received, there are feelings of either joy or misery. Behind these changing unrealities, there is something which is permanent, which is Pure Consciousness, giving power to these subtle and gross bodies. Consciousness covered by subtle and gross bodies is a human being. The Atman is covered by a cloud as it were. The task in spiritual life is to remove the cloud and perceive the Reality in us.

We have too much body-consciousness. We think of others also in terms of bodily relationships (father, mother, friends etc.). It is of the utmost importance to think of everyone in terms of the Atman. Is 'our' Atman the only Reality? The reality of others also is the same Atman. Our Self is a ray of light and the light is Paramatman. Every other ray must be given its importance. The ray has no existence without the light. So He is the Soul of our souls, of all souls.

As time passes, objects lose their beauty. We think too much of the body, which also perishes in course of time. After all, it is made up of flesh, bones, blood and filth. A body is merely these things. Think of your body as a skeleton, and then you will no longer have any attraction for it. There are people who grow physically but not mentally. Their childish mentality remains till their death. If the spiritual consciousness is not awakened, what is the use of existence?

We waste much energy trying to appear what we are actually not. We use make-up to appear different from what we are. Girish Babu used to wonder at the actresses when he saw the difference in them after make-up. It is not that we should look ugly, but too much care in this respect is not good. Beauty of the soul should be cultivated. Abraham Lincoln was an ugly person. A gentleman going to meet him with his small daughter warned her not to comment on his appearance in the President's presence. Lincoln met the child with a loving heart and the child was so deeply touched by his kindness that she said: 'But Papa, he is not ugly. He is beautiful.' Beauty should come from within. A man said to Lincoln that his portrait had been painted beautifully. Lincoln replied that the beauty was of his heart and not of his body.

The Asura and the Deva are both in us. A struggle is always going on within us between the Asura and the Deva. But there is the Atman also as the witness, who is eternally connected with the Paramatman. We must conquer the Asura with the help of the Deva, after which, we have to go beyond both of them. The Atman must always be conscious of Paramatman. That is our task in life. Sri Ramakrishna worshipped the Mother's image and she revealed to Him Her Presence in everything. That is the great vision we should all strive for.

Self Separate from Body and Mind

The self should be realised. The body changes, the mind changes. The mind, unless trained to be one-pointed through concentration, undergoes constant changes. A careful observer can see these changes in himself. To observe a change, there should be a changeless factor behind the changing things. The Upanishads contain the allegory of two birds living in the same tree, one on the lower branch eating

the bitter and sweet fruits thereof and the other one simply
watching. There is a changeless observer in this tree of the
body. When you lose your temper and act rashly, you
suddenly become conscious of your temper and say: 'What
am I doing?' You will notice that there is a spectator in your
mind. You feel that something in you is watching all your
good thoughts as well as your bad ones. If you become
introspective, first the mind becomes the seer and the body
becomes the object. You become more introspective, and
then the Buddhi, the higher aspect of the mind becomes the
seer and the lower mind and thoughts become objects. Then
you think; 'This good thought should be strengthened,
that bad one should be expelled', etc. How could you
discriminate thus unless there was the witness deep within
you? Go deeper and deeper and when the mind becomes
pure, and the intellect becomes perfect, the Atman which is
within us would shine forth and you would see not only what
is inside but also what is outside. Sometimes when you
identify yourself with your mind, you lose discrimination. In
calm moments you can be the witness of all the changes
going on in your mind. During these bright moments we
feel as if a light shines within and in that light we discover
what has been happening within ourselves.

We constantly refer to 'I'. Who is this 'I?' There is one
'I' which is beyond both body and mind. It is born from
the underlying Consciousness in us. One can reach that
Consciousness by tracing the source of 'I' in one-self. We
should get hold of that 'I' in us; We should feel restless in
order to know this 'I'. This restlessness is a good sign. It is
not like the restlessness arising from not attaining
sense-objects.

The Self has no age; it is unaffected by diseases and
old age; it is beginning less, endless, eternal and immortal.
The body changes, so does the mind. They undergo constant
changes. The Atman is there, changeless amidst these various
changes. This world, fashioned by ignorance, is illusory and

our whole trouble comes from mistaking the illusory for the real. Can we say that this world does not exist? No, it has a changing reality, a temporary existence. Every other thing changes, but not so the Atman. We take this body to be real and mistake the body for the Atman. Consciousness has been identified with body and mind. Free yourself of this delusion. Then you come to feel that you are different from the body and mind. Putting on a certain garb, you think you are a beggar or a king. But the one who puts on the garb is neither of them. Enquire who he is. When you go deep you will find that you are the Self. The finite and the Infinite are mixed up in us. In the course of evolution of the soul, the Infinite becomes more and more manifested. The reflected light becomes clear to the extent the water becomes clear. The more the mind becomes pure, the more the Self shines. The light shines all the time; we need not force it to shine. Such is the power of japa and meditation on the blissful form of the Lord. It awakens a new consciousness in us.

The Unchanging Reality

Once Indra and Virochana (the King of the Asuras) went to Prajapati to learn the secret of the Immortal Self. They were asked to perform Tapas for 32 years and then to see their faces reflected in a basin of water, and were told that what they saw in the water was the Reality. Both saw their faces reflected, and mistaking the body for the Atman went away. What Prajapati meant was not the body seen by the eyes but the observer seen behind the eyes. The Asura was satisfied and believed the body to be the Atman. But Indra was not satisfied and came again to Prajapati, who sent him for another 32 years of Tapas and then told him that what he saw in dreams was real. Indra was initially satisfied but on further contemplation found both happiness and misery in dreams and so was not satisfied. Again after 32 years of Tapas, Indra was told that he would be one with the Atman in the state of deep sleep. Indra went back but soon found that though he got peace and felt refreshed after deep sleep, he could not get any permanent bliss from it. Hence deep sleep could not be the state of self-realisation. At last Indra was told the nature of the Atman and how to be constantly in that highly spiritual state which is a witness of the waking, dreaming and sleeping states and so on. This is how a man of contemplative nature is gradually led from the level of sense-perception to self-realisation. The body and mind are changing realities; the Self alone is the unchanging Reality.

A certain woodcutter held a shining axe on his shoulder, and was proud of it. Its wooden handle shone too. When he was praised for possessing such a new axe, he said: 'When I was 20 years old I got the axe. I have changed the blade 3 times and the handle 7 times.' This is the state of our body and mind. Do we have the same body from our very birth? We see it changing. The Atman which is changeless sees all these changes. So Yajnavalkya told Maitreyi that one does not love another for the sake of the body or the mind but for the Atman which is permanent. Maitreyi who got this knowledge was a householder. She had led such a pure life from the beginning that she had become fit to receive this knowledge.

A devotee reminded Mahapurush Maharaj of the poor condition of his health. The great Swami was least concerned with his body. Ordinary souls get terrified when reminded of death. They may even die from the shock. But great souls like Swami Shivananda and Holy Mother are different. This body which we glorify is subject to many changes. It takes birth, lives, grows and decays. Behind all this what is that which remains changeless? The spiritual consciousness or Atman. If you feel that you are Atman, you can stand as a witness to all your joys and miseries. Mind and emotions change very quickly but the body lasts longer. Hence we think that the body remains the same. In fact, the body also is ever changing. This body that is full of filth—we think we are that. One should see the body as it is—an inert mass of bones and flesh. We may purify the body externally but within we can never clean it. The wash that we give ourselves through renunciation and knowledge is the one which purifies us: that is real sauca. People are very careful to clean the outside body. But control of the senses is the real cleaning. He who sees is the Atman. He who hears is the Atman. Who cares for whom, if it were not for this Atman? We need this new way of seeing. Who will care for a dead body? Without the power of this Atman we cannot see or do anything. We should know that Atman. No education is complete without Self-knowledge. Most people are engrossed in this perishable body and forget the eternal entity, the Atman, which enlivens the body and mind. There are some psychologists who know that there is a mind, but they don't know about the Self. Only a rare few are aware that there is the unchanging conscious principle behind this changing matter—the Self, the Atman.

Five Sheaths—the Panchakoshas

Our Scriptures say that the Self is covered in five sheaths— namely the sheaths of bliss, knowledge, mind, vital energy (prana), and lastly, the gross body. They are described in other terms as three bodies of man: the causal, the subtle and the gross. The Self is beyond the five sheaths or the three bodies; luminous, without any external aid; shining through the coverings. It is our Reality. We are like spheres of light, covered up by successive coverings. So to go to our true Self, to discover what we are, we have to go deep into ourselves, piercing the five sheaths or the three bodies which stand as obstructions. We think too much of these bodies. As physical bodies, we are only male and female animals. Even if we are able to progress a little, we are caught up by our minds and identify ourselves with the thoughts, feelings and emotions there. However, there is a way. Enter the sanctuary of the heart and feel your consciousness throbbing there. That is the point of Self-consciousness. It permeates the entire body and mind. It is the individual soul, a ray of the Universal

Self. It is the connecting link with God, the all-pervading Consciousness. Merge your body, mind, ego, everything into that Consciousness—God. Keep up the mood you attain just before you fall asleep: the function of the body and mind come to a slow halt, but you yourself are still awake. Guard against falling asleep; the mind is either restless or it falls into sleep. From the heart try to go higher and higher to the very core of Consciousness, where no thoughts exist and only the light of Consciousness shines.

Contact with the Divine

The Transcendent Being is beyond all names and forms and He also can manifest Himself as all creation. Having created the world and also the souls, He enters them. He is the antaryami Purusha, the living entity in all beings, and He also manifests Himself as gods and goddesses, as divine incarnations and as the Ishta devata. Think in this strain and see the presence of God everywhere and in everything; otherwise real progress is not possible. Think of the universe as resting in Him and of Him as immanent in the universe, who dwells in your heart. A devotee says that he would go to Mahapurush Maharaj with so many doubts in his mind but as soon as he is in his presence, all doubts disappear and he feels as if there is nothing to clear up. Why so? In the presence of great souls the mind is elevated. We rise above our petty problems. In their presence we feel something of a higher Presence. We should be able to feel this higher Presence by our sadhana and elevating our minds to a high level. When you are despondent, merge everything in the Infinite. As Sankaracharya says: 'I am that Siva of the nature of pure consciousness and bliss'—give this strong injunction to your mind. We are always clinging to our little personality, this dirty body! Rise above the body, above the mind. But for this, the mind must be prepared.

In 1925 the foundation stone of the Bombay Ashram was laid. When it was completed we invited Swami Shivananda for the opening ceremony. He was suffering from a terrible attack of asthma. Even breathing was very difficult. But he would sit for meditation and then be lost in joy. There was no suffering at all. He used to say that it was the meditation of an old man. When you suffer from headache, if you can forget the head, there will be no headache! Everything else will lose its value after experiencing this Reality. If you come to the stage where our little personality does not exist, you will have great peace. You will have a new outlook. If you have any problems, reveal everything to Him, and there won't be any problem. One may ask, 'He knows all my problems; why should I tell Him at all?' But are you really aware that He knows? If you truly know that He knows, then you won't be worried at all. Your purified mind itself will gain power and will solve the problems for you. Don't depend on outside help. Thinking of, feeling and experiencing the divine presence in you is the remedy. Our troubles arise from our thinking. If we can rise above all the mundane matters in meditation, contact the Divine and come down with a little of that consciousness, and the whole bondage of personality will be loosened.

Micro and Macrocosm

The whole universe is pervaded by the Supreme Reality. Corresponding to the individual body, there is a Cosmic Body—the visible universe. Corresponding to the individual mind, there is a Cosmic Mind—the world of ideas. And corresponding to the individual soul, there is a Cosmic Soul—pure, all-pervading Consciousness. The whole universe is nothing but God. Our task is to tune our individual selves to the Cosmic Self at all the three levels. Our thoughts should be connected with the Cosmic Mind. We begin spiritual life with meditation on the Supreme Spirit as a God with form; weaklings are satisfied with this conception. They are like persons who remain in the cellar, to avoid the trouble of climbing the stairs! You should struggle hard to reach the top, where there is fresh air and sunshine. From the conception of the Lord with form, we must aspire to merge ourselves in the formless aspect of the Lord. There is macrocosm and microcosm. There is Cosmic Mind. So also the Paramatman is the Soul of our souls. The aim of spiritual life is to be one with the over-Soul. There is no other way to the goal than constant practice and detachment

We should always remember that our minds are part of the Cosmic Mind and our souls are part of the Cosmic Soul. Whatever we do, we do it in connection with the Cosmic. It is the Cosmic Energy that flows through us all. The material world is a whirlpool of matter and our bodies are a part of it. Though this is the fact, we are ignorant of it. Identifying ourselves with the ego, we lose the knowledge of this fact. Our lives should be devoted to realising this Truth.

Proceed from the microcosm to the macrocosm. Experiencing the divinity here in yourself, proceed to know the divinity behind the universe. The heart is the gateway to spiritual consciousness; it is the door to the formless and attribute-less Reality. Try to gain that spiritual consciousness. That is the purpose of meditation. Then we know what a great miracle lies hidden in ourselves.

This self-consciousness that is here in this little heart permeates our entire body, mind and soul and the same consciousness pervades the universe. This is a grand meditation. Think of it—one life pulsating in all bodies, minds and souls, and not in my individual body, mind and soul alone! Our bodies and minds are a reflection of that Reality; begin from the reflected image and discover that which is reflected. Begin this inner pilgrimage and go right up to the Supreme Truth. Begin with japa, stotra and mental worship and reach the worship of 'That I am'—*So'ham*.

There is the external sky, the *Mahakasa*. The universe exists in it. Then there is the *Chittakasa* the Cosmic mind and

lastly the *Chidakasa*, the Cosmic Soul. We should try to
identify ourselves with the last, which is all-pervading pure
Consciousness. In identifying ourselves with that, our small
limited personality vanishes and we grow into Universal
Consciousness. This process should be followed gradually.
The Guide of guides, the Supreme Guru, is in yourself. So
why depend on external guides alone? In the beginning it
is essential, but as you advance you should try to stand on
your own feet. As we go on meditating on the form of the
deity, He Himself will reveal His true nature to us in due
course. The body is gross matter, which is surrounded by
mind, subtle matter. Both are *jada*, inert, and both are made
alive by atman. The Universal Being has a physical body,
the Manifested universe. Our bodies are a part of that. Our
subtle bodies are a part of His subtle body, the Cosmic
Mind. And our individual Consciousness is a part of His
Consciousness. The origin of all of us is in Him but because
of identification with body and mind, we forget that.

Relation between Atman and Paramatman

The universe is filled with the light of Divinity. It is like
the sky lit up by the sun. There are some patches of clouds
in the sky which can be compared to the individual souls.
The particles of ice which can be found in the centre of
the clouds are like the gross body of man. They are covered
by particles of water (subtle body) and water-vapour
(the Self). Just as clouds combine with one another and act,
the individual souls act together in life in the role of friends
and relatives. In other words, friends, relatives and others are
only individual souls with the coverings of mind and body
who happen to be together for some time. Essentially,
they are all Atman. The eternal relationship between the
Atman and the Paramatman should be understood and
realised. At first, this identity can be known just intellectually.
To experience this one should do sadhana. The path is
made easy by the Guru.

God should be imagined as vast and infinite. The whole universe is filled with His presence. It is His Light that fills the sky. Atman shines forth everywhere. Think everyone to be a soul. In the ocean, it is not the waves that are real, but the ocean itself. The whole world is an ocean of spirit and individual souls are like waves in it. The waves are the working of the ocean. This idea can be grasped only as a result of a great deal of spiritual practice.

Way to Reach Reality

What is the way to reach Reality? There are two ways. The negative way is to try to get rid of various miseries, physical and mental, and the positive way is to feel the Bliss of the Supreme Spirit. After receiving blows after blows, one turns towards God. Till we realise the unreal nature of the world, insignificant things are treated as significant. Many cannot stand the idea that we are living in a world of impermanence. This world which we consider as very important is forgotten in sleep. The child in sleep does not care even for its mother. Our world concept and values will change when we awake to the Reality. The human desires for liberation, holy company and the strength to strive are the grace of God. The culmination of divine grace is liberation. We are trying to dispel the clouds. As the clouds grow thinner, a little light shines. When a glimpse of the Reality is perceived, we will be enthusiastic to get more and more light, till we are completely enlightened.

A song contains the following lines:—

> '*O Lord! I did not aspire to you*
> *But You wanted me before I sought You.*
> *You Yourself have revealed to me....*'

It is God that attracts us to Him. In fact spiritual life begins after you get a glimpse of God. Till then we are in the preparatory stage. We always long to be united with the Infinite. Why? There can be no finite without the Infinite. God is the ground and the reality of our individuality. But the 'bubble' thinks so much of itself all the time, forgetting the 'ocean', though it has no existence apart from the latter.

Seeing His presence in all is the culmination of all spiritual practices. We should imagine this at the beginning. All the great souls of the past, Sri Ramakrishna, Holy Mother, and their direct disciples have felt and experienced this, and we should have faith in their words. Some say that everything concerning God and spirituality is imagination. Let it be so. Do not people imagine so many other things of the world and also believe in the words of others? If spiritual truths are imaginary then material things also are so. They too are not real. While travelling through a desert in the hot sun one can see mirages in which trees, a lake etc. could be clearly seen. One might have read about them but they are none the less real. But they are only phenomena, not factually real. Likewise, material things also are phenomena, appearing to be real. The jnani begins his spiritual life with the attitude of 'Not this', 'Not this' (this is not real, this is not real). When he is established in Brahman he sees the Lord manifested everywhere and in everything. Sri Ramakrishna has clearly shown this truth to us in His life.

A little injection of *advaita* is essential. One need not fear to follow these *advaitic* principles in practical life. Sri Samkara said: 'I am not the body or the mind. I am not a conglomeration of the five elements. They cannot affect me.' Why should we always think of ourselves in terms of this flesh and blood? Think of the Spirit within. Really, the spirit is condensed and has become subtle things like mind and gross things like the body. The same prana is everywhere. Everything is created from that. This was declared by the ancient Sages. Scientists also agree with it now.

The Upanishads lead us to the Truth by the path of 'not this, not this'. They instruct us that our ordinary perceptions are not real. But when one realises the Truth, one also comes to know that it is the same Truth which is manifested as the

universe. Then one knows that 'everything is That'. Sri Rama
krishna gives an example to illustrate this fact. When we want
to go to the top floor of a house, we go by the staircase,
starting from the lowest landing stage. We approach it, open
the gate and start climbing the different steps, finally reaching
the top floor. There we find the all-pervading bright light.
After reaching the roof we come to know that all the steps
leading to it also are made of the same stuff as the top floor,
and the same light is shining everywhere. We become happy
by enjoying the breeze and light of the terrace. Similarly, we
become satisfied by enjoying the infinite joy and knowledge
of spiritual illumination and also understand that the same
spiritual entity is manifested as the universe. The joys and
sorrows of the world then cease to affect us.

Different Grades of Reality

Many young men approach Sadhus complaining of the
restlessness of mind. Restlessness of the mind is not bad.
Only you should know the cause. Restlessness for attaining
noble objectives is good. Negative restlessness of the mind
is of no value. The yearning to be free, to achieve something
higher in life is a blessing. This divine discontent is quite
different from dissatisfaction caused by unfulfilled worldly
desires. Dissatisfaction in lack of spiritual experience is good.
Follow the spiritual path. Attain something that gives you
peace. Have you seen anyone fully happy in this world?
But still we seek happiness. It is like quenching one's
thirst with the water of the mirage. The world as we see it
is unreal but it has a Reality behind it—just as the mirage
which is unreal is supported by the desert which is real. The
world is not unreal like the horns of a hare; the Reality
behind it is all Bliss and Peace. We should attain that. The
world of name and form exists this moment and does
not exist the next moment. The reality of name and form
differs from the reality of spiritual consciousness. There
are four grades of reality.

1. *Atyantika asat (Tuccha)*—it is completely unreal with no possibility of existence—like the horns of a hare. 2. *Pratibhasika satya*—illusory reality, like seeing a snake in the rope. It is real for the frightened man. 3. *Vyavaharika satya*—this is real for the day-to-day existence in this world. All the various things of the world come in this category. 4. *Paramarthika satya* the Supreme Reality, the ultimate Reality. At the dawn of awakening you realise: 'I am the Atman which has put on the three bodies to play the drama of life.' If you think of the nature of the body you do not feel like living in it, as the Holy Mother said once after coming to the normal plane from samadhi. We have to dwell in this house. Our aim is to awaken the spiritual consciousness and realise our real nature. Live in such a way that there will be no necessity to take another body. Many times we think that we have become saints but soon tumble down from that state.

Reality and Illusion

Reality is not a result of imagination. There is Reality. Since it cannot be defined in precise terms one should not say that It does not exist. It appears as different objects according to our concept. A thief, having stolen something in the night, was running away to hide himself. There was a stump of a tree on his way. He took it for a policeman. A policeman in search of the thief took the same stump for the thief. A woman in search of her lover took it for her beloved. Their perceptions were all incorrect. Yet the existence of the stump could not be denied. We should always remember this fact. Just because we do not perceive Reality or understand It, we should not deny It. Hence one should not rush to the conclusion that the forms of various Gods and Goddesses are all imaginary. It is true that we imagine them in the first instance. But suddenly we get a vision which we would not have consciously thought of at all. Where did it come from? Ordinarily we act at the instance of either the conscious mind or the sub-conscious mind. But these visions come from a different plane. Intuition is beyond both the conscious and sub-conscious minds. All may not get visions but that does not matter. By spiritual practices, one comes to feel His living presence. That is enough. One need not see Him at that stage—but the experience of that living presence would clearly show us that He exists.

Bound by our illusory thoughts, we do not see the truth. One day, a drunkard drank his fill at night, and returning to his car, sat in it but could not find the steering wheel or the brake, so intoxicated he was. In that condition he went and rang up the police to complain that the steering wheel was stolen. By the time the Policeman came, the effect of the drink had diminished a little, and re-entering his car he found the steering wheel and brake in their proper position. Only then did he know that initially he was occupying the wrong seat. All our action should be properly controlled and directed or else there will be a crash. This applies to religion also.

Maya

God is beyond all dualities but all dualities have been manifested by Him. It is all His play. His maya has two aspects *avidya* and *vidya*. He has bound us through His *avidya maya* and He Himself helps us to get out of all entanglements by his Vidya maya. So we should pray to God, the Mother of the universe: 'Mother, I have had enough of your play; now I want you.' The juggler woman has a bag full of small objects which she spreads out and performs magic with them. Captivated by this jugglery, people forget themselves and do not remember the juggler woman. We are absorbed in the Divine Mother's maya and forget the Mother Herself who is the cause of it all, the Truth behind the phenomena.

Our vision is clouded by maya, and though the sun is shining we cannot see it. When we attain realization, we will see the light of our atman piercing through maya. Someone found fault with a sadhu for not observing sandhya The sadhu replied: 'The sun of Consciousness is ever shining in my heart. It has no rising or setting. How can I know whether it is morning or evening?' This is the experience of realised souls like Sri Ramakrishna. It is not easy to know the truth. Mind has the enquiring capacity by which it can unravel the truth but we do not always employ it properly. What the senses tell us may often be not the truth. For example, no object has any colour of its own. The solar light has seven colours in it which we see in objects. We are thus attracted by them. That is how we believe our deceiving eyes. We see the sun rising and setting, but science tells us that the fact is not so. We need a different eye to know real facts.

The sages point out the desert and the mirage as an example of the illusive perception by the senses. This is a wonderful illustration. The eyes tell us that the mirage exists. It has a name and a form but it does not really exist. The reality is the desert. Just as the desert projects and supports the mirage, the infinite projects and supports this universe. As long as we are satisfied by the sight of the mirage, there is no chance of the true knowledge coming to us. We have to doubt the mirage's existence, then only the way will be open for correct knowledge. It is only when the scientist began to doubt the rising and setting of the sun that he could find out the truth. Similarly, sages have discovered the real nature of the self. Just as we believe scientists, we should believe the sages and follow the path shown by them. The mirage is seen when the sun shines brightly. We take the reflected thing to be real, and delude ourselves. A man of realisation sees the world as an appearance, like the mirage; hence he is not attracted by the objects of the world. The things of the world are not real, in the sense that they have only temporary existence, but it does not mean that they do not exist at all. A man of realisation has to live in this world of diversity, but is not affected by it in any way as he knows its real nature. We take the rope for a snake in the darkness and the illusion persists as long as we see a snake in it. We discover the rope when knowledge dawns. We generally put on coloured glasses and take things to be as they appear through them. This is due to ignorance. There is a post on the road. In the dark, a thief takes it to be a policeman. A policeman following the thief takes it to be the thief. A father who has lost his child takes it for his child. In reality it is only a post. So, what is knowledge? It is : knowing a thing in its true nature. Now, try to know yourself; then you will be able to know also about things other than yourself.

The world is all maya, we say. Then why should we perform our duties? Do we really feel the world to be unreal? Till that consciousness arises in us, there is no way but to perform our duties. Daily, for some time at least, we should try to raise our consciousness to the level of the Atman, beyond body and mind. Then everything will be set right of its own accord. In meditation we try to become one with the Ishtam, merging the Atman in the Paramatman. This is the required practice. In the drama of life, we play our part as mother, father, friend, and so on.

If the actress playing the queen's role in a drama thinks that it is real and begins acting like a queen in her everyday life, what would happen? A king in a drama cannot be a king in the world. If they behave like king and queen, they will land in a lunatic asylum! This world has become a mad-house. A bubble sticks to another bubble and both burst. They do not see the ocean behind. People like Sri Ramakrishna saw the ocean in the bubbles too. They could see the All-pervading Reality in the world. Thus the whole conception should change. The deer seeing water in a mirage runs to reach the water and dies at last after a fruitless hunt. In the same way people try to find happiness in the world. They do find it, no doubt, but always mixed with much misery. They do not mind a lot of misery followed by a drop of joy. That has become their fate. People see others suffering in the world but gain no experience from it. As Yudhishthira said, the most wonderful thing in this world is that, though seeing people dying all around us, we still think that we have no death to face. We try to arrange things on a permanent basis. How to remove the delusion and practice self-control? The founder of the Quaker movement suggested to his friend a way of getting rid of the habit of drinking: 'As soon as you hold the filled glass in your hand, drop it.' Yes, that is the way, but is it easy to do? However difficult, it should be done.

Why do we forget God? It is through maya or ignorance. Do you love Him as much as you love the things of the world? It is a strange phenomenon that we believe the unreal to be real and vice versa. After great introspection we feel the spiritual consciousness present in us. We are Atman identified with body and mind. Who is free from this madness? Only men of realisation know this. In the course of our inner evolution, we feel that the world is unreal and we get a glimpse of the illusory nature of the world. Then we become eager to be one with the Reality.

13

The Unreality of the World

The Unreality of the World—Maya

There are different views about the reality of the world. Some say it has a subjective reality. But according to Vedanta, the creation of the world is not a subjective creation, but it springs from Avidya i.e. ignorance, or nescience. The forms of intuition and the categories of thought are all unreal, and the One and the Only Reality stands at the back of the subjective as well as of the objective. *This is an important point to note while studying Vedanta.* All this is a product of maya, everything—all manifestation, the whole empirical world, cosmic ignorance—everything. Therefore one should not have any desire for it. Let us see what scriptures say about it:

All this is a product of maya and maya itself is unreal. Therefore one should not entertain any fear. One should always think of Brahman, think that one is none other than Brahman.

Even the mind with which one fears is unreal.

If one is afraid of hearing the words of the son of a childless woman, then alone this world is real.

If the hare has got horns, then alone this world is real.

If an elephant can be killed with the horns of a hare then let this world be real.

If one is satisfied by drinking the water of the mirage, then only this world is real.

If the castle in the air is a reality, then only this world also exists.

If the blue colour of the sky is a reality, then only this world too would be real.

139

If a man who died a month back, can return to his old body, then alone this world is real.

If the milk that comes out of the cow's udder, can go back, then only this world is real.

If it is possible for a lotus to grow inside a blazing fire, then let this world be real.

If it is possible for an ignorant man to fathom the depths of the heart of a man of knowledge, then only this world is real.

Meditate that you are no other than the Sat-Chit-Ananda, and that this world does not exist.[1]

We have another funny way of expressing the unreality of the world:

The son of a childless woman, having had a bath in the waters of a mirage, carrying in his hand a bow made of the horns of a hare, put on a garland made of the flowers hanging in the sky. If such a son is real, then alone this world exists.[2]

Before this diversified world came into existence, the One existed without a second. He is the One without any colour, but He by virtue of His inscrutable power brings into existence this diversified world with many colours.[3]

Sankaracharya says:

Maya is the inscrutable power of the Lord. We cannot find out its beginning. It consists of the gunas that bring into existence this manifold world. It is neither existent nor non-existent, nor a combination of both.[4]

Sri Ramakrishna has said: The snake itself is not poisoned by the venom that is in its fangs, but when it bites another, the poison kills. Even so there is maya in the Lord,

---

1. Although such ideas replete in Yoga-Vasishtha, the exact reference could not be traced.
2. cf. Laghu Yoga-Vasishtha 3.7.
3. Chhandogya Upanishad 6.2.1 and 6.4.1.
4. Vivekachudamani, 108/109.

but it does not affect Him, while the same maya causes the delusion of the whole universe.[1] As a cloud covers the sun, so maya conceals God. When the cloud moves away, the sun is seen. When maya is removed, God becomes manifest. On a serene and perfectly cloudless sky a cloud may suddenly appear and darken the whole atmosphere. Then suddenly, it may be driven off by the wind. Even so is maya. Maya suddenly covers the serene atmosphere of consciousness, creates the visible universe, and is again dispersed by the breath of the Lord.[2]

How to Transcend Maya?

There is a song in which it is said:
O Lord, if Thou existest, pervading the whole universe,
Why is it that I do not find Thee,
Even though I call on Thee so much?
I see, someone has blindfolded my eyes
And that is why I cannot see Thee.
Pray, remove the bandage of maya and open my eyes.

This bandage of maya is to be removed and so long as there is this bandage of maya on our eyes, the phenomenal world appears real. We need a new sight to see the face of Truth. We must purify ourselves—our body, our mind, our desires —because without purification the face of Truth can never be seen. Without purification the phenomenal world can never be transcended, the bandage of maya can never be removed.

'Know this maya to be the cause of this universe, and the Lord Himself to be the author of maya.'[3] Maya is eternally dependent on God, the Great Juggler. It is His jugglery that has brought into existence this phenomenal world. He Himself can never be deceived by His own tricks. The poison of the snake does not hurt it. This is the answer to the question:

1. Gospel, 1997, p. 102.
2. Ibid., p. 169.
3. Shvetashvatara Upanishad, 3.1.

'Does this maya delude God?' God and His inscrutable maya are never separate, but He is not affected by His maya. It is to be transcended by the spiritual aspirant.

In order to transcend this maya, this jugglery of the Lord, the aspirant must pass through strict ethical discipline. He must purify his body and mind and must be steady and patient in his spiritual practices, surrendering the fruits to the Lord. He must be prepared to die in the struggle. The weakling and the dabbler have no place in spiritual life.

The surest way to get rid of maya is to take shelter under the Lord, who is its author. Since the Great Juggler is never deceived Himself by His tricks, if we take shelter at His feet, we too shall see His jugglery as jugglery and no longer as something real. The devotee seeks the protection of God. The *jnani* seeks the protection of the Guru. The Guru is an illumined soul, and the illumined person has become one with God. Thus it is equivalent to seeking the protection of God. That is why, really speaking, there is scarcely any difference between the approach of the *bhakta* or the devotee and the *jnani*, and the means to get rid of maya are more or less the same.

Sri Krishna says:

This maya of Mine is very hard to cross. They alone are able to cross it who take shelter under me.[1]

In Shvetashvatara Upanishad it is said: 'There is one unborn being, red, white, and black, producing manifold offspring of the same nature as itself.[2] This is the symbolic expression for the three gunas of Prakriti. The *sattva* is represented by white, the *rajas* by red and the *tamas* by black, all of which are to be transcended by the spiritual aspirant because they all belong to the great jugglery of the phenomenal world. You must reach the state of perfect colourlessness;

---

1. Bhagavad Gita, 7.14.
2. 4.1.

even being white won't do. Even the state of pure sattva is not the ultimate goal, though every aspirant must pass through it on his way to Truth.

The Sankhyas give the following illustrations: Prakriti, primal matter, is a very ugly dancing girl that has put on a beautiful garment to enchant the soul. The moment her true nature and looks are discovered, the dancing girl, Prakriti, feels ashamed and runs away, thus freeing the soul from her presence and allurements.

The World Dream

What is this life after all? Why are we just acting in this world like actors? We are sleeping, as it were, in the waking state. All this is a dream, true, but the dreamer should never forget himself. All this is thought, true, but who is the thinking entity? The Vedantic teacher wants us to know that all this is dreaming, but the dreamer should never forget himself. He should do away with his dreaming and realize his reality. This is the purport of Vedanta, and this must never be lost sight of.

So long as the dreamer goes on dreaming the dream, the dream is a reality. When the dreamer somehow gets a glimpse of it being a dream, only then the question arises how to break this dream. But this can never be done before the dreamer begins to doubt the dream.

We do not become the Self; we are It already, though unconscious of It. The waking state is nothing more than a kind of dream when seen from the highest state, the fourth, and steps are to be taken to get rid of this dream and reach the super-conscious state. Our goal is to make the ideal real, and what used to be real to us, must become unreal. The worldly dream only appears to be real so long as we are not awake, so long as the vision of the Atman hasn't come to us. And our waking state has no greater reality than our dream-state. Both are unreal.

The Three States of Consciousness

On account of one state of consciousness succeeding another, not one of them—neither the waking state, nor the dream state, nor the state of deep sleep—can be said to be real. Nothing that belongs to the realm of relativity, the changing, the fleeting, can ever be said to be real. At the most, its reality is a secondary one and wholly dependent on the sole reality of the Self, the substratum of all these states of consciousness. The unchanging Self that witnesses the three states of consciousness is called *vishva*, *taijasa* and *prajna*, in waking, dream and sleep respectively, and is wholly unaffected by them.

In deep sleep, consciousness is present. After waking from sleep, we say, 'I knew nothing'. But to enable us to say, 'I knew nothing,' consciousness must have been present. One cannot therefore, predicate a time when consciousness is not.

A comparative analysis and the frequent meditation on the experiences of dream and wakefulness will lead one, step by step, to the realization of the unreality of the empirical world. The objective world perceived in the waking state stands on the same footing of unreality as the world we perceive in a dream. The world in a dream appears to the dreamer just as real as the world in the waking state erroneously believed to be real by the person who is perceiving it. The objects seen in a dream are just as liable to cause joy and suffering to the dreamer as those perceived in the world of the waking state.

The goal of the true Vedantin is just to break all the upadhis (limiting adjuncts) and to attain to the fourth state, the super-conscious, to which no name can be given, and which has been described as 'the One without a second'. You must never lose sight of the fact that the aim of Vedanta is to enable the *jiva* (individual soul) to get rid of maya and his limited consciousness and then to realize his oneness with the Supreme Self *even in the waking state*. The whole sadhana (spiritual practice) is meant for one's own realization of the highest consciousness.

After the dawn of real jnana (knowledge) the empirical world may still continue to be perceived, but it will not affect the enlightened person as it did before. He will estimate it at its true value, as relative, fleeting, shadowy, unreal, and will not be affected by the pleasures or the miseries of life. On waking from our dream, we still remember the dream, but we never give it the place of reality, however pleasant or unpleasant the dream may have been.

For the ordinary person there exist only three states of consciousness: deep sleep, dream and the waking state, but Vedanta knows four states and stresses the fourth state of consciousness, the super-conscious. And something of that super-conscious state must be brought into the waking state of ordinary life by the aspirant.

Ignorance and Superimposition

In a red hot iron-ball it is not the iron-ball that burns, but the fire in it, which might just as well be in a lead ball or in a piece of wood. The fire-principle as such may be associated with a red-hot iron ball or with a red-hot brick or with lava or it may even appear in the form of a flame. But what really burns is the fire-principle. The burning principle does not belong to the limiting adjunct, but to the principle itself. Similarly the body and mind appear conscious but the consciousness belongs solely to the Atman or soul.

The moment you take the rope to be a serpent, different feelings are aroused in you: fear, the thought of killing it and how to kill it, etc. etc. The moment you take the piece of glass for a diamond, greed comes and fills you, creating the desire to possess it. If you take the mother-of-pearl to be silver, the same thing happens. If you think that the body is a reality, lust and the desire for physical enjoyment are roused in you. Always, the first error creates all the subsequent errors and all the lies that build up our lives. That is why the first error must be annihilated.

And this first ignorance is something tremendously real. It is very far from being a mere imagination like the son of a barren woman or the horns of a hare. This ignorance is real, not a mere imagination. It does not belong to the category of imagination at all. The perception of the snake in place of the rope is not false in the sense of there being nothing to account for the appearance of the snake. The rope forms the substratum, the basis, on which is superimposed the idea of the snake. The snake is in no way based on a mere nothing. Maya is not illusion in the sense of mere nothingness.

The empirical world has no existence apart from Consciousness with a capital 'C', and is unreal, because it is insentient, dead, inert and fleeting, a mere reflection of reflections. Consciousness (Atman) is not the cause of the phenomenal world, nor is the phenomenal world an effect. When a rope is mistaken for a serpent, you do not take the rope to be the cause of the serpent, you do not think that the rope has ever been modified into a snake. It is the absence of proper knowledge that makes one perceive a snake in the rope which has never been modified into a snake. So it is with the Self (Atman) and the universe, the whole world of the manifold.

The Vedantin believes in evolution as a stage, but never as the ultimate goal, and to him even this evolution is merely an appearance, never an absolute reality. Evolution can never be an ultimate fact to the Vedantin. It too is a mere appearance, the rope, which is being taken for the snake. It is true at a certain stage, it is no longer true after we have gone beyond that stage on our path to Truth.

This is not a question of something becoming something else. It is not the milk becoming curds. Then it would lose its true nature. But it is the rope 'becoming' a snake. And when this mistake has been made, when the rope has been mistaken for a snake, then it brings in all the troubles of a real snake; fear etc. etc.

What is unreal, we take to be real; what is insentient, we take to be sentient; what is matter, we take to be spirit. We are always giving some superimposition the place of reality. Sankara says: 'We always take a thing to be what it is not.' And all these false ideas, all these false conceptions, are to be removed by following steadily and patiently the right method.

The reason why we want to live eternally is that our real nature is eternal. First this false identification with the body and all its upadhis (limiting adjuncts) must be got rid of. The body, the mind, the inner organ (antahkarana) etc. can never be eternal, and so long as our identification with them lasts, there can be no eternal life for us.

Whatever becomes the object of your consciousness is maya (a phenomenon) and you must separate the knower from the known, the witness from all things he is witnessing, the perceiver from the things perceived. There must be merciless, clear analysis and clear thinking at every stage of the spiritual journey. When we remove the veil of maya, we find that 'x' and 'y', the knower and the known, are one and the same. That which Kant calls 'space, time and causality,' according to Vedanta, belong to maya and must be transcended.

Physical objects are always percepts, being perceived by one or other of the sense-organs. The sense-organs themselves become percepts to the mind. In its turn the mind becomes a percept to the self which is always the witness or the perceiver and can never become a percept as this would mean a 'regressus ad infinitum'. We must stop somewhere.

We are more or less living on false notions, and therefore these false notions are to be refuted. Truth always brings pain to those who cling to untruth. There are very many people who are terribly afraid of spiritual life lest their dreams be broken. They go on clinging to their pet notions and untruth all their lives. Usually we find people who want to dream false dreams, who are not prepared to meet Truth face to face and stand the pain that is caused by the destruction of their pet ideas. But without this destruction there can never be any spiritual life.

People who have lived for a long time in a perfectly dark room, cannot stand the light when it comes. The owl cannot see in daylight. Now, to us, the darkness is something real, intensely real, until the Light appears. Spiritual Realization means removal of darkness and bringing in of Light, a Light that does not depend on another light for its illumination, a Light that is not reflected light.

Bondage and Freedom

Swami Vivekananda says in one of his poems:
Thine only is the hand that holds
The rope that drags thee on.
Let go thy hold, Sannyasin bold! say—
'Om Tat Sat, Om!'[1]

We do not recognize that the chain is something to be avoided. Rather we cling to it and want to hug it to our hearts' content, but finally, some day, we will have to take a bold step and let go the hold. This holds good with reference to what is gross and also to what is subtle. Let go your hold of all things of the world and your personalities, and hold tight only Brahman and become one with It. Without forging new fetters, we have to break the old ones. That is the very first step, and without breaking them, the goal can never be attained.

1. CW., Vol. 4, The Song of the Sannysin. P. 394.

All these lives we have entangled ourselves into things that are unreal, and now we must follow just the opposite process and dis-entangle ourselves from all these fetters and bonds that our ignorance has created for us. The counter-thought is to be raised, consciously, energetically. In place of the false identification with the body, the mind, the ego, we must raise the thought that we are separate from all these limiting adjuncts, i.e. the body, mind, ego etc. etc. The chain is moving, but holding on to the chain, we are dragged along and go on complaining, 'Ah, the chain is dragging me!', instead of just letting it go. Cease to hold the chain of causality, the chain of life and death! Try to become purer and purer and purer. Do your spiritual exercises steadily, patiently, purposefully, without any break. Then even the practical side of spiritual life will become easy and natural to you.

Once upon a time two men were standing on the bank of a river when they saw a beautiful rug floating past. So one said to the other, 'Jump in and get it. It is such a beautiful rug.' The man did so, swam to the rug, got hold of it, but instead of being able to drag it to the bank, he was dragged along with it. Seeing this, the man on the bank shouted, 'Let go the rug, let it go!' But the other replied, 'I cannot let it go, the rug has got hold of me.' You see, under the rug and hidden by it, was a bear!

The moment we run headlong after objects of enjoyment in order to get hold of them and enjoy them, they get hold of us and begin to suck our blood and life-force. This happens to all who have entangled themselves in the meshes of the illusion of the world.

You must hammer at your encrustations day by day, till some spot becomes soft so that it can be broken even by a light blow. One can do this with a very strong blow, but this is very dangerous if the mind is not yet fully purified and fully prepared. Just go on giving steady and relentless blows to your encrustations. You see, in the case of a tiny bird you can help it to get out of its egg if it is already sufficiently developed. But if you break the shell too early, the poor little bird is bound to die.

In the Vedanta Sutras it is said:

The instruction is that there must be constant repetition of, or dwelling on, the Truth.[1]

If such is the requirement for a person who is well-prepared for a spiritual life, then you must repeat the truth much oftener. This constant repetition of the truth is necessary in order to eradicate the wrong notions that have taken possession of your mind and have coloured it entirely.

---

1. Vedanta Sutras. 4.1.1.

14

Spiritual Progress on Experience

The Inner Journey

The mind is always thinking of gross forms. If you think of the luminous form of the holy personality, the activity of the mind will be turned into new channels. We are pre-occupied with our little-I; now we come to think of something nobler and higher. The blissful form of the holy personality seizes the mind. The mind, which had become *jada*, stone like, by thinking of material objects all the time, now becomes infused with the luminosity and bliss of the divine form. It starts shedding its jada-nature. From the blissful form, go deeper, think of His noble attributes. Do not stop there. Consciousness is the most important thing. My consciousness, though a poor reflection, is part of His consciousness which is one with Infinite Consciousness. The higher you go, the subtler the plane you reach. It is higher and also deeper. As you reach the purer planes, your consciousness expands. So, we start from the gross plane taking the help of a physical symbol, the divine name. Do your japa, consciously, knowingly and intelligently, dwelling on its meaning. Then you come to the threshold of the spiritual plane. You are transported from the mental plane, cut off from the outside world, to the plane of deep meditation. Outer activity becomes distressful. The mind becomes very quiet and reaches the subtle plane. Meditation should be like 'niravacchinna tailadhara'—unbroken stream of oil. Here, even without the help of sound and form, the mind is concentrated. A new inner consciousness awakens. *Bhajan* and *Kirtan* elevate the mind, but that is not a permanent state.

For permanent results, you have to conquer every inch of
the ground and that can be achieved only through steady,
prolonged practice of meditation. Know the technique; you
can then dwell upon the Lord with love and joy. You cannot
stop the function of the mind. Hence give it a new theme—
the Lord, the Divine Mother, the all-pervading Consciousness.
Spiritualise the mind. This is the way from the gross, to the
subtle, to the spiritual.

You go 'within'. What does it mean? Not somewhere
inside this body, but into the mental and spiritual planes of
consciousness. You come to a world vaster than this physical
world. Your little mind gets in tune with the universal. Heart
is the gateway to the plane of consciousness. There are hearts
and hearts—physical, mental, spiritual hearts. These are all
different planes of consciousness, as in concentric circles. Let
our little heart beat in tune with the Cosmic Heart. Know
that the Atman permeates the entire body, but of all the
centers in the body, we feel the concentrated consciousness
more in the heart. Withdraw your mind to the inner Light.
Practice this for a few moments. Then gradually you will have
the experience of 'living Consciousness'. To the extent one's
mind is pure, spiritual practice is successful. Swami
Brahmananda used to tell us: 'As you go on with your
spiritual practice, you will discover what the heart is, how
to go deeper, what to discover.'

In sadhana, we start with external objects and move
towards the inner Reality. The highest state is seeing, 'the
Self in everything and everything in the Self,' (Gita, VI. 29.)
and in that state 'where is delusion, where is sorrow?' (Isa
Upanishad) The journey commencing with image-worship
will lead us to this Supreme Truth. What was the experience
of Sri Ramakrishna? The shrine, the Puja-vessels, everything
appeared as manifestations of the Mother. In this state
the devotee experiences the presence of God within and
without. He attains same-sighted-ness. Great humility comes.
Without going through these stages one cannot come to the

worship of the Formless. Thinking of the external objects all the time and trying to worship the Formless—no, that is not possible. If the external objects are real to us, then for worship also we have to adopt an external object. So we worship a personality with the noblest virtues. When meditation becomes steady and Self-consciousness is awakened, mind subsides and worldly thoughts disappear. All thoughts, even the thought of the deity, disappear. This is how sadhana leads one step by step to the experience of Brahman. Till then one should continue with japa, meditation and spiritual thoughts. We have to proceed from form to the Formless, from name to the Nameless, and from thoughts to the One beyond all thoughts.

The Way to Peace

An aspirant complained to Swami Shivanandaji that though he had been practicing meditation to the best of his ability, he found hardly any joy in it. He was going through the practice as a routine wnich did not give him any joy or peace. This is an eternal complaint. We talk of peace. When we get the thing that we want, we attain some peace for the time being. But immediately thereafter, the mind starts hankering for something else and again we have no peace. Again, when faced by some unpleasant thing, we feel miserable and want to get rid of it. Thus we are ever deprived of peace. The peace we get through enjoyment does not last long. We want lasting peace but the way to peace is very difficult. 'Sharp as the blade of the razor and hard to traverse is the way to self-knowledge,' as the Upanishad says. The Upanishad says further:

Atmanam rathinam viddhi Sariram rathameva tu
Buddhim tu sarathim viddhi Manah pragrahameva cha
Indriyani hayanahuh Vishayamsteshu gocharan

The self is the rider in the chariot of body. Buddhi (intellect) is the charioteer and mind is the rein. Senses are the horses which run along the path of sense-experience.

Now, the fact is that the senses go after the objects of enjoyment. The horses are not under control. The reins are loose. The charioteer is not alert. So the whole chariot is proceeding towards a crash. The task is to make the horses go in the opposite direction—the senses are to be directed inwards. The intellect should be vigilant and keep the mind under control. This path is indeed difficult. But no one forces us to follow it. When we have chosen the path, we should not mind the difficulties. As Swami Brahmananda said: 'Find joy in the struggle.' The peace we will get as a result is worth all the trouble.

The child is under the impression that his mother is omnipotent and feels happy. But after some .time he sees his father scolding the mother, and then the father becomes omnipotent. When he grows still older, he ceases to have any regard for them, by seeing their hypocrisy. He turns to other quarters for love and security. The pursuit of the mirage thus proceeds indefinitely. The love of mother, father or of any earthly relation is nothing compared to the love of the Lord. He is the very source of all love that we see in this world. A drop of His love is found here. So we should feel joy in the struggle to attain Him and His infinite love and peace. But we are not able to give up our petty joys for the sake of the great joy of God—like the child affected by tonsillitis, who is better when he does not eat sweets, but cannot give them up. We are engrossed in the magic of the Mother and are busy with our toys, forgetting Her.

Leaving the abode of peace, *shantiniketan*, people seek *shanti* in *samsara*, like a thirsty man seeking to quench his thirst from the mirage in the desert. Infinite Peace is within us, but we look for it in the world outside, like the musk deer that runs about in search of the perfume, ignorant of the perfume coming from its own body. Everyone wants only peace and blessings but all the time go in the opposite direction—away from eternal peace—getting more and more bound. Along with a drop of worldly peace they get a mass of misery. They become petty-minded. Abiding happiness can be had only in the Lord. If you are to get *brahmajnana* you should hold fast to Him.

We do not practice truth, nonviolence, equanimity of mind etc. We go the wrong way of lust, greed, hatred etc. and then demand peace. How can you get it and if at all you get some peace, what peace is it? Do you want the type of peace which you get after eating nice dishes or enjoying something for which you have to suffer later on? That is not the peace we are looking for. The great ones used to forget their bodily pains by going to that higher plane. For this, there should be great practice. Through meditation we can reach a stage where we do not exist as our small personalities, where our troubles do not exist. It is not sleep. Sleep is only a state of temporary forgetfulness. The mind tries to dwell on the physical plane. It should be raised to a higher plane. Then when you come back from that high plane you can look upon things objectively. Where there is dispassion, detachment, how can there be any trouble? Practice properly. You get tremendous peace thereby.

Animals move with nature. They do not tell lies nor do they eat when not hungry. But human beings do all that. If one so wishes, one can be worse than an animal or greater than the gods. Live a life of discipline. A spiritual seeker is a psychologist. He studies his mind. By spiritual practice morality will be established in us. Sometimes you get a glimpse of the Reality and that memory will ever remain. We will not be happy unless we get it again and again. The soul yearns for it and repeated practice would make that peace a continuous, living experience.

Peace and Bliss

We say we want peace, but we do not have a clear conception of it. Is it the peace of a sleeping man or a stock or a stone? That is the peace of ignorance and inertia. Real peace is something far greater; it is the peace full of consciousness and bliss. Swamiji has composed a poem in which he says: 'We shall set fire to all desires of the heart and there Kali will dance.' But we do not like to burn all our desires and therefore Kali will not manifest Herself there. The difficulty lies there. Desires and presence of God do not co-exist. We should decide whether we want God or sense-objects. No doubt these philosophical sayings are good. But we have to proceed in our own way in order to realise the highest.

How to get peace and bliss in life? The Lord is the source of infinite peace and bliss. By thinking of Him we get a little of His peace and bliss. By selfless work we can get peace. The highest state of peace is moksha. Identifying ourselves with the Reality is the highest state. But it is a long way to go. Till you reach that state, what should you do? As you go higher and higher while climbing a hill, you see a lot of beautiful scenery and feel happier and happier. So also in spiritual life. As you elevate your mind to higher states, you attain more and more peace and bliss. Worshipping sat-chit-ananda, we are lifted above our limited body-mind consciousness. We should feel that we are the reflection of that ananda. By this practice, emotions of anger and hatred are eliminated and waves of harmony are maintained in the mind. The final state of total identification is a great ideal, beyond the reach of many aspirants. So our conception should be. 'He is the Creator, Infinite Light, of which we are beams.' By japa and meditation we should purify the mind. In the North when Sadhus meet each other, they ask: 'Is your vision clear?' meaning the spiritual vision. God is the only Reality; the world has no abiding reality. The mind should never forget this truth. A moment of joy and long hours of misery that is this world.

Joy of Spiritual Practice

By sitting quietly after meditation, much more pleasant thoughts come. We feel joy though we are not in contact with the sense world. Where does it come from? This is the joy arising from worship. We are at peace with ourselves and with others. Joy comes from expansion; petty-mindedness brings misery. Whenever we do some selfless work, what joy we feel! The moment one becomes absorbed in contemplation, one experiences boundless joy. Only glimpses of that joy are experienced in the beginning. Greater joy will be found when one progresses in practice. Swami Brahmanandaji used to pass days and nights in the blissful consciousness of God.

At the end of our daily practice, we shall sit quiet for a while. Morning is the best time for meditation, as then we feel fresh after a good night's sleep. Why do we feel happy at the time of prayer? For the time being other thoughts are repelled. Thinking of the Infinite makes our troubles look insignificant. We will rise far from the lower mind with the help of the repetition of the divine name.

Sri Ramakrishna used to speak of three kinds of joy— vishayananda, brahmananda and bhajanananda. The joy we get from sense enjoyment is vishayananda; it is momentary and is followed by misery. We also get joy when we do bhajan and recite hymns. That is bhajanananda. That is pure, sastric joy. But it is also not permanent. Our aim is to attain transcendental joy termed brahmananda—the joy of Brahman. It is possible to attain it by deep meditation and samadhi. If we succeed in maintaining the experience of the vaster Presence we get immense happiness.

In the first type of joy, the mind dwells on the lower centers. In the second one, the mind starts moving up. In meditation and samadhi, the mind ascends to the highest centers. But the mind wanders from one centre to another, corresponding to different states of consciousness and different states of vibration. The mind feels happy over one thing at one time, and dejected over the same thing at another time. Hence the attitude of the mind is always to be watched. What brings misery to the mind? Desires, jealousy, lust, hatred, anger etc. bring dejection and misery. The task is to remove them by following the advice of Patanjali—namely, counteract bad influences and tendencies by good ones.

The Joy Within

We try to know everything which is outside without ever thinking of ourselves. These external objects are like toys and one gets tired of them. A state comes when the soul yearns for Self realization. The Chhandogya Upanishad narrates how Narada, having studied many Sastras, mantras etc., was yet not happy and went to his Guru for instruction on Self knowledge. This is the hunger of the soul. In spite of all material comforts there is something wanting, a discontent. It is a blessing if this hunger comes at a young age. Then one takes to spiritual practices. The mind should be purified through study and contemplation. When the soul knows that it is a part of the whole, there is satisfaction.

We are all pleasure-seekers but do not know the correct place where we should seek it or the nature of it. The Self is the source of all joy and we should look for Him within ourselves. He is sat-chit-ananda and it is easy to think of Him in one's Ishtam rather than in anything else. If we love our little self so much, how much more we should love the Infinite! The holy name and form lead us to the nameless and formless. If our real nature is misery can we ever have happiness? Our real nature is infinite joy. We bind and limit ourselves. Can the finite exist without the Infinite? The wave without the ocean? Think that you are carrying God within your heart and work with the right spirit. What is needed is sincerity and eagerness. We are distinct from the body and mind and inseparable from the Lord. Repetition of the divine name, dwelling on the meaning and imagining the living picture of the deity leads to the awakening of the Spirit. He incarnates Himself from age to age. One need not seek any help outside since He alone works through one and all. You should pray: 'Reveal to me what You are and what I am.'

Each of us is in a narrow staircase composed of the ego and subtle tendencies. If we go down, it would only be hotter and darker there. One has to go up step by step because pure air and light are at the top, on the roof. While climbing we may get a glimpse of the light and a breath of pure air. That encourages us in our effort. After reaching the top and spending some time there, we may come down. But we shall always remember the roof and the pure air and light prevailing there, as we have tasted their joy. Every day we do enjoy that Bliss while we sleep. But we are not conscious of it at the time of sleep. Meditation is a conscious effort to experience that Bliss. When we fall asleep, we do not care for anyone. One should have the same attitude while sitting for meditation. We should be wide awake. We should also 'raise the anchor'—cut off all the worldly bonds, at least for the time being. Conscious japa of the mantra is an important part of this process of meditation.

Spiritual Progress

For spiritual progress, more than anything else, one should have the blessing, co-operation of one's own mind. There are many deep-rooted samskaras which cannot be eliminated so quickly. Samskaras are created by wrong thinking and action; they can be erased by right thinking and action. Yet some are of the opinion that human nature cannot be changed; but this is not so. It can and does change for the better or for the worse. When we find any wrong tendency in us, we should throw it out at once, but mere wishing will not achieve it. We must start acting, plunging into sadhana. Conscious practice is needed, after which we will see some progress in ourselves.

What is progress? We become more and more selfless in our dealings with others; we feel an inner joy and peace. Think of your mental state in the past and compare it with your present state; you will see the difference wrought by sadhana. Similarly, examine how many times in the day you think of God. How much time is spent in contemplating on Him? Find out what thoughts come to the mind when falling asleep and on waking up. That would give a true indication of the contents of the mind. These are the ways to find out spiritual progress.

By mental purity, it is meant that worldly thoughts will not unduly disturb the mind. Progress in the mental field is both vertical and horizontal—the mind is elevated and it also expands. The outlook widens as we do japa and meditation regularly. Identifying ourselves with the body, mind and ego, we experience pleasure and pain. As we proceed in spiritual practice, bondages will drop and we will begin to be conscious of our real nature. Then the dual experiences like pleasure and pain will not affect us. Neither the body nor the mind is 'I'. Only the Atman shines brightly. As this feeling increase in us, we will experience inner joy and this will lead us to immortality.

Through moral practice we come to know purity; through spiritual practice purity becomes established in us. Both these together lead us to the goal. We gain strength and a state of fearlessness is reached. Spiritual practice can make us pure, but realisation cannot be attained by that alone. Only through the grace of God is realisation possible. Just as age-long darkness in a room is removed as soon as a lamp is lit, so all the impurities are removed when we get the grace of God. And unless the heart is purified, God's grace does not reveal itself. So our effort should be steady and unfailing. The breeze is ever blowing; our only task is to unfurl the sails. To awaken to the presence and grace of God is our task— the task of 'unfurling the sails'. The light of the sun shines everywhere, but it will be reflected only in a clean mirror. As long as the needle is covered with rust, it cannot be attracted by the magnet. The force of attraction is ever there, but the needle does not move in spite of it. Hence the need for purity. Bonds will fall away if the mud of passion and attachment is washed away by repeating the name of the Lord.

The Guru gives instructions to the devotee. He teaches him about various stages in spiritual life. He will guide him and lead him to the goal. When the devotee meets with the Reality, all his doubts vanish. In the course of his sadhana, various spiritual experiences may come to the sadhaka. He may see many visions of the deity and so on. He should not stop at these stages, but proceed further on, to become one with the all-pervading Reality, Brahman. That is the highest stage in which all doubts vanish. The Guru leads the disciple until he reaches that stage. The mind is the greatest Guru; nothing can be done without the help of the mind. The mind is to be purified by the practice of japa and meditation. By such practice our body will become pure. We shall not be victims of minor diseases and the body will become strong and healthy. There will be mental strength and our hearts will expand. When this happens, we come more and more in touch with the Inner Reality. Truth will unfold itself from within. A strange inexpressible joy is experienced. A dumb person having tasted a sweet can obviously not tell anyone about its sweetness. The joy of spiritual awakening is like that. This is the test—as one comes into contact with this Reality; he will feel an inexpressible joy from within. There are two kinds of persons who are happy—those who are engrossed in the world and those who are jnanis. But people who are neither here nor there, the sadhakas are unhappy. They have to be so for the time being, otherwise how can they hope to achieve the highest bliss?

Marks of Spiritual Progress

Some say that they are not progressing, but they do not know what progress is. If our body has become more harmonious, if our mind becomes purer, we should know that we are progressing. We have to watch and see whether our selfishness and egoism are going down.

Some aspirants wish to retire to lonely spots for sadhana. One disciple wanted to give up his work and go away in this manner, sometime ago. Now he says; 'Now there is no such hankering. I do not feel the need for any change of environment. For me longing for solitude is gone now.' He had now become established in japa and meditation.

One who feels the presence of the Lord within and without is an Advaitist. He cannot find fault with others. He thinks that all are Lord's children. We have many drawbacks in us which we do not want to acknowledge. But when we judge others we think that we are superior. Only those who have dirty minds talk ill of others. Whenever you find anybody criticising others, understand that such a person has weaknesses in himself. Therefore the Holy Mother, who had a pure mind, could not find fault with anybody. Such purity is the test of progress. We should find out if our attitude towards others has changed and whether we have gained universal love for all. Thus we can test our progress.

Some blame God if they are unhappy. Is it that the compassionate Lord has become inconsiderate? On the contrary, it means that there is something wrong with us. What is the use of 'rowing without removing the anchor?' It is absolutely essential to remove it at least during meditation. We should cultivate the consciousness that we have no attachment to anything in the world—even to our own bodies. When all forms are seen as embodiments of Light, we cannot maintain the feeling that some forms are 'mine' and some are not.

We enter the sanctuary of the heart and think that the Light of the Atman is everywhere—both inside and outside. We feel the relationship of our soul with the Infinite Spirit whose spark is in each and every one of us. By following the instructions of the Guru in practice, we make this idea our own. As we are body-conscious, we have to think that the Light of the Atman has taken the form of the deity. In the shrine when devotees sit and sing with imagination and fervour, we can feel His actual presence. By regular practice, our understanding becomes clear. A child wants to cross the road, but there is heavy traffic, and it cannot have a clear conception of the whole picture. But an adult crosses the road easily. His vision is clear. Similarly, experience clears our understanding and broadens our view.

Meditation on God with form leads to the knowledge of oneness in time. The aspirant is gradually led to the contemplation of the Formless. Meditation on a divine form, is suited best for most people. There the mind dwells in the heart centre, which is the middle point of the body. Meditating in the heart, the mind rises above the lower centers where it usually wanders attracted by objects of the senses. The highest meditation is on the all-pervading Light of Consciousness. The chosen deity has arisen from that Infinite Light; it should ultimately merge in that.

Question: 'How does it culminate? Is the immanence of God realized in all, or, does everything disappear completely?'

Answer: Both happen. There is no use in discussing these matters idly. One should progress through sadhana. There are some Sadhus who repeat 'I am Brahman', 'That Thou art' etc. and lead a life of idle luxury. It is hypocrisy to talk of religious truths and not live accordingly. We want others to think that we are great devotees. What do we gain thereby? There should be inner transformation and growth. So sadhana is very essential. It gives us the power to understand. We should pray to God to guide our understanding and enlighten our consciousness. The Vedic mantra says: 'Dhiyo yo nah prachodayat.' Swami Vivekananda said: 'Out of those who take to religion, 80% become hypocrites, 15% become mad and only 5% succeed.' Many take to religion but they do not persevere. Religion is not for weaklings. Much strength, inner strength is needed. Mental power and bodily strength are equally essential. If one is bodily weak, he cannot proceed with his spiritual practices. Back pains, reeling of the head, etc. will disturb him. There will always be a tug-of-war between the lower nature and the higher nature. To withstand these struggles and tensions, mental strength is absolutely essential. The best way is that work and worship should go hand in hand.

Sadhana Leads from the Finite to the Infinite

It is impossible to have an idea of the finite without a conception of the Infinite. The manifested phenomena are limited. But there is an unlimited power behind all of them. It may not be possible to have a conception of the Infinite with our brain. The power of the mind is to be increased through sadhana, which is the only way to understand these truths. What do we understand when we hear of the different chakras in the body? The heart is very small—how can we think of a deity seated in it? One should not judge these things in purely physical terms. The deity is manifested in our inner consciousness. By sadhana our understanding capacity increases.

Two Types of Samadhi

Samadhi is of two kinds—*savikalpa* and *nirvikalpa*. Sri Ramakrishna's first experience when He saw the Divine Mother and became unconscious for a long time was *savikalpa* Samadhi, that is, the vision of God with form—seeing the Ishtam face to face. A trace of the ego remains in that state.

In *nirvikalpa* Samadhi, the aspirant loses all consciousness of his individuality and goes beyond the name and form of the deity. His consciousness is totally merged in the divine Consciousness. At the beginning of spiritual life, because of egoism, it is not possible during meditation to see that the whole world is full of His light, without the least consciousness of the individual's body. Our body belongs to the world of matter which is the plane of gross manifestation. Our mind and intellect and their outcome, i.e., thoughts and emotions, are of a subtler plane. Neither body-consciousness nor thoughts and emotions remain in the state of *nirvikalpa* Samadhi. This state is one of perfect union with God and it is the highest state of consciousness.

Once Sri Ramakrishna spoke of the manifestation of Brahman as sound (*sabda Brahman*). Maharaj (Swami Brahmananda) meditated on that theme and that aspect of God was revealed to him. The name of God is sabda Brahman. There are sound waves all over the universe all the time. When we express our ideas through our vocal organs, we tune ourselves with the sabda Brahman and thus we get the sound.

(15)

How to Live in the World

Maintain Peace and Harmony Within

'Charity begins at home.' First of all, everyone should bring into practice all the noble qualities. Then the world will be a better place. There are international movements, community movements and family movements for improving the world. The last mentioned comes first and the others follow. In order to live in harmony in a family, one should improve oneself; one should be at peace with oneself. Those who are in conflict with others always find that they are in conflict with themselves. Going to forests is escapism and useless, as the same mind with all its conflicts and agitation would follow us there. The Yogavasistha narrates the story of a king who gave up his kingdom and retired to a forest to attain peace and happiness and of his queen going to him as a brahmachari and imparting this great truth to him.

We should cultivate the right attitude towards life and the world and for that purpose should always be alert and be thinking of noble things. The Vedic prayer goes thus:

Om bhadram Karnebhih srnuyama devah Bhadram pasyemaksabhiryajatrah ... etc.

We should hear and see good, auspicious, noble things. We should think good thoughts. That is the means of cultivating harmony in mind which is essential for the practice of japa and meditation, The body should not be neglected at all. It should be kept in a healthy, efficient condition. Mind, body and soul should be given equal care and attention. Thinking, feeling and willing should be coordinated. Another famous prayer is:

166

Om apyayantu mamangani vak-pranah-chaksuh, srotram-atho-balam-indriyani cha sarvani.. etc.

Let my body, senses of perception, senses of hearing, speech and vital force be strong. This prayer clearly states the need for giving equal importance to body and mind and maintaining them at an efficient level for the purpose of devoting oneself to God-realisation.

All are Equal

It is the same all-pervading Consciousness which has taken the form of deity and that of the devotee. It resides in all. It has taken different forms. If we could understand and maintain this idea our attitude towards others would change. We would start seeing them as spirit and realise that all are parts of the one all-pervading Consciousness. That Consciousness is flowing through every one. Thus all are equal. If this energy or power stops flowing through a person we say that he is dead.

There is the story of the asuras, men and devas going to Prajapati for spiritual instruction. Sankaracharya interprets these three types as representing the three Gunas to be found in each individual. Devas stand for sattva, human beings for rajas and asuras for tamas. These Gunas exist in the individual in varying proportions. In the spiritual evolution, sattvaguna is to be developed and then this too should be transcended to attain the Absolute. Those that have realised the Infinite see the same Absolute in all and overlook the shortcomings of others and love them. Only mean-minded people magnify others' faults and think highly of themselves

We should always remember that all are equal. But we forget it and think that we are superior to others. We judge others as if we knew everything. We criticise others but cannot tolerate others criticising us. As the Lord resides in all, we should have love for all and try our best to serve all. Sri Ramakrishna saw the Lord manifested in all and could not bear to see others suffering. Swami Vivekananda learnt

H 12

the ideal of service from him and propagated it. This does not mean that we should always be soft. If a child does something wrong, we should correct him. We may even have to beat him sometimes. This does not mean that we hate the child. We only want him to become good. We are fighting for the truth, but people feel hurt if we point out their mistakes. That cannot be helped.

Some complain of the external atmosphere being unfavorable for sadhana. A peaceful atmosphere has to be created in one's own mind.

Supreme Spirit in All

When we enter the abode of the Lord, what can the external atmosphere do to us? We should repeat His Name, dwelling on its meaning. We should think that the same atman forms the core of all physical bodies. The Supreme Spirit in one aspect has taken the forms of all gods and goddesses and in another aspect, the forms of the devotees. This Truth will be ultimately revealed. We should here see the broad-mindedness of the teachers. When Sri Ramakrishna met Sarat Maharaj for the first time, the former sang: 'Lord, you are our everything.' This song has great significance. We should ever remember the fact that God is our all-in-all. Prayers containing such noble ideas should be sung daily and they should be deeply rooted in the heart.

You need not give up the world. Seek the Reality that is in the friend and relative. We want peace which abides. Meditation has an abiding effect in removing our miseries. When you cannot get that abiding peace, you go after fleeting joys. When you cannot get pure water, you quench your thirst with dirty water, and the result is sickness. Set a little time aside every day to develop this understanding of higher Reality. Everyone is very eager to gather information about spiritual practice, but there is no eagerness to do any practice. We render service to sincere people. Those with good samskaras follow the path sincerely.

Don't Depend on Others

We cannot change the outer world. We cannot 'improve' it according to our will. Our own mind should be trained to change its outlook. The aspirant should look into himself rather than try to change others. He should try to depend on himself. In the spiritual path, depending on external help, attaching oneself exclusively to a person, is always dangerous, because such external help is not permanent. One may need such help in the beginning but gradually one should leave it and start depending on oneself. The Blissful Lord is in the heart of our hearts. Think of Him, depend upon Him. He is awaiting our call. When we call on Him sincerely, when we intensely search for the Reality, He starts shining in our hearts. He is the refuge and the guide. Realise His presence in your heart by means of meditation. Depending on external things for our mental peace makes us slaves to circumstances. While meditating on the Infinite, Cosmic Energy flows through us and this works wonders. Try to keep that contact always. Always depend on the Eternal which is the essential thing in us and always abides by us. The world cannot change for you; you have to tune yourself properly, coming in contact with the vaster Presence, and higher Reality. We cannot grumble at the world, we should change ourselves.

A spiritual seeker is a fighter, and a fighter has more courage in a crisis. What does the Lord advise Arjuna? '*Klaibyam masma gamah Partha*' 'Do not become despondent; give up this disdainful weakness of the heart.' Some feel like committing suicide, but what is the use of cutting short the life in an unnatural manner? We have to come again to this world and face the same difficulties. The only result is that many years are lost and progress is hampered. Did the Buddha preach a sermon to Kisa Gotami when she went to him with her son's dead body? He simply asked her to get a handful of mustard seeds from any house where nobody had died so far. And she herself found out the truth and said: 'Oh, this is the nature of the world!' The world cannot be without troubles. Joy and misery go hand in hand. We have to remain in this world which is a mixed world of good, bad and indifferent. It is a world of the three gunas. Hence the world cannot have a different nature. Sattva is less here. Is eternal joy possible in the world? Do you want a cloudless sky and eternal sunshine? Sometimes rajas and sometimes tamas would dominate. There are bright moments when sattva is predominant. When you are really in trouble no human being can help you. Then you have to turn to a higher power. Whether at home or in the monastery, there are many troubles, but you will forget them when you are on a higher plane. The mind can be raised to a higher plane. How? With the help of divine name and divine thought.

The higher mind is distinct from the ordinary, impure mind. The ordinary mind tastes both, good and bad. There is another way of living, living with the higher Self, the Paramatman. That is our Reality. Giving up That, you identify yourself with the unreal and suffer. We ourselves have created all these troubles. The wheel is moving and you are clinging to it. Let go of it! 'Yours is the hand that holds the rope that drags you.' Let go of it and you are free—a simple truth. A new way of thinking and living—that is the task. If we look back upon the troubles we had to face in the past, we really feel astounded and wonder how we could have faced them. But circumstances force us to face them boldly. There is the unused, untapped mind. We think that we are working with full concentration. But in reality only a small portion of the mind is on the work at hand and the rest of the mind goes wandering haphazard. This wasted energy should be conserved. As we go on we find that we have greater capacities. This unused potential is to be developed. The mind is a link between the spirit and body. It can go either way. Turn it towards God, towards the spirit in you. Hari Maharaj always used to repeat Sri Ramakrishna's saying: 'Let the body take care of its pains. Oh my mind! remain in bliss always.' So the mind can be detached from the body. Meditation will enable you to separate yourself from the body. Maintain a little of that experience throughout the day.

How to Face Life?

In worldly life, misery comes to everyone. How are you going to face it? Sermonizing is not enough. We must turn to the real source of peace and joy who is *Parama-prema-rupa, Paramananda-svarupa*. We have cut ourselves off from that, but the soul is longing for it. We see a little of it in the individual and turn to it. Along with that drop of joy we get a mass of misery. And then death stares us in the face. It may come now, it may come after a hundred years, but it has got to come. This does not mean we should always dream of death. We have to fulfil our duties to our relations, but we have also the duty towards the Supreme Being. Do your duties and at the same time come to that Reality which is *Parama-prema-rupa, Paramananda-svarupa*, We have forgotten our real nature; we have to regain its awareness. Arjuna was Nara incarnate, but being embodied, he forgot his real nature. He was in great grief. A war had to be fought so that the power of right might destroy the evil. When there is trouble, we want to renounce the world. Face the realities of the world with dispassion, without identifying yourself with them.

See everything in its proper light in the light of the Self, and everything will be different. Not that there won't be problems, but a new vision will come. Make the Self more real than your problems. The more you go within, the less will be the outside dependence. There is everything within you; you have only to see. Infinite Bliss is our birthright. Fragrance is within, but we search for it outside. Running away is not the solution. Face problems and rise above them. Thinking of the Supreme Spirit who is ever free, assert yourself.

Mind's course should be upward, like the lotus bud arising from mud and water and keeping its head high up.

Unless you are well established in a higher plane you are not safe. See the baby kangaroo. When it is frightened, it jumps into its mother's pouch and from there peeps out, quite safe and serene. So too, we should **be firmly established in the Divine within.** The source of joy and love is within you. Turn to Him for light, love, guidance, joy, and share then with everybody. Instead of always begging, learn to give. We cannot change the environment, but we can certainly develop a new attitude. Connect all your problems with the Lord. Develop your will a little. Repeat the Lord's Name. Life, as it is, is misery, but if we have this attitude full of devotion, we accept everything, good and bad, as happening through His will. Great ones always have this view. You know Kunti's prayer—she prayed only for sorrow, so that the she might remember the Lord always. Let us get over our fear complex, then you will have strength to rise above troubles. Kabir sings: 'It is not a cloudy day when the heavens are cloudy. The cloudy day is that, O mind, when you do not repeat the Lord's Name.'

In the beginning, the environment may disturb us to a considerable extent and we complain about it. But if we attempt to change it drastically we may end in failure. There may be a tendency to go to a solitary place. Very often this is due to escapism. There is no such ideal place in the world which would be entirely free from all disturbances. Every place has its disadvantages and advantages. The environment may be calm and quiet, but if we go there with a troubled mind it may spoil our efforts. We should think: 'The Lord has placed me here, in these surroundings; let me adjust myself to this environment.' In the case of the disciple mentioned earlier, he has adjusted himself to the environment and found interest in japa and meditation. That is a good sign.

Play Your Part in the Great Drama

A great drama is going on. The Author of this drama is directing millions of actors and actresses. God has become all these—Mother, father, husband, child, etc. The Supreme Spirit is neither man nor woman. Then It manifests Itself as the ideal man and woman. Even in the divine play there are Lakshmi-Narayana, Sita-Rama, Radha-Krishna etc.—all divine pairs. They are, so to say, made of 'pure gold'. Base metals are mixed with that, and men and women are created to play the part in the drama of life. The same Supreme Being in one aspect is the thief and in another aspect the watchman who catches the thief. If it is difficult to grasp this idea, here is another one. He is the controller of the souls; the actors and actresses should obey the Director of the drama. Here the Lord is the Director. When one's part is over one must quit the stage, may be early in life or in old age. There is a mighty Will, a mighty Power, working behind this drama of life. People call it the will of the Lord. We have to play our part—neither clinging to life nor being afraid of death. Surrender yourself as completely as you can to the Author of this drama. In the puppet show, the strings are being moved in different directions. The Wirepuller is the Lord. We have to play. And then, in this game, some win and some lose. We are all bound to Him by this string of divine Will. Have you come here of your own sweet will? If so, you would not have come in this way. You are subject to His will and hence you are here. According to our tendencies and capacities, we should play our parts. But He guides. Behind our little wills, there is a Cosmic will, a Cosmic Power. You play your part and come away. Never try to put an end to this drama by force, running away from life or putting an end to this life. That makes matters worse.

Take things in a new light. If happiness is the gift of God, misery also comes from Him. Let us not be pleasure-seekers. We are eternally bound to Him, related to one another through Him. We are *jyotirmaya anu*—a part of that Infinite Light. Our relationship with others should be through that Light. We should surrender ourselves to that Infinite Spirit, Infinite Power who regulates this drama. We may be playing according to our tendencies. But in one aspect He is the Author of this drama. In another aspect He is the antaryami. And if we don't discover this, we come to grief. Misery is a blessing in disguise when it makes us turn towards the Infinite Being. Know how to utilize it. Connect your misery with the thought of God. Say: 'You alone are real, all else is unreal.' A new light will shine in your heart, distinct from body and mind. Be bold. In the Tantric worship, the devotee says: 'Mother, even if You tear me to pieces, I am going to cling to You.' Rakshasas are afraid of the Mother. But not so a devotee. For him, She is all sweetness. We have to go back to the source. '*Yasmin sthito na duhkhena gurunapi vichalyate.*' This describes the state of Supreme Consciousness, attaining which one is not shaken by the heaviest sorrow. In the last days of the Master, His body was emaciated and He was in great pain but still He said: 'I see one Satchidananda everywhere.' What a high state! Follow the path that will lead you to the ultimate Goal. If you cannot think of Him as all-pervading Spirit, think of Him as the Author of this drama, guiding our destiny. 'You are in me and I am in You. You are the Eternal sharer of my joys and sorrows.' Pain or pleasure, follow the path of duty, prayer, and meditation under all circumstances, Then a new light will shine.

Sadhana Should Not Lead to Narrowness

In religious life, selfishness is the most dangerous enemy. In some cases so-called devotees are more selfish than those who are not religious-minded. Why so? A sadhaka, while meditating, tries to draw away his mind from all outward distractions, towards his own self, and dwelling on his own self, he becomes egocentric. Instead of expanding, his mind becomes contracted. What is the remedy? Think of the Infinite through love and emotion, remove the bad qualities. Meditate on the good qualities, on the auspicious attributes of the Lord—Infinite Love and Infinite Compassion. That will make you expand. Meditation on the abstract is difficult; therefore meditate on the holy personality, his purity, love and compassion. Superficial meditation is not useful; one should go deep. There are three stages in sadhana: (1) Meditation on the luminous form of the deity. (2) Meditation on the attributes—purity, love, compassion etc. (3) Meditation on the all-pervasiveness of the Lord. There is the Vedic prayer: '*Dhiyo yo nah prachodayat*.' 'O Lord of all the states of consciousness, guide our understanding and enlighten our consciousness!'

We beg the Lord: 'Give me this, give me that!' but are not prepared to give anything. Without eliminating selfishness, progress is not possible. Selfishness is caused by the ego, which should go. In egoistic minds there is no place for God. Purity, compassion and devotion are absolutely essential. To put it negatively, we should not hate anyone. Positively, we should love others and be kind to them. Many difficulties may come but we have to struggle on; struggle gives us strength. Our behaviour is well-known to those who live with us. One who persists in religious life and has become kind and loving, will also effect a change in others around him. His very behaviour will change them. But if religious men become selfish, it is better not to have such religion at all.

Those who are advanced in spiritual life have wonderful compassion for others. Their attitude towards others undergoes a wonderful change. If it is not so, we can say that they are not religious at all. By giving to others what we have, we feel inner expansion, which brings joy. So, if one progresses really, he will be kinder and kinder, and more compassionate towards others. In some this spiritual progress may be manifested outwardly too, whereas in others there may be no outward manifestation.

Need for Mutual Love in an Organisation

The organisations, as they are, are always weak. If the Church is destroyed everything connected with it is gone.

The ideal is that each home should be a temple. That has been our Indian tradition, the basic idea of Hinduism. Our prayers should be individual. We may also have congregational prayers. If each individual gains spiritually, then he or she can improve the whole house

Once I had a long discussion with a Rabbi. (The official leader of a Jewish congregation is called a Rabbi.) He said: 'Swami, let us start an international organisation for the welfare of humanity.' I replied: 'I do not like the idea.' He was surprised: 'What! Swami, are you not interested in the welfare of the world?' I said that his approach to that problem was through a difficult path. We have to start with the individual. A good individual tries to promote not only his own welfare but that of his family as well. A good family promotes the welfare of the community; and the community, in turn, that of the nation. That is the way to human welfare. The relationship among the members of ordinary groups is just that of social goodwill. But the love that the disciples of Sri Ramakrishna had for one another was a spiritual love. The Master made them realize that the Supreme Being who dwells in everything, dwells in each one of them too. The Rig Veda described Him as, 'The one with a thousand heads, a thousand eyes and a thousand feet,'(Purusha-suktam) and the Gita sang of Him as, 'The One with hands and feet everywhere, with eyes, heads, and mouths everywhere.' (Gita, XIII. 13). He is the one Unity in all this diversity. We are parts of that Universal Being (Virat Purusha). According to the dualists, we are all servants of God. All are children of the One God. Religion practiced correctly will generate this feeling in us.

Once there was a dispute between two sects of Vaishnavas and some people wondered whether the dispute would persist even in the holy abode of the Lord. A wise man said: 'There won't be any quarrel there because all will be busy offering loving service to God and there will be no occasion to fight.' If our heart is centered on seeking the Lord, we shall be only co-operating with one another. The trouble is we think more of ourselves than of the Lord. Somehow selfishness comes up. If I feel I am a part of the greater Whole, my love for my fellow-beings would be established on a strong foundation. The Christian maxim is: 'Love thy neighbour as thyself.' But Vedanta says: 'Serve the Lord in everyone. The Common link that holds us together.'

Some monastic workers asked Mahapurush Maharaj (Swami Shivanandaji) what was the force that kept the Ramakrishna Order bound together. He replied that it was Sri Ramakrishna Himself and the love that He showered on His disciples. What happens usually? A group is formed and soon it is split! It is most difficult to co-operate. In a family, the members are bound together by blood relationship. When you have a number of people from different families, living together, what is the binding link among them? In a spiritual community there should be greater unity and harmony than in an ordinary social group. A common ideal, love for God, community of culture—these hold a spiritual community together. That is unity in diversity. Communities and organisations should have a common ideal. If that bond is strengthened, unity is established. You find greater love among friends than among relatives.

The second question put to Swami Shivanandaji was: How can this love be preserved without degeneration? Everything has its natural course of ups and downs, a wave-like motion. Institutions are not exempt from the operation of this law. Sri Ramakrishna's disciples were souls of great caliber. Ordinary mortals cannot expect to belong to that category. But to the extent we cultivate that high ideal of spirituality, we can love others selflessly and harmony will be established. What is meant by the expression 'attaining spirituality?' It is to become established in the Self which is the Reality in all. The harmony resulting therefrom is different from worldly friendliness which is very fragile. The worldly harmony is gentlemanliness, just a code of conduct. It is not sufficiently deep. Unless there is a change of heart, a change in consciousness, true harmony cannot be established. Learn to be generous. Give the benefit of doubt. We put up a show of generosity but make unfair comments about others when they are not present. There were two Sadhus who had no regard for each other. They had a common devotee. One of them told the devotee: 'That Sadhu is like a cow.' The other Sadhu told the devotee: 'That Sadhu is like a buffalo.' The devotee was hurt by their mutual disregard and wanted to teach them a lesson. That day at meal time he brought grass to one and straw to the other!

It is necessary to think of the well-being of the people around us. The trouble is that our ego is so strong, it keeps us apart. If we work as parts of a great whole, then harmony is easily established. The sublime personality of Sri Rama krishna, his generous and noble heart and his unmatched love—these were what attracted the disciples to him and kept them together. In all communities there should be an individual, a principle, to control and harmonize its different parts. I had referred to the story in the Upanishad about the different sense-organs thinking too much of themselves. When the sense-organs temporarily departed one at a time, nothing very serious happened to the man except that he was blind or deaf for the time being. But when the Prana prepared to depart from the body, then all the senses were paralyzed. So each one should think of himself as well as of others.

The disciples had the Master as their common ideal and they remained bound to him. What happened when the Master disappeared? The disciples were of different temperaments. One had more of Jnana; another, more of Bhakti; a third more of karma, and so on. Each had something to contribute to the Mission, to the training of our character. They were all, as it were parts of a whole and they had the common spiritual ideal of the Master. But if any member of an organization is too egoistic, that organization cannot function properly. That ego is like a disease which would destroy the health of the whole organization.

When one comes to a higher consciousness, one feels that one is a part of the Infinite Spirit Having realised this idea, the saint's love is spontaneously out flowing. And to the extent our experience of the Reality becomes intense, this love also becomes intense. We saw this in the disciples of the Master. They were all parts of the Cosmic Body of Sri Ramakrishna, who was an embodiment of the Infinite Spirit. We noted another point in them—they accorded great dignity to others. We should practice this sadhana: deal with every individual as if you are dealing with God. Give less importance to diversity. It is the One that manifests as many. By serving others, I serve myself. Everything would run smoothly in this way. Sermonizing will not do. Do a little spiritual practice. We are all the time trying to tread on the pride of others. Instead, let us try to see the Lord in us, as well as in others—this is the way to unity. When I dislike another, I dislike my own self, I make myself mean—that is what the Holy Mother taught us.

Examples of Great Men

Realised Souls are God's Instruments

After realising the highest Truth in life, some people engage themselves in selfless service. Sri Ramakrishna was asked by the Divine Mother to remain in 'Bhavamukha'. Though he was actually instructing many, he used to say that he was not giving any instruction. Did he tell a lie? Of course not. He actually felt that it was the Divine Mother who taught the devotees and disciples, using him as Her instrument. Swami Vivekananda wanted to remain in Nirvikalpa Samadhi but the Master said that he had some great work to do and he transferred all his power to him. With the help of that power, Swamiji could achieve such a great deal. This power was gradually withdrawn from him by the Divine Mother. Those who had heard his lectures in the west during his first visit there found a great difference when he visited the west a second time. Swamiji himself felt this. These great lives show us that we have to remain subject to God's will and our greatest duty is to carry out His orders. There are some other great souls when they are in tune with the Divine they cannot perform any active work, but their mere existence and presence will bring forth spiritual vibrations which purify the mental and spiritual world.

The Master used to say that after getting non-dual knowledge one can do whatever one likes. He meant that one cannot then do any evil, as one will always be feeling the divine presence. One then no more thinks of God but feels His living presence, having attained the highest knowledge through discrimination, renunciation, love, devotion and purity. Such men have gone beyond all gunas.

One has to transcend the dullness of tamoguna as well as the passionately active rajo-guna and reach the calm of sattva-guna. One who has transcended all these gunas is above good and evil—all dualities. Sri Chaitanya, the Buddha, Jesus Christ, Sri Ramakrishna, were all tested by God in many ways, but did not succumb to the temptations. They had transcended body-consciousness. Ordinary people give way to wrong actions and become immoral. When realised souls feel that their consciousness is one with the divine Consciousness, they cannot do anything wrong. This is true freedom.

God-like Men and Incarnations

Sages like Narada and Suka are ishvarakotis. They come to the world to fulfill some divine mission. They are born with perfect knowledge, without the veil of maya. An ordinary jiva is called a jivanmukta when he has attained realization through sadhana. He then cannot return to the ordinary plane of consciousness. But Ishvarakotis are born for the good of the world and hence they are able to function on the ordinary plane with the knowledge and power of the higher planes. Their knowledge is not hidden by maya. When Sri Krishna opened His mouth, His mother saw the whole universe in it. Any length of rope was not enough to bind Him. They are above all limitations. Sri Ramakrishna said to young Hari that he could not endure the pain in his throat. But Hari replied: 'I cannot believe it. You are the embodiment of Bliss. How can you feel any pain?' Sri Ramakrishna protested, but Hari would not concede the point. At last Sri Ramakrishna laughed and said: 'You have caught me!' They are always established in Bliss and Peace-Sri Ramakrishna was an incarnation. The Supreme Spirit puts on a body and that is an incarnation. The Lord comes down to the world in a human form just to help the downtrodden. As He puts on a human body, He shows signs of sleep, hunger, disease, etc. Outwardly He may even show anger, but is calm inwardly. His mind ever tends to return to the realm of blessedness, peace and silence. But in order to teach people, He has to bring His mind down to their level. What a sacrifice! But it is the Lord who does it. The very purpose of taking a human form is that.

Ishvarakotis and incarnations come down to help the people and go back to their realm of their own sweet will. They are not reborn as a result of karma; karma has no hold on them. But a jivanmukta may have to experience or undergo certain difficulties as a result of his karma, though he would all the time be aware that he is distinctly different from his body. Only incarnations can transform ordinary souls. They can undo the karma of others. Ordinary teachers cannot do that. Sri Ramakrishna transformed Girish Chandra Ghosh. The Divine Mother had asked Sri Ramakrishna to remain in Bhava-mukha in order to uplift people. Incarnations go through sadhana just to show us the way to liberation.

Some can enjoy divine Bliss in themselves but cannot impart it to others. Sri Ramakrishna used to narrate a story: Three men were walking on a road. On one side there was a high wall and the merry sounds of festivity were coming from the other side of the wall. One of the men climbed the wall and being captivated by what he saw, he cried 'ha!' and jumped down inside. The second one climbed up and followed suit. The third one climbed up. He also wanted to jump down but in order to show the sight to others coming behind him, he controlled himself and sat down on the wall. Incarnations are like the third man. Sri Ramakrishna and His disciples underwent severe sadhana for several years. The Holy Mother did a Panchatapa (meditation in the hot sun, surrounded by blazing fires on all sides). All that was for the good of the world; they had nothing to attain for themselves.

The Uniqueness of Sri Ramakrishna

Even while he was seriously ill, Swami Shivananda used to say: 'So long as I am able to think of the Lord, I am all right.' He had great spiritual experiences during his illness, but there was none with whom he could share them. Can ordinary persons understand the Lord? The Lord incarnates Himself as an ordinary man, but what a tremendous power He manifests! Remember the incidents in the life of Sri Krishna. In order to approach Him we must have a standard. Great men such as Swami Shivananda enable us to get a glimpse of the immense spirituality of the incarnation.

Incarnations are rarely recognised and understood. Many thought Rama to be just a man; only a few Rishis could understand Him. Even Maruti wanted to think of Him as the son of Dasaratha, not as the Supreme Self. When his mind was on different levels of consciousness he had different concepts of Sri Rama. Tulasidas was charmed with Rama's personality. Someone told him that Rama was only a partial incarnation while Krishna was a complete one. Tulasidas replied: 'Till now I have adored him as the son of Dasaratha. Now you say he is an incarnation, whether part or full I don't care. I adore Him all the more.' Tulasidas sometime came down to the personal plane.

And what do we see here in Sri Ramakrishna? Once he goes to the Divine Mother and fans Her and talks to Her. Again we find Him in quite a different mood. He cannot walk on the grass; he cannot pluck a flower thinking that it is a part of the bouquet adorning the whole universe. A boatman is thrashed on the Ganges and Sri Ramakrishna feels the pain on His body! How does it happen? He is one with the universe, one with Satchidananda. Sashi Maharaj used to say that the Master was experiencing tremendous ecstasy during his last days. When he went into Mahasamadhi all his hairs were standing on end, indicating that he was experiencing great bliss. Swami Brahmananda used to say: 'Who can understand Sri Ramakrishna? He was one moment in one plane, next moment in a different plane. Only through his grace can we understand him.'

H 13

Master revealed himself to his disciples and devotees in so many ways. When young Narendranath went to the Master, he wanted to give him a direct experience of the Supreme Being and so he touched him and Narendranath had his first experience of the Supreme Reality. Sri Ramakrishna could not contain the joy of ecstasy within himself. He was eager to share it with others and was always on the look-out for proper persons.

Swami Turiyananda, a great devotee of Vedanta even before he came to the Master, was undergoing severe austerities and always thinking of pure Brahman. Then the Master asked him: 'What does Vedanta teach? Is it not that only Brahman is real and the world unreal?' Swami Turiyananda used to tell us that the moment he said so, he had a glimpse of the highest truth. He moulded the minds of men as a potter moulds pots. Yet such a physically weak man! Once young Rakhal was fighting some bad tendencies and feeling awfully dry. Master touched him and Rakhal saw that the visible universe was melting away. He got frightened and left his place of meditation. Rakhal with spiritual eyes saw the divine presence. The Master said: 'Why did you leave your seat? You were eager to have this experience, yet you could not stand it even for a moment. I have this experience at all times.' All this power was in that frail little frame. He was in tune with the Cosmic Power. The Cosmic mind is manifested through the will and mind of the individual. He practiced even hathayoga to keep his body healthy in order to sustain the divine experience. Who can bear these experiences? Can one assimilate great spiritual experiences without adequate preparation? Hriday was bothering him to give him some experience. When he actually got a little of it, he began shouting 'O Uncle, we are para-brahman. Let us go out and save humanity.' The Master scolded him: 'Why do you shout? I have these experiences always, and you cannot control such trifles!' What a strong mind the Master had!

Totapuri came and offered to teach Him Vedanta and give Him Sannyasa. The Master said: 'I am married.' But does marriage bind one who looked upon his wife as the Divine Mother and worshipped her? Totapuri, wonder-struck at Master's samadhi, exclaimed: 'What divine maya is this!' Ramakrishna experienced the totality of Reality. Totapuri did not have the complete experience; he had not realised the immanent aspect of the Divine—what Sri Ramakrishna called Mother. The sages described the Reality in both positive and negative terms. Sometimes they sang: 'You are neither man nor woman' etc. and again they sang: 'You are man and you are woman.' The Supreme Being is both transcendent and immanent. Afflicted by dysentery, he went to the Ganga to drown himself. Then came the revelation—One Spirit everywhere! Before this Totapuri had realised the impersonal and transcendental aspects of the Reality, not the personal and immanent. Here the disciple became the Guru of the Guru!

After experiencing the highest aspect of Reality, dysentery was consuming the Master's body. He was ever aware of the Supreme. He retained full consciousness of the Reality even while living in the world. This is the power of the man—who can understand Him? Swami Shivananda and Swami Brahmananda were eager to share their inner experience of joy with others. Sri Ramakrishna also wanted to transmit what He had gained. But this was not eagerness to have disciples, but only the eagerness to share their experiences. We cannot see the ultimate Truth with this mind. To the extent we purify our mind, to that extent the divine eye is opened and He manifests Himself. But, we can keep up the thought that I am the Atman or that the Reality is very close to me and I am part of That. Theoretically we have the capacity to realise the Truth but the mind is bound by its limitations. The Reality is within but the mind has been turned outwards. How can it see the indwelling Being when it does not look in that direction at all? The mind is always

after lust, anger, hatred, jealousy etc. Clouds after clouds have
gathered and you complain that even after such a long period
of sadhana you have no visions. We hide all the secrets of
life, and pose as great devotees. Inside is one thing and
outside another thing. Always feeding our little ego. Always
seeing evil in others. We have become like the fly which
sits on festering sores and occasionally on flowers. Instead
of meditating on virtues we are always meditating on vice.
Life's whole course should change. Without moral purity
none can progress. An anchored boat will not move even
if you row desperately. Swami Vivekananda has said: 'The
case of people who have seen Sri Ramakrishna and have not
acquired a little of that renunciation, is as good as a monkey
witnessing a show.'

In this incarnation the Lord and His consort were veritable
embodiments of renunciation and simplicity. When the Mother
visited the Gavipuram temple at Bangalore, there was one
well-dressed lady with her wearing many ornaments. One
woman took her to be the Holy Mother, prostrated before
her and all others like sheep followed her!

Master Mahashay was astonished at Sri Ramakrishna's
moods. When he came one day, the Master was lost in
ecstasy over the Divine Mother. Another day, he was in
samadhi and yet another day he was cracking jokes with the
youngsters. The Master was unpredictable. One never knew
in what spiritual mood he would be. That is why Swami
Vivekananda refused to write the Master's biography. He said
that he did not know him fully! Sarat Maharaj wrote the Lila
Prasanga but said that it was an imperfect approach. The
Master would say that visions were obstructions in non-dual
experience. Such a Cosmic Being he was, with such powers;
how could he impart his experiences to those who were not
his equals?

Many disciples saw him after his Mahasamadhi. Holy
Mother saw him many times. I have seen in the West that
devotees had his vision. Swami Saradananda went to the

West and was a lady's guest. She had seen Sri Ramakrishna in a vision and when she saw the Master's picture in Swami Saradananda's book, she cried: 'I have seen the holy man in a vision!' In the case of the Holy Mother also, such incidents are recorded. Girish Babu would never agree to see the Mother as he felt his sinful eyes were unworthy of seeing Her sacred form. Once he went to Jayrambati and when he actually saw Her, he exclaimed: 'Ma! I have seen you before!' When he was seriously ill in his youth. Mother had appeared in a vision and cured him. At this exclamation Mother smiled. Can we understand anything? Just with the small measuring tape of our minds, we try to measure these Great Ones. The only course is, pray to the Lord: 'Give us enlightenment, enlighten our consciousness.'

Sri Ramakrishna was seen by Mathur Babu as Kali and Siva, it was not in that little body of Sri Ramakrishna that he saw all this. The infinite Spirit had manifested as Sri Ramakrishna. The worshipper and the worshipped are the twofold manifestations of the same. If you come to Sri Ramakrishna, you have to accept that any divine name and form will take you to the Infinite. Having come to Sri Ramakrishna, you cannot maintain any narrow outlook as of Ghantakarna, who could never accept that Vishnu and Siva were essentially two aspects of the one Being.

When you read the Gospel, you would find that many people, following different creeds and paths came to Sri Ramakrishna. Each used to think: 'The Master follows our path.' His grace enabled them to progress on the path of liberation. Sri Ramakrishna used to say, 'If you think of me, you are thinking of God, because when I look within, I don't find anything but the Infinite Spirit in this (body).'

Sri Ramakrishna liked Adhyatma Ramayana very much. He had a wonderful memory: he was a 'srutidhara'. He could remember what he had heard but once. Swami Vivekananda had to read things twice to remember them. This memory is due to the power of the mind. They had perfect control over their minds. Sadhana is the only way to develop such power. With each japa we increase the power of the mind. But we must use our will-power, unlike some who tell their beads but allow their minds to wander. What kind of japa is that? One should do it with full attention and continuously. Those who have done sadhana have a wonderful power of concentration. They can retain what they have learnt. Swami Turiyananda could repeat whole passages by heart.

Sri Ramakrishna first heard what the great saints of different sects had to teach. Then one day he put on a garland of flowers representing all the scriptures and danced for a while. One should absorb the essence of the teachings of all great men. They show us the path. We have to digest them and put them into practice.

The Life and Message of the Buddha

The Buddha Purnima is considered a thrice blessed day because Buddha was born, renounced and got illumination on that day. When he was born, astrologers predicted that if he were prevented from seeing misery, old age and death, he would be a great king, or else he would get tremendous renunciation and would be a king all the same, but in the spiritual realm. His father tried in vain to keep his son in a fool's paradise. As Fate would have it, one day he saw a very old man and came to know that a similar change would come on all in due course of time. Then he saw a sick person, a dead body, and so forth. Thereafter he could not be kept tied to the world and to its temptations. He took to a life of renunciation, from self-indulgence to extreme austerity. His health broke down. Then he realised the need for the middle path. In due course he attained illumination and lived a noble life of knowledge, renunciation and compassion. He preached nothing new. What our ancient sages had preached, he made them living truths again in his time.

When God incarnates, He generates a great spiritual current. Many attain illumination by joining that current.

Swami Shivananda and other disciples, when they were with the Master at the Cossipore garden house, were fired by the Buddha's spirit. They did not fully believe in a personal God. Were they atheists? No; they did not care for the God of theology who merely fulfilled all desires. They believed in a higher transcendental Reality free from all modifications, beyond all names and forms. They were thirsting to attain the transcendental state of consciousness. Our conception of jiva and Iswata brings the mind to body consciousness. They wanted to go beyond that. After passing away, the Master once appeared before Mahapurush Maharaj and said: 'The Guru is everything, there is nothing beyond Him.' Sri Ramakrishna did not mean His own form when He mentioned the Guru. He referred to the Supreme Being, the real Guru. He taught Swami Vivekananda and others the reality of all divine forms. He broke their one-sided-ness. Sri Ramakrishna could not be one-sided. In His all comprehensiveness, He saw that the same transcendental Being manifests Himself as all. He transcends names and forms and personalities and is beyond all speech. He saw the same power being manifested in all. In one aspect He manifests Himself as all gods and goddesses and in another aspect as the world of manifold forms. Other teachers generally stress only one aspect of the Reality suited to their own religion.

Critics say that the Buddha attained a state of annihilation (Nirvana). How can annihilation bring so much joy and peace and compassion? Men of realisation are very compassionate. It is the transcendental consciousness that made the Buddha never to waver from compassion, sympathy and love. Our sympathy is egocentric and not spontaneous. There is no bargaining in the illumined souls. Out of their realisation, the spirit of service is born.

The Buddha came to help mankind. The great ones come down to the level of ordinary beings to understand their feelings and console them. A bereaved father came to

Sri Ramakrishna direct from the cremation ground, quite inconsolable. Sri Ramakrishna did not preach him a sermon, but came down to his plane and showed him great sympathy, saying it was quite natural to grieve over a departed son. By and by, Sri Ramakrishna sang in a lofty mood the song: 'Oh! Jiva, get ready to fight; take to arms against the enemy, Death' etc. The man was greatly consoled and said: 'That is why I came to you direct from the burning ghat.' From the stand point of pure knowledge one may ask, since the world is unreal, why should there be sympathy and compassion at all? Why should you help anyone? No doubt the world seen physically is unreal. The physical personality is unreal. But behind such personality there is a mind and a soul. Till the mind is illumined, it is liable to be afflicted by sorrow. Seeing this sorrow in others, illumined souls try to remove it, even though they themselves are beyond all sorrow. We should work in the world in this spirit.

Part - II

Part - II

(17)

Notes on Drig Drishya Viveka

Drig Drishya Viveka or An Inquiry into the Nature of the Seer and the Seen is an acknowledged prakarana treatise of the Vedanta philosophy, ascribed to Sankaracharya. A prakarana treatise explains the chief purport of Vedanta, viz. the identity of the jiva and Brahman by following a particular line of argument.

These are the notes of Swami Yatiswarananda's classes on the Drig Drishya Viveka, given to earnest spiritual aspirants at Campfer, Germany, in 1935. These class-notes do not contain a word-by-word explanation. Such a commentary by Swami Nikhilananda has been published by Advaita Ashrama, Calcutta. It is obvious from a perusal of these notes that the Swami selected some slokas for detailed discussion while rapidly skipping through others. For instance, though the subject of different kinds of samadhi has been discussed in eight slokas (22 to 29), the Swami has not explained all of them. Instead he has preferred to stress the importance of preliminary disciplines, without which the discussion on samadhi has no meaning, except to satisfy the intellectual curiosity of the reader. His emphasis has been on the practical side of the philosophy of Advaita Vedanta. The interested reader would benefit from reading these notes along with Swami Nikhilananda's translation and notes. —Ed.

Introduction

In Monistic Vedanta the idea is to realize the Truth in a most natural way by trying to analyze what is real and what is unreal, what is Self and what is non-self. Everything else is only a step towards this form of analysis. In this form of

193

Advaita sadhana we do not find any place for God, nor is any place needed for Him. This is the direct path which can be followed only by the very few. But in the preliminary stage there must be unconditional obedience to and unconditional service of the Guru, looking upon one's Guru as the Divine.

Naturally, the dualists are very much against this form of sadhana. The dualist's attitude is always narrower, more fanatical than that of the true monist. Theirs is the greatest condemnation of others. You find it among the Christians, among the Jews, among the Mohammedans, among the Hindus—in all dualistic sects and teachings. They cannot find the point of unity, so they stress diversity all the more and cling to their pet-idols. However, all the sects find their synthesis in the path of Advaita. Dualism (Dvaita), Qualified Non-Dualism (Vishisht-advaita), all these are stepping-stones, on our way to the Real. The Real is that which existed in the past, exists in the present and will exist in future without undergoing any change.

There are two kinds of eternals: The world that is ever-changing; and Brahman that is unchanging. 'Beginning' really means coming from a cause: 'destruction' means going back to the cause, and the whole process is a cyclic one, so far as the phenomenon is concerned. When a candle is being burnt, really speaking, it does not become annihilated; it only undergoes a process of transformation. The oxygen, hydrogen etc. it contains appear in a different form. That is all. Anything that is material passes through these changes. To be beyond phenomena is to be free.

The idea of freedom is not an illusion, It comes from the very depths of our being, never from reason. Lower reason can only end in scepticism, because what is ordinarily called reason, can never take us to the truth; but the higher reason, the purified reason, can reveal the truth to us. It is not Kant's reason, but the highest intuitive vision that reveals the Truth directly.

Vedantic treatises such as the *Drig Drishya Viveka* are concerned with the task of developing that higher reason in us. Ours is gross reason, but that reason can be made finer and finer by going through a process of steady, prolonged purification and strict ethical culture in thought, word and deed. Philosophy is not mere empty speculation with no bearing on life. It is the pursuit of knowledge that reveals the Truth to us directly. When a person is emancipated from all bonds, when lust no longer finds any place in his mind, and when he has become truthful in character, then he attains Brahman.

All the different practices prepare the soul for perceiving the Truth directly. Intelligent and intensive study of the scriptures and deep reflection on their teachings also sharpen the intellect and make a better instrument out of it. To the extent the intellect helps clear and definite thinking, it is an aid, and not intellectualism.

In both Yoga and Advaita Vedanta, very great stress is laid on clear thinking, on not identifying oneself with the non-self, with the phenomenon. When the modifications of the mind are controlled, the Self ceases to identify Itself with the non-self, or the phenomenon. Even what is called samadhi clarifies the understanding, the discriminative faculty. When a man comes down from samadhi he should be able to separate the Self from the non-self.

The jnani does not want to be full of emotions, to be swept away by his feelings. No, being wide-awake, possessing the fullest control over his impulses and feelings, he wants to separate Truth from falsehood, the Real from the phenomenal, and then be one with Truth. But prayer, japam, meditation, concentration, purification of the food one takes in through all one's senses, all these help in having the direct vision of the Truth. Direct vision means to be one with It. The drop of water becomes one with the ocean. The light reflected in the particle of sand becomes one with the indivisible eternal light.

Until you fall into deep sleep or until you die, devote yourself whole-heartedly to discrimination between the Real and the unreal, the immutable and the phenomenal.

Instead of wasting energy in brooding over the fact that you have not yet reached the highest state, you had better give more attention and energy to moving towards the goal and avoiding everything that is a hindrance on your path. The means should be looked upon as the very goal, for the time being, i.e. the same attention and intensity should be given to the means as to the goal.

Clear and definite thinking becomes natural after some realization. Make it a point to be always as wide-awake as possible. Don't allow yourself to think hazy and indefinite thoughts, to have hazy and indefinite feelings, to act in a hesitating, undecided way.

If I identify myself with the body, then naturally, to me comes desire for sense-enjoyment in every form, gross and subtle. So we find what a great mischief this false identification can do. Through this false identification all our troubles arise. A man and a woman meet; seeing their man-form, or woman-form, they fall in love, believe that they are 'meant for each other', the 'eternal companions'. Then after a time they realize their mistake, disappointment comes, all romance melts away, and finally they part. This is the way of the world. So long as any such relation is taken to be real, everything else follows as a matter of course. Really speaking, it is a wonder that things are not worse than they are! You go on creating endless troubles for yourself, committing endless mistakes again and again, and then you complain and wail about your misfortune and life. What else can you expect? Life is not a path strewn with roses, and there is no such thing as lasting happiness on the relative plane. The same holds true in the case of parents, friends, etc. The moment you want to have direct connection with anybody, you are gone. Through the Divine you are in touch with all others, but never in a personal way. Just look back at the past. How many friends, relatives, parents etc., were there and where have they gone? They are all gone far away. Love has come and gone, and what a great attachment we used to feel for all of them! But always after a time, this so-called eternal relation reveals its true nature, and our whole life suddenly changes.

Clear-cut analysis of ourselves and our motives is very troublesome, but it is most essential, and to the extent our mind becomes pure, the better it becomes. We must stand as the dispassionate witness of all our thoughts, feelings and activities and never identify ourselves with any of them. The whole life is a series of identifications with what is unreal and ephemeral.

First have the higher limitations: 'I am a monk. All this is beneath my dignity.' But later on, you will have to give up this attitude which is good for you now, because it is also a bondage. In order to get rid of the lower limitations, we take the help of the higher ones, but even these higher limitations are to be transcended after making the best use of them. And the sense of dignity is always a great help for every aspirant. 'I am an aspirant. This is beneath my dignity. I should not behave in such a way.' Or, 'I am a monk. It is beneath my dignity to do this etc. For the beginner, this attitude is essential.'

Unless people have got enough stamina, have already advanced to some extent in their dispassion for the world and worldly pleasures, they should not even dabble in Vedanta. If they study this without strict preparation, they would be only dabblers, nothing more than that. They can never approach spiritual life without being prepared to pay the full price. Many cannot even stand this uncompromising attitude.

Even denying oneself something for the sake of asceticism, like meat or tea or tobacco or anything else, is good, and should be practised now and then by the aspirant. You see, there is asceticism and asceticism. But even the lower asceticism has its value. Thus do we learn to control ourselves fully and all our cravings and likings. Only thus can we become masters of ourselves and our impulses. Besides, real one-pointedness and will-power become strengthened, the brain does not get weak. The very moment I find I like something particularly, I should practise this kind of asceticism. And we should do this consciously, with a purpose. By doing this, we develop more and more renunciation and dispassion, and cease to identify ourselves with our desires and cravings. Without consciously developing dispassion and true renunciation, no spiritual life will be of any use. Our whole attitude has to be changed, so we should consciously take the attitude of the witness and deny ourselves some of our pet wishes like meat or tea or tobacco or whatever else. Not that those things are bad in themselves, but this practice is a very useful one and gives the aspirant much greater strength and stamina. Naturally, intoxicants like alcohol or any other drugs should be avoided by all aspirants.

We should never allow ourselves to live in a fool's paradise. We can remain unaffected only when we rise to a higher plane of consciousness, when we stand aloof from the world's play as the eternal witness. The ocean is always there, whether the play of the waves and wavelets goes on or not, whether there are mountain-high waves or tiny ripples or perfect calm. We are really the ocean, not the wave or the bubble. We must cease to identify ourselves with the *upadhis* (limiting adjuncts) and rest in our true and eternal Self.

The Perceiver and the Perceived

1. *The form is perceived and the eye is its perceiver. It (eye) is perceived and the mind is its perceiver. The mind with its modifications is perceived and the Witness (the Self) is verily the perceiver. But It (the Witness) is not perceived (by any other).*

This sloka describes, in brief, the steps we have to pass through. From the gross we come to the subtle, from the subtle to the causal, from the causal, taking a long jump, to the Truth.

The Brihadaranyaka Upanishad says:

He is never seen, but is the Witness. He is never heard, but is the Hearer. He is never thought but is the Thinker. He is never known but is the Knower. There is no other seer but Him. There is no other hearer but Him. There is no other thinker than Him. There is no other knower but Him. Everything else but Him is mortal.(3.7.23)

The seer is always a sentient entity and the seen is always a material entity. This is the general rule.

Because everything seen is non-sentient or material, the question naturally arises: How can the eye, the mind etc. which are, strictly speaking, all material, ever be seers? This is because of the reflection of consciousness in them. They can never be seers in the real sense of the term. The Self alone is the real source of consciousness.

Sankaracharya says:

The seer and the seen are always different. The real seer is Brahman, and the seen is maya.

From a lower stage we can only get a very rough and distorted glimpse of the Truth. We perceive things but we have got an apperception of ourselves. We are all self-conscious entities. All these limited forms of consciousness are expressions of an infinite consciousness. Our so-called subject is not the ultimate subject, but a mixture of subject and object. It is a relative subject, and on further analysis the subject will become the object.

You see, it is this: First we try to be the witness, i.e. first we are partly the doer and partly the witness, whereas the ignorant person thinks himself to be only the doer. As one advances, one becomes more and more detached and awakened, more and more the witness of everything, losing the 'doer-mentality'.

How to be wide-awake? To the extent we try to shift our centre of consciousness from the body, mind and the senses to the Self, we become more and more wide-awake and conscious in every moment. To the extent we consciously separate the seer and the seen in ourselves, to that extent we are able to separate the seer and the seen in outside things and others. To the dreamy man, the soul is not actually dead, but it is not his centre of consciousness.

The subject-matter of the first sloka is explained in detail in the following slokas.

2. *The forms (objects of perception) appear as various on account of such distinction as blue, yellow, gross, subtle, short, long, etc. The eye, on the other hand, sees them, itself remaining one and the same.*

That which is changing constantly, is perceived by that which is comparatively steady. The eye is changeless in a relative sense. Vedanta aims at realizing the *Sat,* that which does not change, which exists ever the same under all circumstances, at all times. A similar passage, describing the status of the senses is found in the Katha Upanishad:

The senses, they say, are the horses, and their roads are the sense-objects. The wise call Him the enjoyer when he is united with the body, senses and mind. (1.3.4)

When we call ourselves the enjoyer, this is a complex, for the enjoyer is not something elemental, but is a complex of mind, senses and body.

To the extent we lessen our body-consciousness, cease to think of ourselves and others in terms of men or women, to the extent we are able to separate the Self in us from the non-self, the Eternal from the phenomenal, to that extent we are able to do this in others also. This clear discrimination comes as a result of one's ethical culture and different practices. Even if we can minimize to some extent our identification with the body, it will mean such a blessing to us. Advaita Vedanta just aims at breaking down this false identification between the Self and the non-self.

The eye, on account of its changeable nature, is an object and its perceiver is the mind:

3. *Such characteristics of the eye as blindness, sharpness, or dullness, the mind is able to cognize because it is a unity. This also applies to (whatever is perceived through) the ear, skin, etc.*

The mind perceives all the different changes of the different senses. When we get some stimuli from outside, and our thought is awakened, it is with the help of the mind that we perceive these outside things, and so an aspect of the mind is the seer.

When I identify myself with the senses, I am the doer; when I identify myself with the mind, I am the enjoyer, but all this is illusion. Really speaking, I am neither the doer nor the enjoyer, but the Self that stands as the eternal witness of the mind. As the Katha Upanishad says,

By mind alone this is to be realized, and there is no difference here. From death to death he goes, who sees as if there is difference here.(2.1.11)

One who is always of unrestrained mind and devoid of right understanding, his senses become uncontrollable like the wicked horses of a charioteer.(1.3.5)

And he who is devoid of proper understanding, thoughtless, and always impure, never attains that goal, and gets into the round of births and deaths.(1.3.7)

But he who is always of restrained mind and has right understanding, his senses are controllable like the good horses of a charioteer.(1.3.6)

He who is intelligent, ever pure and with the mind controlled, reaches that goal whence none is born again.(1.3.8)

Mind also, like other sense-organs, is an object perceived by another. This is indicated in the following sloka:

    **4. *Consciousness illumines (such other mental
states as) desire, determination and doubt, belief
and non-belief, constancy and its opposite, modesty,
understanding, fear and others, because it (Consciousness) is a unity.***

The mind appears to be the perceiver; but when we
try to understand its workings, we find that it is just like a
lake that is constantly bursting into waves. However, the
conscious perceiver is eternally unchanging. The greatest
point in the Vedantic analysis is this conscious Self, which
exists ever the same in the midst of all changes and
modifications. This consciousness is like a thread that joins
all our perceptions and experiences together.

We constantly identify ourselves with the modifications
of our mind, such as lust, anger, hatred, etc. It is this
identification with the modifications of our mind that must
be undermined and finally destroyed. How to do this? A
certain passion or desire rises all of a sudden in my mind.
I just stand as the Witness of that passion, of that particular
desire, and this attitude enables me to control it, not to
become enslaved, not to be swept off my feet and carried
along the stream of sense-enjoyment or hatred. Ordinarily,
there is too much of identification with the seen, so the
ordinary person cannot disentangle himself in time and gets
swept away and suffers misery again and again. To the extent
we grow through our striving, through our ethical culture,
through our japam and meditation and prayer, to that extent
there will be less and less identification with the seen, with
the phenomenon, and greater and greater identification with
the seer, the Eternal Subject.

One has to watch one's mind, how one identifies oneself,
sometimes fully, sometimes partly, with either the body or
the mind or the senses. This identification is always due to

sense-desires and attachment in a gross or subtle form. One has to rid oneself of these in order to realise the Atman.

The Katha Upanishad says,

Know that the soul is the master of the chariot who sits within it, and the body the chariot. Consider the intellect as the charioteer, and the mind as the rein.(1.3.3)

The man who has intelligence for his charioteer and the mind as the well-controlled rein—he attains the end of the journey, that supreme place of the Divine.(1.3.9)

So long as one is embodied, thoughts may still arise, but a realised soul is completely detached from them and just remains the witness of his thoughts.

That the mind undergoes changes is known to all. Because of its changeable nature, the mind is an object of perception and Consciousness is the perceiver. Consciousness perceives all these states because it is a unity. These states, though distinct in nature, become unified in Consciousness or Self:

5. *This Consciousness does neither rise nor set. It does not increase; nor does it suffer decay. Being self-luminous, it illumines everything else without any other aid.*

In the midst of this whirl of life, consciousness as such remains unchanged.

In Vedanta our life should be as wide-wake as possible; it should be as conscious as possible in a higher sense. To the extent we are able to take the side of the seer, we are able to have control. The moment the seer is wholly awakened, there can never be any form of desire, neither gross nor subtle. In fact, witnessing itself belongs to the domain of the phenomenon; but this attitude of witnessing is the highest rung of the ladder. Beyond that is the Absolute.

The Nature of Buddhi or Intelligence

> **6.** *Buddhi appears to possess luminosity on account of the reflection of Consciousness in it. Intelligence (Buddhi) is of two kinds. One is designated egoity (ahamkriti), the other as mind (antahkarana).*

The primal cause of all things, subjective and objective, is maya or Prakriti. And this undergoes various modifications when it comes in contact with the Self. First, as a result of ignorance, there comes an identification of consciousness with what is called *Buddhi*, intelligence. *Buddhi* is that product of maya or Prakriti which reflects the light of the Self. The light of *Buddhi*, therefore, is not its own, but reflected or borrowed from the Self. The luminosity is something that is inherent in us.

Buddhi divides itself as egoity on the subjective side and the inner organ (*antah-karana*) which is both objective and instrumental. *Buddhi* is that which precedes what we call our 'I-ness' and the inner organ. 'I-ness' is the very root of all egoism, higher and lower. When the first reflection of consciousness on the undifferentiated *Buddhi* becomes differentiated, each differentiated entity begins to reflect consciousness.

The Consciousness of *Buddhi* and Ego is Borrowed Consciousness

> **7.** *In the opinion of the wise the identity of the reflection (of Consciousness) and of ego is like the identity of the fire and the (heated) iron ball. The body having been identified with the ego (which has already identified itself with the reflection of Consciousness) passes for a conscious entity.*

Our ego becomes conscious because it gets identified with the reflection of consciousness in the undifferentiated *Buddhi*. The ego or so-called subject is a combination of consciousness and subtle matter. Subject consciousness does not arise when the Self is reflected on the undifferentiated *Buddhi*. It is only when the ego comes into existence that we have the notion of subject and object. The jiva, the individualized soul, is consciousness identified with the ego. Thus the insentient appears to be sentient, the object appears to be the subject owing to the presence of consciousness.

When we say, 'The iron-ball burns the fingers,' what is it that burns? The ball? No, it is the fire in the ball, not the ball. The burning quality belongs to the fire, not to the ball. The fire and the ball have become one, but the relation between fire and ball is not a permanent one. Fire can always be separated from the ball. Just as fire and the ball can be separated, Pure Consciousness and the ego can be separated, and although they appear to be identified completely and give us the notion of the subject, this is not so in reality. Consciousness has not become the ego, nor does it depend on the ego. It is because of the initial mistake that all other mistakes and wrong notions follow as a matter of course.

The (relative) subject sometimes identifies itself with the mind, sometimes with the senses, sometimes with the body. Our personality has its various sheaths. Inside, in the innermost sheath is placed the light, and this light passes from the innermost sheath to the outer sheaths. Unless this light passes through the inner sheaths, it can never come to the outer at all. The first reflection of the sun is on the cloud. After the sun has been reflected on the cloud, there is a thick cloud that intercepts the light. But in spite of that the light that percolates through everything is still there. Part of the vapour may become water, part even ice, but the particles are always there.

Different Forms of Identification of the Ego

8. *The identification of the ego with the reflection of Consciousness, the body and the Witness are of three kinds, namely, natural, due to karma, and due to ignorance, respectively.*

There are different forms of identification: (1) 'I am the knower'; (2) 'I am a human being'; (3) 'I am (I exist).'

All these are cases of the identification of the Self with what is non-self, of the seer, with what belongs to the seen. When one says, 'I am', or 'I exist', one has already individualized oneself. This means falling off from the Advaita Consciousness, because from the standpoint of the One, there is no question of 'I' at all, or of subject and object; it is a transcendental state. When one becomes finite, with limited consciousness, a complex has already been formed of the Self and the non-self, the seer and the seen.

The identification of the 'I-ness' with the witness is based only upon ignorance and nothing else. The ego becomes the centre of this individualized consciousness. It identifies itself with the Witness Consciousness.

When ignorance has become an accomplished fact, the next mistake is natural or innate. And from this innate identification which is false there arises the identification with the body, with which the soul becomes associated owing to its past karma. This ego identifies itself with the other reflections of consciousness—the body, the mind and so on. First there is the undifferentiated state. Then comes the differentiated state, and in that there is the order we have noted here.

How the Identifications of the Ego End

9. *The mutual identification of the ego and the reflection of Consciousness, which is natural, does not cease so long as they are taken to be real. The other two identifications disappear after the wearing out of the result of karma and the attainment of the knowledge of the highest Reality respectively.*

The task is, how to get rid of this ego? Unless we get rid of this ego and all these false identifications, there is no salvation for us. It is through right knowledge and clear analysis, revealing the true nature of consciousness, that this identification can be removed. The identification of the ego can be put to an end with the attainment of real knowledge which discriminates clearly between Pure Consciousness and the ego which is only a product of ignorance. The ego is regarded as the product of ignorance because it originates from undifferentiated *Buddhi* reflecting Consciousness.

Roughly speaking, this *Buddhi* is synonymous with maya. The unanalyzed *Buddhi* of the ignorant appears to be sentient, but on further analysis it is found out to be non-sentient. Subject, object, means of perception, are all modifications of maya or Prakriti. So long as ignorance continues, the mutual identification of the ego with the reflection of consciousness continues. So long as the bubble-form continues, the individuation of the water-substance is inevitable.

Our connection with the body continues so long as the karma that has brought it into existence is not fully exhausted. When the karma is exhausted, there comes dissociation between the body and the soul. All identifications are put an end to with the dawn of the highest knowledge, in which the individualized soul realizes its true nature as Brahman and Brahman only. This knowledge can be attained even when one lives in the body but does not identify oneself with the body. And in order to attain this, strict ethical culture, spiritual discipline, studies etc. are necessary. But they are the means, not the end. They do not bring about illumination, but prepare the way, remove the obstacles and obstructions which stand in the way, do the necessary cleansing and scrubbing; so that the light of highest knowledge can manifest itself clearly through this instrument. Everything that takes place, takes place in Consciousness. It is in this Infinite indivisible Consciousness, which is eternally One, that all this cosmic play is going on.

The Three States

10. *In the state of deep sleep, when (the thought of) ego disappears, the body also becomes unconscious. The state in which there is the half manifestation of the ego is called the dream state and the full manifestation of the ego is the state of waking.*

The subject-consciousness is manifest in our waking state and also in the dream state. The conscious manifestation of the ego disappears in deep sleep, not that the ego disappears completely. The identification has taken place previously, but there we are not conscious of it. We become conscious of it only during the waking state and the dream state.

Just as in deep sleep there is no conscious identification, similarly, when consciousness reflects itself on undifferentiated *Buddhi*, there is no conscious identification, because consciousness has not yet become individualized.

11. *The inner organ (mind) which is itself but a modification (vritti) identifying itself with the reflection of Consciousness imagines various ideas in dream. And the same inner organ (identifying itself with the body) imagines objects external to itself in the waking state with respect to the sense organs.*

From the standpoint of the waking state, dream experiences are unreal. Similarly, from the standpoint of the super-conscious state no waking experience possesses any ultimate reality, i.e. they are just as unreal as the dream experiences seen from the waking state. In fact, the waking state, seen from the fourth state (*Turiya*, or super-conscious), in no way possesses any greater reality than the state of dream or deep sleep. There is nothing to prove the reality of the things experienced in our so-called waking state. All experiences of the waking state are imaginations, but only when seen from the fourth state. From the standpoint of the fourth state of existence, waking, dreaming and deep sleep belong, strictly speaking, to the same category though on the relative plane, the plane of manifestation, they may have slightly differing values.

As a matter of fact, our waking state is often partly a dream state. Very few of us are ever fully in the waking state. Our so-called waking experiences are formed of our subjective ideas of the 'thing in itself' lying outside the subject. And all these are coloured cosmic ignorance. The outside world is not wholly created by our imagination, though our imagination does form a great part of our idea of this so-called 'outside world'. Similarly, in the dream state one may be conscious of the subtler mental world, but this is not always the case. Sometimes dreams are purely subjective, sometimes a combination of subjective and objective.

12. *The subtle body, which is the material cause of the mind, and egoism is one and of the nature of insentiency. It moves in the three states and is born and it dies.*

When the gross body is asleep, the subtle body is awake and dreams. The subtle body here means the entire mind-stuff. In deep sleep it too, may be asleep but it is and continues to be until illumination dawns on a person. So it is only through the highest knowledge that this subtle body can be made to perish. There is one great point to note: anything that is non-self, is non-sentient. And this subtle body that rises from maya through the medium of *Buddhi* partakes of this insentience, but it appears to be sentient, because of the reflection of the Self or Consciousness.

Maya

13. *Two powers, undoubtedly, are predicated of maya, viz. those of projecting and veiling. The projecting power creates everything from the subtle body to the gross universe.*

Maya is the power of Brahman and wholly under the control of Brahman. As Sri Ramakrishna says, the poison does not affect the snake, it only affects others. Maya is not illusion, but the cause of our empirical experiences. So long as we are in maya, we go on taking the phenomenon to be real. Maya on the one side veils the Truth and on the other side projects the phenomenon out of it.

All these, *prakriti, maya, avidya, ajnana,* are synonyms of Primal Matter, illumined by Brahman or Atman or Consciousness. It is the cause of all things material, including the mind. At first *prakriti* is in a perfectly balanced state. Then, in the course of evolution, this balance is disturbed, and there comes into existence the *Buddhi* of Vedanta or the *Mahat* of Sankhya, but this is still undifferentiated. Next comes into existence the ego or subject and the inner organ consisting of *manas* or volition and doubt, *Buddhi* or determinative faculty, and *chitta*, the faculty of memory. This *Buddhi* is differentiated *Buddhi*, as distinct from the undifferentiated *Buddhi* which precedes it.

From the relative standpoint maya or *prakriti* is eternal, but from the Absolute standpoint it doesn't exist. Even if something is false, but is taken to be real, it has a definite effect, and we feel it. However, when we recognise *prakriti* for what it is, these effects cease to have any hold over us. The Sankhyas give this funny illustration: *prakriti* is an ugly, hideous-looking dancing girl. And when she, on close examination, is found out to be what she really is, a very ugly, old and very dirty creature, then she just runs away, feeling terribly ashamed.

The Nature of Creation

14. *The manifesting of all names and forms in the entity which is Existence-Consciousness-Bliss and which is the same as Brahman, like the foams, etc., in the ocean, is known as creation.*

The light of the sun falls on the still, calm ocean. This light has, as it were, become one with this undifferentiated ocean. Then, all of a sudden, the ocean bursts into waves and bubbles, and individual existence begins. But then each single wave and bubble is reflecting the same undivided and indivisible light of the sun.

The significance of name and form in Vedanta is best understood by means of an illustration. A pot before it was made did not exist. The Vedantic teacher says, this was not non-existence, but existence in a subtle form. The Vedantin always stresses the substance, but the worldly-minded stress the form and run after the form, and do not bother at all about the substance. Because the Vedantin stresses the substance, he does not take the form very seriously or gives it a great place in his consciousness. Before the pot was made, its pot-form was non-existent. And after it is broken, it also becomes non-existent. The non-existence spoken of here, is not absolute non-existence (like the horns of a hare or the son of a barren woman), but the non-existence of a particular form before its appearance.

15. *The other power (of maya) conceals the distinction between the perceiver and the perceived objects, which are cognized within the body, as well as the distinction between Brahman and the phenomenal universe which is perceived outside (one's own body). This power (shakti) is the cause of the phenomenal universe. Maya is the cause of the undifferentiated Buddhi from which the internal organs and also gross objects have their rise.*

This maya first produces the macrocosm. The macrocosm divides itself into the microcosm. The relation between these two is akin to the relation of the whole to its parts.

There are various theories regarding the creation of the world:

1. Theory of atomic agglomeration: In atomic agglomeration good and bad exist

eternally. Atoms build up our mind and body. There is God, and there are we, the souls.

2. Theory of evolution: In evolution, what we call good and what we call bad, and all opposites, have their origin from a common primeval force or energy, or primordial matter that is the matrix of all things mental as well as physical. Evolution proceeds through contact of matter and spirit, *Prakriti* and *Purusha*. Previously we had pluralism, now we have got the dualism of matter and soul, *Prakriti* and *Purusha*.

3. Theory of reality and appearance: According to the third school, there is

absolutely no dualism of matter and spirit. It is the spirit that, through its inscrutable power of ignorance, appears as the phenomenon, like a snake in a rope. And when this ignorance hides the face of Truth, then evolution proceeds as a matter of course.

4. The phenomenon is not created at all. There is no phenomenon, and there has

never been any phenomenon, any manifestation.

The last theory is so high that we need not bother about it now. But there is such a perception from the highest standpoint.

The Problem of Evil

In this context, let us discuss briefly the concepts of good and evil. Although we cannot explain rationally what is the cause of good and evil, there is a way to transcend both. But so long as we cling to our personalities, so long as we want to find a cause for the unreal phenomenon, instead of attributing what we call good to God and what we call evil to evil powers, it is more rational and far more scientific to attribute both to a Cosmic Power that manifests

Itself in this phenomenal world of relativity, in which good and evil are eternally inseparable. What we call good is so only from the standpoint of relativity, never in any absolute sense. And the same is true of evil also and they both belong to the domain of maya. Although this phenomenon takes place in the noumenon, or in other words, although the reality appears to be the phenomenal existence, It remains wholly untouched by good and evil, for It is transcendental— and this is the only solution. You do not attribute your good and evil to the Divine, but to ignorance, that is the power of the Divine, that is wholly dependent on the Divine, but by which the Divine is unaffected.

Really speaking, the only way to escape the conclusion that God is the cause of evil is to attribute evil to ignorance, because of which the Truth is hidden, and the whole phenomenal existence is brought into being. Good and evil belong only to the domain of the phenomenon, never to the domain of reality.

It is no use discussing such problems eternally. So long as you are in maya, it exists and continues to exist. As soon as you are out of it, it has no existence at all. So Buddha very rightly said, 'Why bother about it? When the house is on fire, just extinguish the fire and do not discuss its cause.'

The Vedantic teacher tries to explain the cause of both, relative good and relative evil, by his explanation of 'Appearance and Reality'. And, at the same time, he shows us also the way to transcend all relativity, be it good or evil, and to reach the Reality as such. He advises us first to rise above evil with the help of relative good, and then to attain to the transcendental state which is eternally untouched by both relative good and relative evil.

Maya in Relation to Jiva or the Empirical Self

16. *The subtle body (Lingam) which exists in close proximity to the Witness (Sakshin), identifying itself*

*with the gross body becomes the embodied empirical
self, on account of its being affected by the reflection
of Consciousness.*

Our whole thought-world as well as the outside world,
including our gross body, that we perceive with our senses,
belong to the phenomenal world. It is because of the power
of ignorance called maya that we are not able to find which
is the true subject and which is the true object; which is the
real perceiver, knower, and which is the real perceived,
known.

The root cause of all our troubles lies deep below the
surface of our consciousness. First of all, the Self is covered
over by ignorance, giving rise to the subtle body. Then, when
we become forgetful of our true nature and identify ourselves
with the different limiting adjuncts *(upadhis)*, all subsequent
mistakes are committed. Owing to this superimposition we
become the doer, the actor, man or woman, the enjoyer etc.
If we are able to know our true nature, which is eternally
the Self, we become neither man nor woman, neither doer
nor actor, nor enjoyer; and then there is neither freedom nor
bondage for us as we are ever free and immutable.

The whole secret here is to have as clear a brain as
possible, to find out the subject and the object, to give up
all superimpositions of the non-self, and realize our eternal
nature, that which we really are.

17. *The character of an embodied self appears through
false superimposition in the Sakshin also. With the
disappearance of the veiling power, the distinction
(between the seer and the object) becomes clear and
with it the jiva character of the Sakshin (Witness)
disappears.*

In one state, the veiling power (maya) is; in another state
it is not, it ceases to be. When true knowledge dawns on
the aspirant, it ceases to be; during ignorance it is. So where
does it come from? We can never say it is real, nor can we

say that it is unreal. It has neither existence nor non-existence. When we are in it, it appears to be real. When we are out of it, it ceases to be. So its nature can never be known, but maya can be transcended.

Our vision of the many is not illusory. For a time it exists, but when all disturbance stops, it is gone. What we see is not the reality, but an appearance that is taken for the reality. It is this one real that appears to be the many on the subjective side, as well as the many on the objective side. This can easily be understood with the help of Kant's ideas, as explained by Swamiji. Let X denote the subject and Y denote the object of perception. Since the mind comes in between X and Y for perception to be complete, we have in reality, X plus mind (subjective) and Y plus mind (objective). If we take away the mind, X and Y become one and the same, the Absolute. According to Vedanta, mind belongs wholly to the phenomenal plane, mind is matter, and as such ceases to be when the highest knowledge dawns. (It should be pointed out that Kant did not go this far. According to Kant, time, space and causation are part of the subjective world, whereas in Vedanta, time, space and causation are partly subjective and partly objective. In the final count, time, space and causation become part of the transient existence.)

Universal or Cosmic Maya

Where does maya exist? Is it in Brahman or in the individualized self? The previous two *slokas* described the character of maya at the individual level. A fundamental tenet of Vedanta says that the microcosm (individual) and the macrocosm (universe) are built along the same lines. The next two verses discuss the nature of universal or cosmic maya.

18. *Similarly, Brahman, through the influence of the power that conceals the distinction between It and the phenomenal universe, appears as endowed with the attributes of change.*

The same thing is appearing in one form as the seer, in another as the seen. This is not only so in our inner world, but also in the outside world. Maya is the cause. And it is this maya that brings about this bifurcation into subject and object.

In order to trace the Sakshin (witness) we take the individualized soul. On the other side, when we try to trace the reality at the back of the phenomenal world, we come to the same Brahman. When the true nature of the Self is concealed by the veiling power, then comes into existence the individualized soul associated with the body, mind, senses, etc. Similarly, in a cosmic sense, the true nature of infinite existence is hidden from view and appears to us as the outside world. So this concealing power of ignorance brings into existence on one side the jiva, and on the other side this world of name and form.

The phenomenon is the Absolute coming to us through the distorting medium of time, space and causation. All changes really belong to maya, but we, through ignorance, attribute these changes to Brahman which is eternally beyond all change and mutability. What we see now is not Brahman, but only changes.

The one undivided and indivisible Existence appears, through the power of maya, to be many, both subjective and objective, just as the one Self appears to be many selves. Brahman also appears to be this whole diversified world. It is Brahman that seems to bring this phenomenal world into existence with the help of maya. But, really speaking it does not bring anything into existence at all. That which is eternally one and indivisible can never become the many, but it can *appear* to be the many.

This makes one wonder, 'Which is more powerful: Maya or Brahman?' If maya is more powerful, then this phenomenon can never be transcended. But maya is fully dependent on Brahman. It is a power of Brahman. The poison of the snake is dependent on the snake and never poisons the snake itself. So, maya will cease to effect its hold, once the distinction between maya and Brahman becomes clear. This is explained in the next verse:

19. *In this case also, the distinction between Brahman and the phenomenal universe becomes clear with the disappearance of the veiling power. Therefore, change is perceived in the phenomenal universe, but never in Brahman.*

Brahman becomes the cause of this phenomenal world only on the relative plane and only from the relative standpoint. Something that is different in nature cannot be the cause of something different. The Absolute can never become relative, and, if it becomes so, it is only an appearance, an appearance that is taken to be real owing to the veiling power, maya.

Consider an ocean, where the water-substance appears to undergo modifications. But the nature of the substance can never be changed. What we call the foam or the wave is a combination of the water-substance and something other than water which gives the same substance different forms, different appearances.

Our ideal is to transcend the phenomenon and not to be fooled by it. We should not give it any real reality, only an empirical reality. Maya is Brahman in a way, and maya's existence is temporary, whereas Brahman is eternal. I want the Absolute Reality, not this world of phenomena, not the empirical reality.

The phenomenal world means constant change. I want that which does not change. I want neither good nor bad. I do not want nature's smiles nor do I want nature's frowns. I do not want personal relations with the many or one of the many, but I want the One only and through the One, all. I want that which does not change under any circumstances. I am not satisfied with this world of change and changing relationships. Security can be had only in that which never changes, not in that which is constantly and eternally changing and fleeting.

The Five Characteristics

20. *Every entity has five characteristics, viz., existence, cognizability, attractiveness, form and name. Of these, the first three belong to Brahman and the next two to the world.*

With reference to outside things we see: the thing is, presents itself to us, becomes attractive for some reason or other. With reference to ourselves we see: we want to exist eternally. Moreover, we do not want to live like stocks and stones, but as intelligent, conscious, blissful beings. This is the common yearning of all human beings.

But then we are such fools and go on clinging so much to names and forms, that we want to seek the Infinite in the finite. We want to realize eternity in time. We want to have infinity in space. We want to realize abiding peace in the midst of misery and change and falsehood. So we find our task an impossible one. What is really necessary is this: we should cease longing for the impossible. This giving up is giving up the attachment to this life and all that it implies. Then we have to transcend name and form, transcend all limitations and pet desires, and then alone it is possible for us to realize Existence-Knowledge-Bliss Absolute.

Our self-love is an aspect of this love for Brahman, but then it is all upside down, all distorted. The soul's love for itself is transferred to the body and the mind, then to some other body and mind, not ours, and then there comes confusion and bondage. In everything we see the attraction of the Self, but we misunderstand it and begin our search in a very wrong and misleading direction.

We should recognise this during our spiritual practices, too. Even if we try to practise concentration on any image or sound, we should always recognize the image, the sound, etc. as a symbol of the Divine. Even if we make our own mind the object of concentration, we should try to see the Self reflected in the mind. So our mind too becomes a symbol of the Divine. Look upon mind as Brahman.

The ideal is to try to rise above the name and form of the object of concentration that is within or outside. The objects of concentration should take us nearer and nearer to the Reality.

Consciousness Reflected in Nature

The one undivided and indivisible substance, because of the diversity of names and forms, appears diversified. If we take away the forms of the bubbles and the waves, and then even the form of the ocean, which too is but a form of the water-substance, nothing but this substance is left, and the goal is attained. This is the task before us.

21. *The attributes of Existence, Consciousness, and Bliss are equally present in the Akasa (ether), air, fire, water and earth as well as in Gods, animals and men etc. Names and forms make one differ from the other.*

When we take the name and form to be real, the Reality disappears, and then all our troubles arise. In order to recognize the unreality of name and form, we must first of all have right intellectual knowledge and discrimination. But that is not enough. We must also practise concentration that enables us to rise above names and forms, above the whole phenomenon. The idea is to transcend name and form, not only inside, but outside also.

We can never really give up name and form, because they are intimately associated with our false personality, with the So-and-So, belonging to such-and-such a place that we imagine ourselves to be. But we can become indifferent to name and form and this false personality of ours, and assert what lies at the back of ourselves as well as at the back of all names and forms.

First we see name and form, and name and form are the only reality. Then we see the Self reflecting Itself on forms. Then comes a time when names and forms disappear altogether. The Self alone, one and undivided, exists in all Its glory.

This is, emphatically, not the same as seeing the Divine in physical nature. In fact, seeing the Divine in nature is very far from being the highest experience—it may even be dangerous. So Christ, Buddha, Krishna, Ramakrishna, etc., do not make much of all this Cosmic Consciousness, because it is a manifestation of consciousness on the physical plane.

Phenomenal reality is not a primary, but a secondary reality and should always be taken as such. Art at its very best and highest is merely a reflection of a reflection of a reflection of the Truth. It can never show us the Truth however great it may be.

The danger of seeing the Divine in nature (i.e. seeing nature and not the Divine, because that is what it comes to mostly—admiring the beauty, the physical beauty, gross and subtle of nature) and the danger of getting physical Cosmic Visions, is to set too high a value on the physical world. This leads one away from the Truth and gets one entangled all the more in the meshes of the phenomenon, of maya, of Cosmic Ignorance. So however elevating these visions may seem to be, they are a great danger to aspirants in most cases and should rather be avoided by stressing the Ultimate Essence and not the manifestation, gross or subtle.

Nature may be elevating to some, but this feeling of elevation mostly contains physical elements and thus does not lead us to the Truth. But if we stress the Divine and not the expression of the Divine through nature, there is less danger of slipping one's foot and being caught in the net of ignorance.

From the true spiritual standpoint, the transcendental experience is always higher than any Cosmic Experience however grand it may seem to be, because Reality transcends even the Cosmic. Cosmic always means phenomenal, always means ignorance.

In some cases one may not have any experience easily, because one does not care for physical experiences, but wants to have them on a higher plane only. In other cases, for those who are ready to have experiences on a lower plane, experience is an easy thing but has no high value at all, whatever the experiencer may think. It will serve to make people all the more conscious of their personality and of the outside world of phenomena.

We should do our practices steadily and regularly, never missing a day, and then let the fruits of these practices take care of themselves. Strict discipline, strict ethical culture, study etc. are necessary; then let the rest come of itself and take care of itself. Do not bother your heads too much about visions and experiences; they have no higher value if you have not prepared yourselves properly through strict training and discipline and discrimination.

The Six Kinds of Samadhi

> **22.** *Having become indifferent to name and form and being devoted to Satchidananda, one should always practise concentration either within the heart or outside.*

First of all there must be clear thinking, then clear feeling, willing and activity. That is why it is essential to have serious studies, to think deeply, to exercise the brain and ponder deeply over the problems. If this is not done everyday as one of the items of sadhana, one cannot make any considerable progress, and there is always the danger of the brain becoming muddled through outside stimuli owing to a lack of right discrimination. The higher centres do not work properly. Without very clear and definite thinking, no clear activity is possible. And every aspirant has to be as wide awake as possible, has to know his weak and strong points, his attractions and aversions, and act accordingly. Too much time is being wasted in idle talks with people, instead of studying some good books and thinking over what is written in them. All this is a useless waste of time and opportunity.

Thought always comes before action. Therefore we should be always on our guard with a drawn sword. We should attack the thought-world and not allow ourselves to be drawn into muddled feelings and associations. To the extent we really purify our mind, the whole outer activity, all attractions and aversions, would change.

It is very helpful even to repeat the words that speak of this clear thinking again and again. Through habit we are able to think of the higher things more and more. Daily repetition of these ideas with a highly concentrated mind is very essential for every aspirant. Too little work is being done in that direction. There is too much of indiscriminate mixing with all sorts of people, too much of idle talking, and too little of private studies and deep thinking. The only way to colour our whole mind and drive all these ideas deep into our consciousness, is steady study, repetition of these truths and deep steady thinking.

23. *Two kinds of samadhi to be practised in the heart (within one's self) are known as Savikalpa and Nirvikalpa. Savikalpa Samadhi is again divided into two classes, according to its association with a cognizable object or a sound (as an object).*

Sankaracharya says, 'The seer is Brahman, and the seen is maya.' And again, 'Brahman alone is real. The world is unreal. The jiva is no other than Brahman.'

Meditation on this is subjective concentration. But in objective concentration the aspirant has to think that the world, freed from name and form, is also Brahman.

All these forms of Savikalpa Samadhi are with thoughts, but the highest form is beyond all sound and beyond all thought. To reach that highest state we take the help of sound-symbols, and finally rise above them. When one is able to transcend the world of name and form, as also all forms of thought and individual consciousness, and becomes identified with Infinite Consciousness, then only is the highest form of samadhi reached. Savikalpa Samadhi is only a step.

But these higher forms of samadhi can only be attained after long years of strict ethical culture, and they can never be attained without brahmacharya in thought, word and deed.

24. *Desire etc., centred in the mind are to be treated as (cognizable) objects. Meditate on Consciousness as their Witness. This is what is called Savikalpa Samadhi associated with (cognizable) objects.*

25. *I am Existence-Consciousness-Bliss, unattached, self-luminous and free from duality. This is known as the (other kind of) Savikalpa Samadhi associated with sound (object).*

Ordinarily, we identify ourselves with the desires arising in our mind. But the aspirant has to think: 'I am not the wave. I am the witness. This thought rises in my mind. I dissociate myself from the thought. I am not the thought, nor the thinking faculty, I am the witness.' If the aspirant consciously practises this attitude for some time, the thought would be there, the thought would rise, but there won't be any identification with the thought.

Desire may be made the object of one's concentration, just like one's own mind and its movements. Sound may be made the object of concentration, too. But the attitude of the witness has to be always stressed and is to be kept up: 'I am the witness, I stand aloof and watch all this.'

We think we are men or women, attached, ignorant, bound to the world and the senses, to this whole world of dualism and slavery, but the aspirant has to raise the contrary current of thought and rise above all duality and all the pairs of opposites. First of all we have got to pass through the world of imagination. This helps one awaken one's innate freedom, the freedom that is our very nature. Swamiji says that a hero does not forget his duty, whether the world remains or dissolves.

There is always the light of the soul in the innermost recesses of our being. But without strict ethical culture, we can never dis-cover this. We are in touch with the highest consciousness, but we do not know it. It is veiled by layers and layers of filth and dirt, physical and mental.

It takes a long time to store the necessary energy for higher spiritual practices. You see the thundering cloud, but the energy has been collecting all the time without your perceiving it. We must restrain all the outgoing tendencies of our mind, subtle and gross, and force it to settle down to serious study and thinking. There is no other way.

And all this clear thinking is possible only when we lead a perfectly pure life in thought, word and deed, when we are able to shift our consciousness to a higher centre and no longer allow it to dwell on worldly thoughts and worldly people, however subtle their attraction may be. We should go on doggedly, perseveringly with our practices and daily routines and see that we are not unguarded, not lacking in discrimination. We should not allow our mind to deceive us with any plausible arguments hiding our gross and subtle desires for enjoyment.

26. *But the Nirvikalpa Samadhi is that in which the mind becomes steady like the (unflickering flame of a) light kept in a place free from wind and in which the student becomes indifferent to both objects and sounds on account of his complete absorption in the bliss of the realization of the Self.*

In one of his poems, Sankaracharya says,

> *I am not the body,*
> *there is no birth or death for me.*
> *I am not the mind,*
> *there is no pleasure or pain for me.*
> *I am not the doer,*
> *so there is no bondage or freedom for me.*

It is when we shift the centre of our consciousness from the body and the mind to the Self that we become really free.

'I am the body; no, I am the Self. I am bound; no, I am free. I am a man; no, I am the Self. I am a woman; no, I am the Self. I am finite; no, I am infinite. I am limited; no, there are no limits for me.' This way of thinking has to be practised more and more by every aspirant.

27. *The first kind of samadhi is possible with the help of any external object as it is with the help of an internal object. In that samadhi the name and form are separated from what is Pure Existence (Brahman).*

One usually gives the universe the place of Reality. This attitude must be thoroughly undermined and changed. Otherwise one cannot progress. Nothing phenomenal is real, nothing phenomenal is of any consequence. You just stand as the witness of the play. Do not identify yourself with it. The Real is never the cause of anything.

In spite of intellectual conviction and rejection of the manifestation, both good and bad, the heart still refuses to grasp this fully.

One must learn to watch one's mind consciously, standing as the witness, aloof from all its movements. Desire arises in my mind. What then? I stand as the witness of that particular desire, calm, unruffled, not identifying myself with it or with my mind in any way. We have to see that we separate Consciousness from things that are really insentient by their very nature, e.g. from our desires, impulses, cravings, that are insentient. We must try to separate the Self from matter. Even our mind with all its desires etc. is nothing but matter. Whatever is non-self comes under *drishya*, the seen, or matter; as distinct from *drig*, the seer that sees, watches and recognizes it. So all desires, all impulses, good or bad, are *drishya*, matter, things seen.

Then one comes in touch with that undivided and indivisible Consciousness that divides Itself into the subject and the objective world through the power of maya. We find such meditations in the Brihadaranyaka Upanishad:

He who inhabits the earth, but is within it, whom the earth does not know, whose body the earth is, and who controls the earth from within, is the Internal Ruler, my own Immortal Self.(3.7.3)

The idea is to transcend name and form, not only inside, but outside also.

We may also take up some holy form of a saint or a prophet. The formless aspect, with or without attributes, may appeal to us intellectually, but when we come to practise we find that it doesn't work. Very few people are able to begin their sadhana in this way, whatever their intellectual learnings may be. First of all they say, 'Oh, the formless appeal to me. I do not want any anthropomorphic form.' But after a time, they themselves find out that they are not able to make any progress at all, and they come back to the form and can be given a form. But first they must find this out for themselves. So I just let them try for a time. So long as the child is a child, it has to take the help of the kindergarten, but we, being children, want to take up the attitude of the grown-ups and have the formless. It sounds all very grand and satisfies our intellect, but what can we do so long as we are still children? So it is better to have a form to cling to and to concentrate upon.

To the extent we rise above name and form in the subjective world, we rise above name and form in the objective world. To the extent we rise above name and form in the objective world, we rise above name and form in the subjective world.

> **28.** *The entity which is (always) of the same nature and unlimited (by time, space, etc.) and which is characterized by Existence-Consciousness-Bliss, is verily Brahman. Such uninterrupted reflection is called the intermediate absorption, that is, the Savikalpa Samadhi associated with sound (object).*

This is the main thing in Monistic Vedanta: One tries to get hold of this unchanging consciousness. No individualized consciousness is possible, unless there be at least an indefinite glimpse of the infinite consciousness.

Echoes of this idea can be found in western philosophy. Herbert Spencer says, 'Besides that definite consciousness of which logic formulates the laws, there is an indefinite consciousness which cannot be formulated.' Kant also says, 'All empirical consciousness has a necessary relation to a transcendental consciousness which precedes all our single experiences, i.e. the consciousness of our own self as the original apperception.'

> **29.** *The insensibility of the mind (to external objects) as before, on account of the experience of Bliss, is designated as the third kind of samadhi (Nirvikalpa). The practitioner should uninterruptedly spend his time in these six kinds of samadhi.*

Here we get a glimpse of the goal. Here alone one comes to be identified with the Infinite Consciousness, free from all thoughts and objects. Here the individuality as well as the world gets merged in Brahman in which all names and forms, subjective as well as objective, are lost. This is an experience in which the dualism of subject and object is transcended, in which even the functioning of the mind

stops completely, and the Pure Consciousness of the Self
exists as it is.

It is, really speaking, contentless Consciousness.
Ordinarily, in our consciousness, there are things that we
are conscious of, but here there is nothing objective that
we are conscious of in any way.

In the most purified personality, this Infinite
Consciousness is realised first; then the mind melts away.
The pitcher is broken. Then comes the light in the presence
of which all darkness disappears.

Result of Realization

30. *With the disappearance of the attachment to the
body and with the realization of the Supreme Self, to
whatever object the mind is directed one experiences
samadhi.*

Even samadhi is only a step and nothing final. There
is a state that comes even after samadhi and is much higher
than samadhi. And this alone is the Ultimate goal of the
Vedantin. For him, mere attaining of samadhi won't do.

The Vedantin teaches us in very clear terms: 'Don't care
very much for samadhi even, but try to have this infinite
consciousness even in your conscious state.'

First of all one comes in touch with Brahman only
through steadfast concentration, but when one comes down
to the sense plane, the sense world, one sees the same
Brahman, and the whole world appears to be a shadow, a
mere nothing.

Herein lies the test: If one has really experienced
Brahman consciousness through concentration, one is able
to retain something of this consciousness when one comes
in touch with the phenomenal world. But if it is only a
hallucination or one's own imagination, one's outlook
towards the things of the senses and one's desires are not
changed.

When one comes down for the first time, one might be a little unbalanced and upset. One is not quite able to adjust. The sense of proportion might be missing, when one comes down to this world after some experience. Later on this becomes more and more natural, producing less and less of unsettlement.

When the finite gets rid of its limitations and superimpositions, it becomes infinite, i.e. it attains again to its true, eternal, immutable nature. As Swamiji says, 'I see Thy face when I see all faces.' We have lost this sense of reality as a result of the veiling power, as a result of the outgoing tendencies of our minds. We should try to see the permanent element at the back of all impermanent names and forms.

31. *By beholding Him who is high and low, the fetters of the heart are broken, all doubts are solved and all his karmas (activities and their effects) wear away.*

Sometimes stress is laid on the objective aspect, sometimes on the subjective one, but the subjective and the objective can be combined. The subjective test of samadhi is that one feels the presence of the Reality and knows clearly without any shade of doubt that it is the Reality. The objective test is a life of purity, of selflessness, of introspection, of divine Consciousness.

The man of Self-realization recognizes the same Divinity in and through all. Then only he becomes perfectly fearless, a hero. Previously the phenomenon wants to allure him, to capture him, but when it becomes like a shadow, it loses all its influence on him. Then the phenomenon with all its glamour can no longer capture you, no longer frighten you. What was real, has become unreal. What was ideal, has become real. What was real, relatively speaking, has become an empty shadow. This is *jIvanmukti*, emancipation while in life.

JIvanmukti is characterised by karma releasing its hold on us. There are three kinds of karma:

1. That which has begun to bear fruit.

2. That which is accumulated.

3. That which is being done now and the results of which are going to be worked out in the future.

Once the arrow is shot, it cannot be made to return to the quiver. But the unshot arrows need not be shot or even taken out of the quiver. If one stops rowing, the boat is still driven on for some time, impelled by its own past momentum. The state of the *jivanmukti*. is very similar to this. The body goes on moving due to its past momentum, but karma has ceased to have any hold over him.

Views about Jiva

32. *There are three conceptions of jiva (Consciousness), namely, as that limited (by) Prana, etc., as that presented (in the mind) and the third one Consciousness as imagined in dream (to have assumed the forms of man, etc.). Among them the first one is the real nature.*

33. *Limitation is illusory but that which appears to be limited is real. The jivahood (of the Self) is due to the super-imposition of the illusory attributes. But really it has the nature of Brahman.*

One school thinks that the soul is a part of Brahman, even in a spatial sense. So the individuals are both different and non-different from Brahman; like sparks and fire.

Another school holds that the individual soul bound by the *upadhis* [limiting adjuncts] of body, senses, mind, ego etc. is different from Brahman, though through meditation and knowledge it becomes one with the highest Self. For this school the individualized state is real, for the time being.

Another school thinks that the individualized soul is absolutely identical with Brahman which in some way or other presents Itself as the individualized soul. Sankara takes this third view. And he takes the text that the jiva is a part of the highest Reality to mean: 'a part, as it were'. So Brahman which is not composed of parts cannot have parts in the literal sense. All these are only appearances, not realities. The jiva is an entity imagined in a dream which appears to be real as long as the dream lasts. Even in this interpretation, greater stress is laid on the *upadhis* than on the Reality that appears to be limited by them. But limitation does not mean anything; it is nothing, when seen from the higher standpoint. The illusory nature appears to be real only so long as the charm of maya lasts.

The very first necessity in spiritual life is to attune the individual to the universal in some form or another . So even if the ego exists, it exists not as an independent entity, but as something dependent on the Cosmic Existence (Being).

We identify ourselves with the body, then there is birth and death. We identify ourselves with the mind, then we get pain and pleasure. Our misery is unavoidable, brought about solely by ourselves through false ideas, false conceptions of ourselves, as well as of others and things.

Why should there not be misery and suffering in this world, when our whole life is based on falsehood, on insincerity, on what is not truth? The more of suffering and misery and pain, the better. That will give us a good shaking and finally wake us up. We think that we are men, women, bodies, personalities, so-and-so, belonging to such-and-such a place, which are all lies, all falsehood, which we are not. Everything in our life is based on falsehood, on false foundations, and then, one day the whole superstructure falls down, and we suffer. Why not? The sooner this happens, the better. Blessed pain, blessed suffering.

It is only when we get wholly tired of the many, that our soul yearns for the One, and then only real spiritual life can be begun. It is only when we get really tired of the phenomenal world and nature's beauty, that our soul hankers

H 16

after Self-realization. So long as the glamour of the phenomenon holds us and binds us, there can be no real and sincere spiritual life, whatever plausible arguments our mind may be inventing to deceive us.

Unless the seed of ignorance is burnt through knowledge and discrimination, there is no safety. The burnt rope alone can never bind again. The burnt seed alone can never sprout again. With the dawn of knowledge the jiva realizes that he is not the jiva at all, that he is the Self.

Jiva and Jagat

34. *Such Vedic statements as 'That Thou Art' etc. declare the identity of partless Brahman with the jiva who appears as such from the standpoint of the 'Theory of limitation' (Avacchedavada). But it does not agree with the other two views (of jiva).*

If by 'thou' we mean the individualized self, and by 'that' the manifest world, 'thou' can never be equal to 'that'. The true meaning is that the Reality in the individualized soul (jiva) as distinct from the limitations of names and forms that bring about the individuality, and the Reality as distinct from names and forms that bring about the diversity in the phenomenal world, are one and the same. You can never be He, but the substance in you can be He, and is He. The Brahman element is there in the jiva; only it is limited by different upadhis (limiting adjuncts).

What we are concerned with in the case of the jiva is the reflected consciousness, reflecting itself in the subtle body. The reflected light is always there, and from this reflected light we must pass on to the real Light. We can proceed towards it only with the help of the reflection.

The sun's light is reflected on the water. And with the help of this reflection we try to find out the light of the sun.

Taking hold of the reflection, you must find out that which is reflected. So in the individualized soul, there is the reflected light, always, and the jiva is this light identified with the mind, the body, the senses etc.

Our real Self is consciousness as such, i.e. the unreflected consciousness. But this we can reach only with the help of reflected consciousness. The highest state is the state of existence, without thought, but with consciousness.

35. *Maya which has the double aspect of projection and concealment is in Brahman. It limits the indivisible nature of Brahman and makes It (Brahman) appear as the world and the embodied being.*

Brahman is neither subject nor object, but through maya comes this distinction of the subject and the object, which is, really speaking unreal, non-existent. And the world of subject and object is the world of name and form, the world of changes and instability, the world of birth, existence, growth, modification, decay and destruction.

How to see Brahman in the phenomenal world? The only way is first to see the Self (Brahman) in our little individual world. The jiva in his true nature is Brahman and nothing but Brahman. Similarly, the manifest world is Brahman and nothing but Brahman in its true nature.

To the extent, through our practices and strict ethical culture, this veiling power becomes thinner and thinner, and we become better reflectors of the Light, the distinction between Brahman and the phenomenal world also becomes clearer and clearer. And when the veiling power is finally destroyed, the phonomenal world completely disappears.

36. *It is because the fallacious presentation of consciousness (chidabhasa) located in the Buddhi performs various actions and enjoys their results, that it is called jiva. And all this, consisting of the elements and their products, which are of the nature of the objects of enjoyment, is called Jagat (universe).*

Jiva is Brahman appearing through maya. Through maya, Reality appears to be bifurcated into the individualized soul and the universe or into subject and object, but really speaking there has never been any subject or object.

The jiva freed from all upadhis is the same as this universe freed from all upadhis. The Reality behind the jiva is the same as the Reality behind the universe.

When we are in maya, the duality of the soul and the universe is a reality. In the jiva, the individual, there is the false self and the true Self. The false self is to be separated from the true Self by stages.

The individualized soul consists of the real light, real consciousness, identified with the limiting adjuncts, and to the extent we rise above the limitations of our personality we get a better and better glimpse of the real Consciousness in us.

37. *These two, dating from time without beginning, have (only) empirical existence and exist till one attains liberation. Therefore both are called empirical.*

Now, to us, our personality is intensely real, whatever it may be from the Absolute standpoint. But this reality is not a primary reality, but a secondary reality. It is neither absolute nor illusory.

The jiva is nothing but a complex: the body, senses, mind, ego, etc. He becomes the doer, the enjoyer. The limitless, through the limitations of names and forms, appears to be finite. And the soul regards its finite nature as real. This is a wrong conception. The function of the scriptures is to remove this wrong conception. This is their meaning and purpose. Scriptures have their use so long as we are in avidya (ignorance). With jnana or *vidya*, scriptures become useless, but that does not matter. Then we no longer need them, but before that stage is reached, they are necessary as stepping stones to the highest knowledge and realization. Afterwards we even want them to become useless. Then they no longer serve any purpose. With the dawn of the highest knowledge, the Vedas cease to be Vedas. Vedanta is the only religion that says that there comes a time in the life of the aspirant or sincere seeker after Truth when even the scriptures lose their importance and are no longer necessary. No other religion has had the courage to say this.

To the enlightened one who has known the Self, all the Vedas are of so much use as a reservoir is when there is flood everywhere.

(Bhagavad Gita II.46)

Scriptures are of no use for the illumined soul, but they have their use for those living in ignorance. This is a very bold statement, but we want the ideal to cease to be an ideal, we want the scriptures to cease to be scriptures. The ideal must one day become real, otherwise the ideal is of no use at all.

Jiva as Conceived in the Three States

38. *Sleep, said to be associated with Consciousness wrongly presented (in the mind) and of the nature of concealment and projection, at first covers the (empirical) individual self and the cognized universe, but then imagines them (in dream) afresh.*

There is cosmic ignorance as well as individual ignorance. We come in touch with cosmic ignorance in deep sleep. But when we awake, we have a thicker veil of untruth, of unreality, hiding Truth, in spite of our waking consciousness. In deep sleep we forget most of these limiting adjuncts, but fall unconscious, but when we come back to this waking state, we come with all our limitations, all the *upadhis*, and also create things that are awful. So seen from a particular standpoint, even the state of deep sleep is not so bad as our waking state.

Our individualized personality is a product of this maya that veils the Truth and at the same time creates this whole phenomenon out of it. And when this individualized soul (jiva) has come into existence, being a product of maya, it just follows these two powers, the veiling power as well as the creative power, and then we begin to create what is false and limiting and untrue and go on increasing our bondage more and more.

Now our task is to remove this veiling power little by little. Our whole mind is clouded and covered by masses of filth and dirt which have to be removed. Our whole way of thinking and looking at things has to be overhauled. All this dirt has to be removed layer after layer, then the Truth that is within shines more and more brilliantly of itself.

> **39.** *These two objects (namely, the perceiving self and the perceived world) are illusory on account of their having existed only during the period of (dream) experience. It is because no one after waking up from dream sees those objects when one dreams again.*

Here the author takes up dream. Dream is imaginary and as such has got less value than the phenomenon, because in the phenomenon we see an amount of persistence which we miss in dreams. Generally, we do not see the same dream day after day. The phenomenal world has its changes, no doubt, but in it there are common points which we notice from day to day. That which has got greater persistence than something else, has to that extent got greater reality too, i.e. it is more real than that something else, whatever its reality, when seen from the standpoint of the Ultimate Truth may be.

The test of Truth is persistence. Therefore, judged from the standpoint of the waking state, the dream-world and the dream-self are illusory. Generally, our dream-self and the dream-world are not repeated again and again in exactly the same manner, though in exceptional cases both may be repeated.

> **40.** *He who is the illusory jiva (pratibhasika jiva) thinks the illusory world as real but the empirical jiva thinks (that world) as unreal.*

There are three selves: the dream-self, the waking self, the illumined self. Accordingly, there are three realities, dream reality, phenomenal reality and absolute reality.

If the whole phenomenal existence is unreal, no greater reality can be given to the waking states than to the other states. But so long as we take the phenomenon to be real, we inevitably put greater stress on the waking state than on the dream state or the state of deep sleep.

The dream state is a state in which the waking consciousness is concealed for the soul. And waking consciousness here implies empirical individuality and empirical world. The waking state is called phenomenal; the dream state illusory, but then illusory only when seen from the waking standpoint.

You see, now the author has made you swallow a bait and drags you up. He takes you step by step. 'You hold your dream-state is unreal, don't you? Now, from which state do you take it to be unreal? From the waking state, isn't it? All right, but let us take just one step farther. There is an experience from which the waking state is seen to be illusory too. So you have to concede my point.'

41. *He who is the empirical jiva (Vyavaharika jiva) sees this empirical world as real. But the real jiva knows it to be unreal.*

The jiva takes the phenomenal world to be real, but the real jiva who rises to the superconscious plane takes this empirical world to be unreal.

As for you, reject the good manifestations as well as the bad manifestations. Reject everything belonging to the phenomenal world. Regard all manifestations, people, things, thoughts, ideas, as mere empty nothings, mere shadows that have nothing to do with your reality. For you this is the best attitude: rejection of everything phenomenal. Your intellect grasps this idea, but your heart does not respond to it. Feelings, good or bad, are roused in you by manifestations, and here your whole attitude has to be changed.

Why care for what happens? What is it to you what happens outside? What is a person after all? What is a mere puny man? What does he or she matter? What is a mere phase in the lives of nations? They come and go, but then for you, for your heart, they are still being given the value of something real. And that is wrong. That has to be changed. Cut off all connection with what is manifestation and rest in that alone which is Real.

In no way can what is Real ever be the cause of anything. So the Reality is not the cause of the phenomenal world at all. The rope has never been the cause of the snake. The Reality remains ever unchanged and immutable, wholly beyond the domain of cause and effect. Cut off all connection with your personality which is just as unreal as everything else that is phenomenal. By the relative, your personality is affected, not you yourself.

One need not believe in the God of the theist at all. But the phenomenon, people, things, thoughts, ideas, all these must become unreal, fleeting, unimportant, of no consequence, to you. That is very important. So here there must be a change in your whole attitude.

Sankara, in his *Vivekachudamani* says:

How can the body, being a pack of bones, covered with flesh, and full of filth, and highly impure, be the self-existent Atman, the Knower which is ever distinct from it?(158)

It is the foolish man who identifies himself with a mass of skin, flesh, fat, bones and filth, while the man of discrimination knows his own Self, the only Reality that there is, as distinct from the body.(159)

We are such slaves and cowards, caught in the meshes of illusion and constantly entangling ourselves more and more through our attachments, likes and dislikes and terrible clinging to life. We are constantly living in fear, in some form or other, sometimes fear for the sake of ourselves, sometimes for the sake of others. And we come to have fear, because we look upon this world with its diverse manifestation, its men and women etc. as real; and we get rid of it, to the extent that the world, including our own body and mind, is recognised as something phenomenal, something shadowy, and thus unreal. This is a very vital point in spiritual life, even in the case of the dualist. The true dualist never gives the world the place of primary reality, but makes it wholly dependent on the Lord.

42. *But the paramarthika jiva (Real jiva) knows its identity with Brahman to be (alone) real. He does not see the other, (if he sees the other) he knows it to be illusory.*

Sankara says in the *Vivekachudamani,*

The fool thinks he is the body; the book-learned man identifies himself with the mixture of body and soul; while the sage possessed of realization due to discrimination looks upon the eternal Atman as his own Self, and thinks, 'I am Brahman.'(160)

Our waking state, our dream state, our state of deep sleep, all become relative, possessing different degrees of reality from the higher standpoint.

The difference between the waking state and the dream state is made only from the standpoint of the waking state, but from the higher standpoint, that of the fourth state, the superconscious state, both are equally illusory and deceptive and fall under the same category. In fact, what we call empirical consciousness is no better than dream consciousness.

The being who passes through all these states, is different from these states, the witness of all these states, but never identical with them. And we do not derive the dream state fully from the waking state, nor the waking state fully from the deep sleep state. These are three states for the soul, not that one is fully derived from the other. From one standpoint there may be causality, from another standpoint there is no causality at all. Sequence does not always mean causality. If one thing follows after another, it does not always mean that there is causality. As *Gaudapada's Karika* says:

Nothing is produced either of itself or of another, nor is anything in fact produced, whether it be being, non-being, or either.(4.22)

Negation of Apparent Identification of Seer with Seen

43-44. *As such characteristics of water as sweetness, fluidity and coldness appear to inhere in the waves, and then also in the foams of which the waves are the substratum, so also Existence, Consciousness and Bliss which are the (natural characteristics of sakshin) appear to inhere in the vyavaharika jiva on account of its relation (with sakshin) and through it similarly inhere in the pratibhasika jiva.*

There is a reality of primary importance and a reality of secondary importance which is always wholly dependent on the first reality. If you get a glimpse of this primary reality, you feel there is an Eternal Unchanging Principle in the midst of all these changing states, in the midst of deep sleep, dream and waking. In the midst of all these changing events too, there is an Eternal Principle that ever remains the same at all times, under all circumstances, the same in the past, present and future.

The jiva who witnesses the three states, is realized as such in a fourth state. In the fourth state the jiva realizes that it is one with Brahman. In this state the soul is freed from all limitations. The jiva transcends the empirical self as well as the whole empirical world. And if it happens to come down to some extent to the empirical state, it does so with a new illumination, a new consciousness, because of which it looks upon the empirical self as well as the whole empirical world as equally unreal.

The deep sleep state gives us just a little glimpse of the fourth state. In both, the duality of the subject and object disappears, but one is a state of ignorance, the other a state of knowledge. In deep sleep the seed of the waking state lies dormant, but is not burnt. In the fourth state the seed is destroyed and burnt away, so that it can never sprout again.

45. *With the disappearance of the foam (in the wave), its characteristics such as fluidity, etc., merge in the wave; again with the disappearance of the wave in the water these characteristics merge, as before, in the water.*

The wave freed from its wave-form, the ripple freed from its ripple-form, the ocean freed from its ocean-form, all become the same water-substance, but the wave keeping its wave-form can never become the ocean. This is the mistake generally made by western critics and Christian missionaries when talking about Sankara's teachings and Advaita Vedanta. At first sight there appear to be two entities, but what is really meant is the one entity at the back of both these limitations.

As I said, the substance in the bubble freed from the bubble-form is the same as the water-substance. Light reflected in a particle of sand freed from the form of that particle is the same as the one indivisible eternal Light.

46. *With the disappearance of the pratibhasika jiva (in the vyavaharika jiva) Existence, Consciousness and Bliss (which are its characteristics) merge in the vyavaharika jiva. When that also disappears (in sakshin) these characteristics (finally) merge in sakshin.*

Here name and form disappear, but the essential nature of the Self remains unchanged. 'I am He', really means: 'I, freed from all limiting adjuncts, am the same as the One Indivisible and Undivided Infinite Existence-Knowledge-Bliss Absolute.'

Once I had a very interesting discussion with Swami Turiyananda about the reality of the world. I asked him, 'Sir, is the world real?' Then he just thought a few moments and said, 'I cannot call it real.' And in their case (the realized ones), these are not empty theories or high-sounding words, but facts of experience which we too can verify if we really care to follow the path steadily and one-pointedly to the very end.

(18)

Notes on Yoga Sutras

These notes are based on Swami Yatiswarananda's notes of his class-talks on *Uddhava Gita* and *Vedanta-Sara*, which were taken down at Weisbaden, Germany in 1934. During these classes, he digressed to explain some of the issues with the help of *Patanjali's Yoga Sutras*. It is obvious that the Swami Commented on only those sutras that were of immediate relevance to the audience. —**Editor.**

Swami Vivekananda beautifully describes his own experience in his *Hymn of Samadhi*[1]:

> Lo! The sun is not, nor the comely moon,
> All light extinct; in the great void of space
> Floats shadow-like the image universe.
> In the void of mind involute, there floats
> The fleeting universe, rises and floats,
> Sinks again, ceaseless, in the current 'I'.
> Slowly, slowly, the shadow-multitude
> Entered the primal womb, and flows no more,
> Void merged into void,
> beyond speech and mind!
> Whose heart understands, he verily does.

This hymn describes the state of Nirvikalpa Samadhi which cannot be expressed, but must be experienced. Here, Swamiji has only tried to give a glimpse of his own experience.

Having established the doctrine of the Self, the Vedantic teacher places before us the path we have to follow, the

---
1. C.W., Vol. 4, p. 498

disciplines we have to pass through to attain the goal. This consists of the four yogas.

In Karma Yoga and Raja Yoga there should be a tremendous play of the will-power. Jnana Yoga represents the cognitive faculty more than anything else. Bhakti Yoga implies more of the faculty of feeling. In Raja Yoga we find great play of the will, but directed inwards. In Karma Yoga there is a greater play of the will on external things, while in Raja Yoga the whole sadhana is mostly internal. The radii are different, but they all lead to the same centre. The paths the aspirants have to follow may be different, but the goal these paths lead to is one and the same. We all meet at the goal, but not on the path.

The Nature of the Mind

Yoga has been defined as restraining the mind-stuff from taking various forms.[1]

There are different states of the mind: one is the wandering, another dull or forgetful; the third disturbed but occasionally steady; the fourth one-pointed; and finally we get the completely restrained mind in which we realise ourselves as the Atman or pure consciousness. We all more or less pass through the first four states, but the fifth is beyond our reach. The ideal of Yoga is to reach the fifth state in which all the thoughts are restrained.

Swamiji used to give a funny example. He said, the mind is like a monkey that is drunk, bitten by a scorpion, and into which a ghost has entered. This is the state of our ordinary mind. And this is brought about by too much rajas or too much activity without any higher goal or ideal. As distinct from this there is the dull state where we are overcome by tamas in which one either falls asleep or remains in a very indolent passive mood.

---

1. Patanjali Yoga Sutras 1.2

There is too much of attachment and impulse due to rajas or too much lethargy and dullness due to tamas, which prevent spiritual progress. Without genuine non-attachment and control of our impulses, without the highest sattvic activity of our entire being, nothing can be attained. Outwardly, sattva may appear like tamas, but inwardly it is very, very different. It is the highest state of purified activity. It may be very subtle activity, but it is tremendously intense activity, whereas tamas is inertness, dullness, lethargy and much lower than the hectic state of rajas.

Overcoming both, the state of tamas and that of rajas, we should try to make the mind steady, at least for some time, although at other times, owing to its inherent rajas, it will be restless and roving. This we cannot stop at the beginning. Through steady and continued practice for a very long time we shall make the mind one-pointed in the end, and this not merely during meditation, but also at other times.

There are five classes of modifications (vrittis), some painful and others not painful.[1]

Thought of any kind, whether good or bad, is an obstruction when the goal is to still the mind. So, in a way, every thought, even a good thought, is a danger. Any mental modification is an obstacle to Yoga.

Memory is when the vrittis (modifications of the mind) of perceived objects, do not slip away, and through impressions, come back to consciousness.[2]

How troublesome memory is we all know. Whatever you have done or seen in your life will come up during the practices and has to be effaced before you proceed on your way to Truth. There is no other way to go. Very often we see how our memory is our most troublesome enemy.

---

1. ibid. 1.5
2. ibid. 1.11

Control of Mind

Their control is by practice and non-attachment.[1]

Just as on one side, there should be steady spiritual practice, on the other side, there should be the practice of discrimination: 'I am not the body, I am not the mind, I am neither a man nor a woman, I am not So-and-so', etc. Very strong countercurrents have to be raised in our consciousness to gain non-attachment and aloofness, the attitude of the witness.

Practice is continuous struggle to keep the vrittis perfectly restrained.

It becomes firmly grounded by long constant efforts with great love for the goal to be attained.[2]

Whatever you have to do at the beginning, do it with a vengeance, thoroughly, because if you do it now in a haphazard way, all your thoughts and experiences will be clinging to you all the way. One should follow the spiritual path without caring for the results. Stick to the rules of the game but do not care whether you win or lose. That is the right attitude for your practices.

We may have to wait for a long time, even for a very long one in some cases, if we want the fruits of our labour. As we can attain the fruits only after a long time, why worry about the results before we have done something? People always want to get things without paying the price. That is not possible in spiritual life. And even if there are no results at all, it is better to have tried, to have striven, than to have led a useless, aimless life that leads nowhere.

That effect which comes to those who have given up their thirst after objects either seen or heard and which attempts to control the objects is non-attachment.[3]

---

1. ibid. 1.12
2. ibid. 1.13, 14
3. ibid. 1.15

That is extreme non-attachment which gives up even the qualities and comes from the knowledge of the real nature of the Purusha (Spiritual Entity) [1]

One has reached the state of perfect non-attachment when one refuses to be attached to any modification of matter, e.g. mind and its modifications and the like.

Japam

One of the most efficient means for attaining success in Yoga is single-minded devotion to the Divine. So Patanjali, the great psychologist that he is, says:-

Success is speedy also by devotion to Ishvara. [2]

His manifesting word is OM. [3]

The repetition of this and meditating on its meaning is the way. [4]

'OM' is the most universal symbol. There may be other words which the aspirant can repeat, but along with the repetition of the sound-symbol one must think of the Divine. It should not be done in a merely mechanical, thoughtless way, if it is to be effective. Repeating the sound-symbol while still clinging to one's passions and attachments and desires and not trying to renounce them is useless. If done in a purely mechanical way, without changing one's attitudes towards persons and things, without giving up one's passions and desires, without true meditation, japam or the repetition of the sound-symbol will have very little effect. If one allows oneself to be attracted or repelled by others, if one just follows one's impulses, no amount of japam will be of any use. We simply become parrots and nothing more.

Along with the repetition of the sound and thinking of the Divine, we may also have some visualisation. We live

1. ibid. 1.16
2. ibid. 1.23
3. ibid. 1.27
4. ibid. 1.28

H 17

in a world of sounds, so a central sound is to be brought in. We live in a world of thoughts, so a central thought is to be brought in. We live in a world of forms, so a central form is to be brought in. We live in a world of pictures, so a central picture is to be brought in. And all others have to be subordinated to that sound or thought or picture or form. It is then that we are able to introduce some order into the chaotic inner world in which we live. There are sound vibrations that bring about a disturbance of the mind, and as opposed to these there are other vibrations to help the mind and the body attain a more or less rhythmic state. And herein lies the great utility of the repetition of the holy symbols.

More important than the sound, of course, is the thought. But if we repeat the sound with an amount of concentration and intensity, we are made to think of the thought through the law of association. What we need now is to bring about some order in ourselves. Now the brain moves one way, our limbs follow another course, and with regard to the body, there is no order at all in the different nerve-currents. And, as long as such a state continues, it is not possible to have higher meditation. For this reason the aspirant is asked to have first of all some fixed centre of consciousness, from which to order and direct the different nerve-currents. Without first putting our house in order it is not possible to have meditation. Through japam, one may be able to polarize one's body and make it fit for the different practices.

Obstacles in the Spiritual Path

It is said in Patanjali's Yoga Sutras that the repetition of Om along with thinking of its meaning leads to the destruction of obstacles on the spiritual path.

From that is gained the knowledge of introspection, and the destruction of obstacles.[1]

For the attainment of perfect concentration and illumination all the obstacles, physical and mental, must be removed,

---

1. Patanjali Yoga Sutras, 1.29

and then the truth flashes forth in all its glory. We should remove both the cloud and our blindness. Our eyes should not be closed. It is not possible to see the sun with closed eyes, even if there is no cloud. Spiritual life means removing all the obstacles lying in the way of our vision of Reality.

There are obstacles in the beginning, in the middle, and in the end. Really speaking, the whole path is beset with obstacles, nothing but obstacles all the way, and all these obstacles are to be surmounted to attain success. Real spiritual life is very difficult and cannot be had without paying the price.

Inertia must be conquered through activity, i.e. tamas through rajas. Then we pass on to the sattvic state which is the highest rung of the ladder before we reach the terrace.

The obstructions to yoga are: killing, falsehood, lack of straightforwardness, lack of continence, covetousness, physical and mental impurity, dissatisfaction, a tendency to go in for pleasures of the body, a tendency to dwell on sense-impressions without deep thinking and deep studies, and in a general way a tendency to worship one's body and that of others without caring for the Divine. These are the great obstructions.

Sometimes at the beginning we come across hindrances which prevent us altogether from taking to the spiritual life. There are many cases like that. In the lower layers of the mind of such a person there are too many obstructions. In the higher layers there are less, but may be something goes wrong. Theoretically everybody can take to spiritual life. Practically this is not the case. If the samskaras of a person are too bad, if there are too many obstructions in the lower layers of his mind, then nothing can be done. In that case, he will proceed upto a certain stage and then slip his foot and fall back into his old ruts.

There are troubles of three kinds: Cosmic troubles, troubles coming from other beings and troubles arising from within oneself. Very often, cosmic currents become obstacles for us. Just try to meditate during a thunderstorm with flashes of lightning and heavy peals of thunder! Other difficulties arise from contact with people whose bent of mind is worldly, who are attached to lust and gold, who try to prevent you from taking to spiritual life and rouse all the old impressions lying dormant in you. That is why every aspirant has to be continually on the alert with sword drawn, as it were, and should always use the utmost discrimination in his contact with other people.

When we ascend to the upper layers, life becomes less troublesome, but the higher we rise, the greater is the chance of falling.

Knowing these obstructions to be enemies, we should overcome them as much as possible and learn to be fully aware of them by being as wide-awake as possible at all times. Our life must become a conscious life, not a life of impulses and subconscious desires.

There are other obstructions that may come to some at the beginning of Yoga, to others even in the course of their practice of Yoga. So Patanjali says,

Disease, mental inactivity, doubt, indifference, laziness, the tendency to pursue sense enjoyments, stupor, false perceptions, non-attaining concentration, and falling away from that when attained on account of restlessness, are the obstructing distractions.[1]

During our spiritual practices, during the time of sadhana, sometimes the body gets out of order, the whole system becomes awfully heated. Any organ of the body may go out of order for some time. Sometimes we may get lung-trouble, throat-trouble, heart-trouble, in fact any organ may be affected, but all this is only a phase if we observe strict ethical culture. Only we should see that such phases do not continue

---

1. ibid. 1.30

too long. Anyhow, all these are passing phases that come to all aspirants, sooner or later. One should go on with one's spiritual practices doggedly, steadily, without any break, even if these obstructions, physical as well as mental, come on the way. They have to be surmounted, and we should never feel any unnecessary depression if they come.

One may even come to doubt the utility of spiritual life and spiritual practices. One may become so full of scepticism that one may not see the utility of spiritual life, at least for some time. And if, at such a time, one gives up one's practices, one falls away from Yoga. One may give up spiritual life or the attempt at it, altogether. So this doubt, this scepticism, is one of the greatest obstructions for the beginner. As soon as we succumb to doubt, to a depressive mood, we become our greatest enemy.

Besides, it may happen that during our practices a desire may arise in a very strong, virulent and concentrated form. Such desires were lying in seed-form in our mind, and then under favourable circumstances they begin to sprout. With great patience, the aspirant should first put them down and then eliminate them. Sometimes we may liken the desires to gout or to rheumatism. We try to control desire in one form, but it appears in some other form. Now the point is how to rid ourselves of all these obstructions.

How to Overcome Obstacles

These troubles come to one and all, but without bothering too much about them, get rid of them. Meditate on the Holy Name, meditate on its meaning (OM). As a result of japam, this repetition and practice, comes destruction of the obstacles. These are the reactions that come to all. They are the price we have to pay for the higher life.

To remedy this, the practice of one subject should be made.[1]

---

1. ibid. 1.32

We have so many ideas and ambitions in our mind, and it is not possible to have all these ambitions satisfied. We must have some central thought, some central desire as the pivot, as it were, and subordinate all other desires to this desire. Everything should be looked upon only as a means to attaining this. We should never forget this central thought, this central desire, in our life and all our activities should be subordinated to this at all times and made to serve it in every possible way.

Regular practice along a certain, definite line must be done; one must not dig the well at different places. Each aspirant must stick doggedly to his own line of sadhana and not bother about that of others.

If we see some people very happy and prosperous, we may feel jealous. If we see some evil or impurity, we may feel righteous anger. So Patanjali says,

Friendship, mercy, gladness and indifference, being thought of in regard to subjects, happy, unhappy, good and evil pacify the chitta.[1]

This way of thinking calms the mind and has to be practised. If one always sees evil in others, one has a taste for evil and impurity. In such cases, all reactions the person shows are negative ones, and negative reactions are as bad and as great obstructions as positive ones. Whether I do a thing or like to talk about it or listen to it, does not make any great difference. Whether I am full of righteous anger at another's evil or impurity or rejoice in it, does not make much difference. It is merely a negative reaction, showing a taste for the thing as such, and will always act as a great obstruction in the path of the aspirant.

This process of mental purification or sublimation is an eternal process, and we have to continue it all through life. Without it nothing can be achieved, sublimation of all one's feelings and desires being the very foundation of all forms of spiritual life.

---

1. ibid. 1.33

Obstructions at Higher Levels

Good thoughts are to be roused in the mind when evil thoughts arise, and then concentration is to be practised. By samadhi all impressions, all obstructions are removed.

The resulting impression from this samadhi obstructs all other impressions.[1]

Savikalpa Samadhi is meant here, because the resulting impression of this samadhi eats up all other impressions that are lying in the mind. Therefore its effect is so clear and transforming. In the course of practice, the aspirant may develop psychic powers.

These (i.e the siddhis) are obstacles to samadhi but they are powers in the worldly state.[2]

Here Patanjali mentions the danger of all supernatural or psychic powers and their development. The aspirant should scrupulously avoid developing such powers, and if they come, he should not pay attention to them at all but calmly proceed on his way. All these powers are for enjoyment, not for emancipation, and he who gets entangled in their meshes will never be able to reach the goal.

In spiritual life, a lot of sportsman's spirit and attitude is necessary. One must be 'sporting'. If hindrances come, what to do? Let me face the obstructions! The greater the obstacle, the greater should be the will to overcome it, to proceed doggedly along one's path. Take the whole thing in the sportsman's spirit. 'What great fun all this is!'

Steps of Yoga

Yoga has eight steps:

Yama, Niyama, Asana, Pranayama, Pratyahara, Dharana, Dhyana and Samadhi are the eight limbs of Yoga.[3]

---

1. ibid. 1.50
2. ibid. 3.38
3. Patanjali's Yoga Sutras 2.29.

Ethical Culture

Ethical culture, continence, Asana (posture), and Pranayama prepare body and mind for concentration. First of all train the body and mind; otherwise meditation will remain a hopeless task for you. The instrument with which we are going to practise spiritual disciplines must be fit. If a knife is blunt, it does not cut; if it is too soft, it breaks; so the steel must be tempered in the right manner to get a good knife.

Anyone can get deep concentration. But concentration, as such has no spiritual value, without the necessary mental and physical purification. The worldly man, by concentrating on his worldly affairs, can attain to his end and prosper in his worldly affairs. But this kind of concentration will never make him spiritual. The man whose mind is concentrated on lust and gold may thereby reach his end. But this takes him further and further away from the Divine and gets him more and more entangled in the meshes of lust, anger and greed, and the multiplicity of worldly desires.

We must learn to create the proper atmosphere around us by avoiding all harmful associations, all disturbing influences that might come to us from others, all associations which might awaken old, harmful memories. We should be very careful in this if we want to progress. If we scrupulously create the proper atmosphere around us by avoiding all harmful contact with worldly people, worldly ideas and old associations, we get an amount of support even when the mind tends to go down. This may lead us ultimately even to illumination. There are higher cosmic states of vibration, and by consciously creating these within us, we come in touch with them, and they are very helpful to us in our spiritual life. There are many different layers of vibrations, and we should try to attune ourselves to the higher ones. One should know how to switch on that inner state in us that brings us in touch with that plane outside.

We should constantly watch the movements of our mind and become fully conscious of them without identifying ourselves with them. This greatly helps us in pursuing the analytic method and in separating the non-self from the Self. There is no Vedanta without becoming wide-awake and conscious and learning to use one's powers of discrimination. Clear thinking, clear feeling and clear action must be created if one wishes to attain the goal. There must be an amount of true dispassion and non-attachment to persons and things, a certain aloofness which enables us to see things and persons as they are, not as they appear to be while covered over with our subjective desires, gross or subtle.

Asana

Posture is that which is firm and pleasant.[1]

The first sadhana is to keep body and brain cool. Ordinarily, people do not stress the fitness of the body. The first dharma is to take care of the body, to make it a fit instrument for spiritual practice, otherwise you will not be able to enter the gates of spiritual life. People often commit a serious mistake by not caring enough for the body and not keeping it in a fit condition.

In Asana [posture], the backbone is the most important thing. Sit with folded legs in as easy a posture as possible. The folded legs steady the backbone and give it a firm support. Backbone must be perfectly straight; head, neck and back forming a straight, unbroken line. The sitting posture is the most helpful one. Trying to meditate in a lying posture is not advisable as it easily induces sleep and drowsiness. It is said,

Placing the body in a straight posture, with the chest, throat and head held erect, making the organs enter the mind, the sage crosses all the fearful currents by means of the raft of Brahman.[2]

---

1. Ibid., 2.46.
2. Svetaswatara Upanishad, 2.8.

It is a very bad habit to move any limb, one's legs etc. during meditation. Any movement shows an undisciplined mind and restlessness of the body which has to be curbed. With an undisciplined mind and an undisciplined body nothing can be achieved.

Pranayama

Controlling the motion of the exhalation and the inhalation follows after this.[1]

Breath and heart-beat should be rhythmic. This can be attained by composing the mind and keeping it calm and serene. The yogi's breath is very rhythmic when he sits for meditation. The retention of breath comes later. Pranayama is for calming the mind and minimizing wastage of energy through irregular breathing. But the breath as such has no spiritual value.

Control of breath is not advisable for most people. On the contrary, it is decidedly dangerous for most people. If the general nervous current is not balanced, or if a person has not led a perfectly pure life for a long time, the control of breath can bring about great disorder and even insanity, or a serious nervous breakdown. Let one try to breathe as lightly as possible and to be conscious of this breath. Nothing more for most people! Real Pranayama requires a long moral and ethical preparation.

Sense-retraction or Pratyahara

The drawing in of the organs (Pratyahara) is by their giving up their own objects and taking the form of the mind stuff, as it were.[2]

When the body and the mind have been trained and made somewhat rhythmic, it becomes possible to draw the mind away from sense-objects. The things that attract may

---

1. Yoga Sutras, 2.49.
2. Ibid., 2.54.

not necessarily be physical or in the physical world. They may be either partly or fully in the mental world. Our mind is like a lake and innumerable waves rise out of it. When the waves arise, we should try to withdraw, so that without getting support the waves subside of themselves.

First of all, we must try to bring back our wandering mind to ourselves, and if we have already practiced the (effortless) posture and rhythmic breathing, i.e. being fully conscious of the breath, we are able to bring the mind under our control.

Dharana and Dhyana

Dharana is holding the mind on to some particular object.[1]

An unbroken flow of knowledge in that object is dhyana.[2]

In dharana the mind holds on to some object either inside or outside the body. Instead of having many waves, let us create one wave and then repeat the same wave. And with concentration there also comes the question of the centre of consciousness. If one day the mind does not go up, just touch the point of one's centre of consciousness with one's hand and feel it more strongly. Sometimes this is very efficacious. It can also be done while telling our beads.

Yogic and Vedantic Samadhi

We should make a distinction between the yogic term 'samadhi' and the term 'samadhi' when used in Vedanta. Samadhi, as such, in Yoga, need not necessarily be anything spiritual. Vedantic Samadhi must always be connected with something spiritual or with the Divine. The great psychologist Patanjali speaks of concentration and samadhi in a general way. Yogic Samadhi can be practised on anything out-and-out worldly, or even sensual. There may be some such thing

1. Yoga Sutras, 3.1.
2. Ibid., 3.2.

as samadhi on a book or on a person connected with our desires. Samadhi can even be on something utterly impure and animal. All these forms of samadhi are not spiritual and have no spiritual value whatever. The Vedantin who has some other end in view, whose attitude is different, has no place in his scheme for this kind of Yogic Samadhi, i.e. he does not give such forms of concentration the name of 'samadhi'. The yogi does. So we should always see by whom the term is used.

The true Vedantin says, 'I do not care for your Yogic Samadhi, or for any form of concentration that is not connected with the Divine and has not the Divine as its goal.' On the practical side, the Vedantin makes use of all the methods of Yoga, but he gives them all a higher turn. In a way, Vedanta is the fulfilment of Yoga. All these forms of concentration should be on the Divine in some form or other. Otherwise the practices won't have any spiritual value.

Samadhi with Seed (Sabija Samadhi) [1]

Samadhi on the Divine with self-consciousness contains what may be called 'seeds of desires' which may germinate again at any time. It is only when one transcends this individual consciousness that all the seeds are completely destroyed, completely burned.

We need not consider the state of Nirvikalpa Samadhi. It is still far off. First of all there is concentration leading to absorption (samadhi) with self-consciousness. And even that is a very high state not attained by everybody.

In the spiritual path, our idea should be to purify the mind as much as possible along with the steady practice of concentration, not on material things, but on the Divine with form or without form. And both these processes combined bring about a great purity of the mind. And even if the desires lying hidden in seed-form in the depths of the mind try to

---

1. Yoga Sutras, 1.17.

assert themselves, the aspirant is able to control them and steadily proceed, towards the goal.

If we do not set fire to our desires, they remain in seed-form in our mind and are sure to create untold troubles for us at some time. Great concentration on worldly thoughts and objects would lead to what would look like samadhi, but this would be samadhi with seeds in which all our desires lie hidden and may manifest at any time when this concentration ceases to exist.

Individual Self in Vedantic & Yogic Teaching

The concentration, called right knowledge is that which is followed by reasoning, discrimination, bliss, unqualified egoism.[1]

Here we should read Swami Vivekananda's commentary very carefully. The objects of meditation may be either the gross objects or the subtle objects. Mind and thoughts and even the ego may become the objects of meditation.

In Yoga philosophy, there is a cosmological theory. First of all there is the 'contact' between the Purusha and the principle of matter, Prakriti. When this contact takes place, then matter begins to evolve from subtler states to grosser states. Before this evolution, the material principle remains in a stable, completely undifferentiated state. Later on comes the differentiation into subtle matter and gross matter. On analyzing the human personality, first we find this body which consists of different particles. Then come the senses, but the eye or ear is only an instrument, not the real sense. The real senses are the subtle organs of perception which manifest themselves through the eye or the ear, etc. which may be called their seat. Next comes the mind, and then the ego, and beyond the ego there is the individualised self. This individualised self, according to Vedanta, is a manifestation of the Infinite. In Yoga there is no conception of the Infinite.

---

1. Yoga Sutras, 1.46.

They do not go beyond the individualised self. So Patanjali, the teacher of Yoga, believes in an infinite number of souls. The Vedantin says, 'Yes, my friend, there is an infinite number of souls, but all these are nothing but the manifestation of the one Principle of Consciousness, which is inseparable from Eternal Existence and Eternal Bliss.'

Various Kinds of Samadhi [1]

Now we come to the various aspects of concentration leading to different samadhis. Patanjali speaks of four kinds of concentration with self-consciousness. In the first kind of meditation, external gross elements are the objects. And in the same kind of meditation, when one struggles to take the gross element out of time and space, and thinks of it as it is, this is called *Nirvitarka* Samadhi, the first being called *Savitarka* Samadhi (i.e. respectively 'without question' and 'with question').

We make the external gross element the object of our meditation and first think of it in time and space. Then we may be so concentrated that in the midst of our concentration we forget for the time being the sense of time and space. And when meditation goes a step higher and takes subtle matter as the object and thinks of it as in time and space, it is called *Savichara*, i.e. with discrimination. When, in this meditation one rises beyond the conception of time and space, one attains to that samadhi which may be called 'without discrimination', *Nirvichara*. What actually happens is this. One does not transcend the sense of time and space completely because both belong to the mind and not to the object. So, in us, in our mind, there still exists the sense of time and space, but for the time being it is forgotten.

The next stage is reached when one takes up the thinking organ (the mind) as the object of meditation. Eliminating indolence and activity, the aspirant may think of

---

1. Yoga Sutras, 1.42-45.

this internal organ as endowed with what is called 'sattva', and then he realises what is called 'Blissful Samadhi' or *Sananda* Samadhi. When the meditation becomes very 'ripe' and 'concentrated', when all ideas of gross and fine materials are given up and when the pure ego alone remains as the object of meditation, it is called *Sasmita* Samadhi. The man who has attained to this does not identify himself with the gross body or with the mind and is said to be 'bereft of body' (vi-deha). When even this ego is transcended and along with it all subject-object relationship, then one realises the highest superconsciousness, having no touch whatever with things material, either in their gross or in their subtle aspects.

First we have meditation on gross matter, and meditating on gross matter we may still associate it with time and space and then rise above the sense of time and space. While meditating on subtle matter one may think of it as existing in time and space. Then one may take it out of time and space. One may make the purified mind as the object of meditation, and ultimately one may come to what is called 'Purusha' or Self or Pure Individualised Consciousness.

Vedanta proceeds a step further and holds that this pure consciousness of the individual is nothing but a manifestation of Transcendental Consciousness or Absolute Consciousness, the realisation of which is the ultimate goal of every true spiritual aspirant. In Vedanta, the teacher takes up all the yogic ideas but gives them a higher turn.

Spiritual Teachings

These *Spiritual Teachings* have been culled out from the *Reminiscences of Swami Yatiswarananda* by the Late Pravrajika Saradaprana of the Sarada Math, Dakshineswar, Calcutta. They have been rearranged according to topics and are being published with her kind permission. —**Editor.**

Purity

Swami Brahmanandaji used to say, 'Find joy in the struggle.' Since then, I have been struggling and discovering that through the struggle alone we grow and the greater the struggle following the correct lines, the greater is the progress. The main task of this struggle is to purify ourselves, our body, mind and ego. The ego should be in tune with the divine Will and follow its biddings with devotion and steadfastness. I am a born fighter and so I am prepared to face any number of problems and find solutions for them through the grace of the Lord whom we are trying to serve.

To the extent the mirror of the mind is clear, to that extent the Light Divine shines forth in all its pristine glory.

Purity is the sine qua non of all spiritual life and whoever is not prepared to pay the price to the full, in terms of inner struggle, will fall away from the ideal, sooner or later.

Our true self is pure by itself. One feels impure only when one identifies oneself with the body and mind. The soul is pure by its nature.

The mind takes up the colour which is near it. Suppose there is a prism and coloured lights, red, yellow etc., are kept on its sides. The prism takes up these colours and we cannot see its real colour anymore. Similarly, our minds have taken up the colours that surround it and it has forgotten its real colour. But when these colours are taken away, the real colour can be made out.

We can lead a pure spiritual life, but we don't want to do it. You have tendencies—good and bad, because you yourself have sown their seed. You alone are responsible for them. Let us not waste our time in thinking about why I am like this, how it came to be, what I did and how and how much. Let us improve ourselves. A man was shot by an arrow. When someone went to remove it, the man said, 'Wait! Let me first find out who shot the arrow, why he shot at me, how, etc.' By the time he could know all that he would die. Let us not waste our time, but try to remove our impurities. Impurities are in the mind, and we blame the atmosphere.

We complain too much about our environment. We really do not want to do anything—always complaining about the environment. Well, suppose we change the environment—the same complaint will be there. We don't find anywhere an ideal environment. You have to practise meditation right here. Don't you try to sleep in the midst of the most troublesome environment? Similarly, you have to try to practise meditation whatever be the nature of the environment. How? By withdrawing ourselves from all the outside disturbances just as we do before we fall into sleep.

If you watch carefully, you will be surprised to see how many useless thoughts have entered your mind. Even if you are very careful, you will find that in the course of a day you have gathered at least some dirt and some bad impressions in the mind. Therefore something of the prayerful mood must be maintained throughout the day. There must be an undercurrent of thought about the Divine even when we are engaged in our daily duties. This flow helps us tremendously in spiritual life. Have divine thoughts while going to bed and on rising in the morning. This prevents the rising of impure thoughts and greatly helps concentration. After arati we do not switch-off all the lights—we keep one burning. Similarly, after japa, we must keep the thought of God during rest of the day.

We have work. It should be done with all concentration. But there is such a time when we are not working, and the mind is wandering from one thought to another, thinking all sorts of things. This is to be stopped and the time utilised, filling idle moments with the Lord's Name and holy thoughts. One hour of meditation is not enough. We must try to maintain the spiritual mood for the rest of the day. This is essential.

Purification of the Mind

How to purify the mind? Let us be systematic in our thinking. There are steps to be taken.

1.*Moral life and ethical culture*: We must have moral and pure thoughts, feelings and actions. The food that we take daily through our mouths should be pure, earned by honest means. Also the food that we take through our senses—what we see, what we hear or what we speak—should be pure. This purifies our minds to some extent.

2.*Service*: We have come to play a part in our life and that part is to be played well. All work that we do should be done as an act of service to the Lord—a dedication to the Lord. This is *nishkama karma*—selfless service.

3.*Spiritual practices*: These two steps are not wholly sufficient for purifying the mind and body. Japa and meditation are also needed. Success largely depends on the regularity and intensity of our spiritual practices.

These are the three steps for purifying the mind; moral life—ethical culture, selfless service and spiritual practices— japa and meditation. A pure mind alone reflects Brahman. The impure mind reflects desires, worldly thoughts, people, etc.

When the mind is to some extent purified, we may get a glimpse of the higher truths. But actually the painful struggle starts when we get a glimpse, because once experienced, the mind longs for it.

Patanjali's Scheme of Purification

This consists of *yama* and *niyama*. What is *yama*? *Yama* includes *ahimsa* (non-violence), *satya* (truth), *asteya* (non-stealing), *brahmacharya* (continence) and *aparigraha* (non-receiving of gifts from others).

Ahimsa (non-violence) is not only non-killing or not harbouring any ill feelings towards others whether they are good or bad, but on the positive side, it includes having good feelings, love, sympathy etc. for all fellow beings.

Satya (truth): One should practise truth in thought, word, and deed.

Asteya (non-stealing): This must not be taken in the gross sense only. Anything that we wish to possess at the cost of anybody else or anything that we get by unfair means is stealing.

Brahmacharya (continence): Without brahmacharya there can be no real spiritual life. Mind and body are to be purified.

Aparigraha (non-receiving of gifts from others): This does not mean absolute non-acceptance of any gift from others. It is not possible. So, we must give much more than we receive. If you have no money to give, then give love, service, knowledge, etc. *Aparigraha* also includes giving up the tendency to hoard things.

What is *niyama*? *Saucha* (purity of body and mind), *santosha* (contentment), *tapas* (austerity), *svadhyaya* (self-study) and *isvara-pranidhana* (self surrender to God).

Saucha (purity of body and mind): The body is a temple of God and should therefore be kept clean; bad thoughts are to be eliminated.

Santosha (contentment): We must be satisfied with our physical environment, adjust ourselves to the things in this world. No grumbling and complaining. You may, however, feel dissatisfied with your spiritual progress. If you can attain both quality and quantity, it will be very good but never quantity at the cost of quality.

Tapas (austerity): We are becoming too soft with ourselves. We must reduce the body consciousness. We must have control over our senses.

Svadhyaya (study): It means reflecting on what you study and making it your own. We read The Gospel of Sri Ramakrishna and we say, 'I have read two pages or one page.' But it is mere reading. Even now I read The Gospel daily. We must dwell on the spirit of the scriptures. There is danger in mere reading of the scriptures. We get high ideas and get indigestion. *Svadhyaya* includes not only the study of books but also the study of one's own mind.

Isvarapranidhana (self surrender to God): Surrender your all—body, mind and soul to Him. This removes the subtlest form of impurity i.e., egoism. We always say: I do, I do this— always I, I; egocentric. Instead of it, say, 'O Lord, take away my I; let me abide in Thee and not remain myself any longer. *Shakali tomari ichha...*'

There is a song, 'We are like dolls; if He wants us to stand, we stand; if He wants us to sit, we sit; if He wants us to lie down, we lie down.'

Once I got a letter from a devotee. The letter was full of statements, 'I can't meditate, I try so much...but I find etc' So I asked my assistant to count how many times 'I' was written. It was 48 times! I told my assistant to write back, 'When there is so much 'I', how can you meditate?'

Purificatory disciplines are only phases of spiritual life, but they are not spiritual life.

True spiritual life is not a negation but the greatest and most fearless affirmation of our very Self, not subject to sin, weakness, ignorance, bondage, desires, wants, etc. but eternally free, eternally full of bliss and knowledge. 'I am He' is the greatest affirmation of Truth ever thought and realized in the world of man.

Danger of Falling

One should follow the steps that lead to the terrace and then, stand there under the pure sky and breathe pure air. Some people reach the second or third floor and remain there. In their case, spiritual progress is arrested. While going higher and higher, one should be very careful, lest he should fall.

It is relatively easier to eradicate the grosser desires and *samskaras* on the conscious level and one feels supremely happy and confident on the narrow and difficult spiritual path. It is at such times that the aspirant is caught unawares when the subtle *samskaras* from the subconscious and unconscious level start surfacing. These are more harmful and dangerous and if the seeker is not alert and vigilant, he is sure to fall from the heights he has reached. Be wide awake; be wide awake.

While going higher one should be very careful lest we should fall. Chances of falling are greater as one goes higher and higher. Once a Dutch man came to India. Before he met me, he went to the Himalayas with some Swamis. The road there is very narrow and one has to be very careful in climbing. This man was very fond of taking snaps. One day as he was taking snaps, he slipped and fell down—he was finished. So also in spiritual life, one has to be very careful.

Dangers on the Path

A great helicopter engineer came to meet me when I was in Philadelphia. He came to attend one of my lectures. Then he asked for an interview to which I readily agreed. He came one morning without any formality and said, 'Swamiji, do you know I practice yoga?' I asked him, 'What yoga do you practice?' He said, 'Oh, I have got Vivekananda's Raja Yoga. I have practised *asana.*' He went and sat on a carpet and practised *padmasana* to perfection. I became inquisitive and asked him, 'What do you see within?' He answered, 'I get wonderful ideas about helicopters!' This is not something to laugh at. His mind is working on that plane. All these objective, scientific truths are there in the cosmic mind. But the spiritual seeker does not stop there. His ambition is to realise the Supreme Spirit. He goes higher and higher, beyond the plane of the gross, beyond the plane of the mind and realises that he is a spiritual being who is inseparable from the Infinite Spirit.

In Germany, one man used to practise withdrawing the mind from the senses and produce a sort of sleepy state. He asked me one day, 'Swami, I have attained samadhi. Is there a state higher than samadhi?' Then I gave him some instructions and encouraged him to get rid of this negative feeling. Instead of being on the negative side, be on the positive side—repetition of the mantra and visualizing the blissful form of the deity in the normal state, thinking of Him with a little love, etc. Then there is no danger.

There are two dangers in spiritual life.

1. *Fanaticism*: When one follows a particular path, worshipping a particular deity, one is likely to be very fanatical, having a narrow outlook about one's deity etc. Therefore it is very good to salute great teachers and saints of all the countries of the world. The mind becomes broad. Accept all the gods and goddesses as different manifestations of same Supreme Spirit. I have heard people criticising, 'Oh, in Sri Ramakrishna Ashrama they sing all sorts of songs.' Vaishnavas resent *Siva kirtana.* Now this is the solution.

A bubble has got a mighty wave beneath it. It clings to it. Another bubble has another mighty wave beneath it and it clings to it. But are they all not the same ocean? Sri Ramakrishna is breaking the narrowness of our minds, but many cannot stand the purity and vigour of spiritual life. This fanaticism is a great obstacle in spiritual life.

2. *Egocentricity*: Religious selfishness—I am not bothered about what happens to others. Many times I have found that, at least in the beginning of spiritual life, religious people become more selfish than ordinary people—more body conscious and more self-centred. Unless and until this ego breaks a little, one cannot expand and likes and dislikes can't go. So it is good to pray also for the welfare of all. This has a broadening effect on our mind.

Do not be like the selfish devotee of the following story: Two religious friends were living together. One was of an active temperament and used to ask his friend to arrange seats and plates but the friend always used to reply, 'I am doing japa!' However, as soon as the former would lay out the plates etc. and serve the food, the latter would stop his japa and come for the meals.

The mark of progress is; are we expanding? Are we more liberal than before? Are we more considerate to our fellow beings? In temples people rush to have a view of the deity, trampling over others! Is this the way to salvation, *moksha*? Never forget *Atmano mokshartham jagat hitaya cha*.

Ignorance

There was an officer who had a number of gold and silver medals—big and small—to his credit, which were displayed on his coat: and the biggest one was a gold medal. A friend of his asked him one day how he had managed to get so -many medals. The officer, pointing to the biggest gold medal, said. 'First this one came by mistake, and then the rest followed.' Seeing the big gold medal awarded to him many other honours, big and small, were conferred upon him.

Due to ignorance (ajnana), came our first and biggest mistake of considering ourselves and others as this body, mind and senses. Then followed all the other mistakes and miseries. Caught in the mesh of *kama, krodha, lobha* and *moha* (lust, anger, greed, attachment) etc., we make our lives and the lives of others miserable.

One late evening, a man, fully drunk, went and sat in his car to drive it. He found all the parts of his car—gear, mirror, steering wheel, etc. missing. He complained to the police. They said they would come a little later. After some time, he went again and sat in the car. He found all the parts intact. How did it happen? Earlier he was fully drunk and had sat at the back of the car. Now when the effect of the drink was gone, he sat in the front seat and found everything all right.

Drunk with the wine of ignorance, *ajnana* we too sit at the back seat of the body and mind and find everything missing in life. When the effect of drink goes, when *ajnana* (ignorance) goes, we sit in the front seat of the Atman and find everything all right. We are ignorant; we have eyes but we behave as though we are blind.

A man was pretending to be blind. He had kept near him a board, 'Please help this blind man.' One lady pitied this man and gave him a 2-shilling note. The man said, 'Lady, please give me two separate notes of 1-shilling each, as it is a bad sign to get one 2-shilling note.' The lady asked in surprise. 'Can you see?' The man replied. 'My friend who plays the part of the blind has gone to a cinema. I used to play the part of a deaf-mute. Since he has gone to see a picture, I am playing his part!' The lady said. 'Then I am that deaf-mute!' and left the place!

Appearance and Reality

We are always guided by our subconscious mind, but is there anything beyond it? You see, all of a sudden we get a glimpse of that which we may not have thought or imagined before. This intuition is beyond both the conscious and sub-conscious mind.

All may not get visions; that does not matter. It is enough to feel His Presence. Though we do not see, we cannot deny the presence of something.

A thief, having stolen something in the night, was running fast to hide himself. Suddenly he saw something in front of him. He thought it was a policeman, but it was the stump of a tree. A woman in search of her lover at night took the stump for her lover. A policeman mistook the stump for a thief while searching for a thief!

Now, their assumptions were all incorrect, but the stump was always there; this cannot be denied. So in meditation also, we may not see a form, but we cannot deny the presence of something.

Discovering Our True Nature

Man has forgotten his divine Nature. The task in spiritual life is to discover mans true nature. If you have *deha buddhi*, start as a child or a servant of God. God will lead you on.

The ideal must be clear and it must be fixed before beginning spiritual disciplines. We must have a very definite idea of the path and of the goal to be attained. In this temple of the body, the devotee and deity are there. Try to bring about their union. Enter your heart and find it filled with the Atman, a part of the Paramatman.

Think of yourself as Atman, a part of the Paramatman, the Infinite. All are Atman. Don't have such a consciousness that this is a man and that is a woman. All are Atman. The Supreme Spirit has assumed all these forms.

All forms are temporary, even the incarnations of God. Meditate on That which remains when all these go away, when the phenomenon disappears.

Pleasant and Unpleasant Aspects of Reality

Which aspect of Holy Mother do you like? Only her love and affection? Remember that she is Kali too. If need be, she will tear open your heart! *Srishti, sthiti* and *pralaya* (creation, preservation and destruction) are three phases of the unreal phenomenon. People are afraid of *pralaya* (destruction).

God is God only when he is the Lord of creation, preservation and destruction, and above all, the God who is also none of these. He is the Reality behind and beyond all this unreal phenomenon. *Srishti, sthiti* and *pralaya*—they come and go, but Satchidananda ever is and as souls we are one with It. The greatest truth is: 'You are the Atman.'

Pleasant and unpleasant, all pairs of opposites always exist side by side in the unreal phenomenon. Why not accept it? Why cling to the pleasant and be afraid of the unpleasant? Why be afraid of death? Life is always followed by death. It is childish not to recognise it. Accept life as it is with all its dualities.

Once I went to take a bath with Swami Turiyananda at Puri. Do you know how to take a bath in the sea? Take the waves, never face to face, but on the side. If the waves are too high, then go low and they pass away. If they are low, jump over then. Never wait for the waves to subside. So too in our lives.

Sublimation

Connect all your desires, directly or indirectly, with the Divine. Give every desire a Godward turn, consciously and knowingly, with an effort of will. If you love somebody and feel greatly attached to him or her, love the Divine in that person and be thereby directly drawn towards the Divine. If done consciously and knowingly, this acts as a great controlling factor, helping us in sublimating our desires. The greatest thing in spiritual life is to transmute our human love into love for the Divine. After your japa and meditation, try to see the Supreme Spirit in you, in Guru Maharaj, in Mother and in all persons who come in touch with you.

When someone tends to annoy you greatly, try to see the good points also in that person along with the bad. You will be surprised to find that good predominates over evil and instead of finding fault; you would rather admire that person greatly. When everything fails, try to see the Divine in him or her and salute the Mother in him or her a few times.

It is certainly possible for a so-called bad person to change into a good one. Atman is ever pure. But owing to ignorance, the soul identifies itself with desires and passions. As the spiritual consciousness awakens, all the desires and passions as well as their objects appear to be unreal and insipid. And the Supreme Spirit is experienced as the Reality—Sat-Chit-Ananda—All in all—the goal of spiritual striving.

During the period of transition, confusion—an amount of confusion—is unavoidable. Hold on to your Ishta Devata and Ishta mantra. All obstacles, physical and psychical, will gradually disappear and true spiritual consciousness will arise.

The trouble with most of the spiritual seekers is that they identify too much with their own body and personality. Unless we succeed in awakening spiritual consciousness in us and consider ourselves as Atman, we can never progress.

Rise above the physical body and the mental world. Rise above all these limitations. Develop *Brahmabuddhi*, develop *Atmabuddhi*.

Whatever be the truth, follow it. An unpleasant truth is always infinitely better than a pleasant falsehood. Even if truth breaks our hearts, let us face it undauntedly.

Different Stages in Evolution

Through meditation, we develop intense introspection, but the trouble is that the aspirant identifies himself or herself too much with the body and worships either a male deity or a female deity. Unless we succeed in awakening Atmabuddhi. we can never progress.

In olden days, there was a school of thought called the Charvaka school. The Charvakas used to believe that there is no soul, no Atman. no life after death. So they did what they liked. Where are those Charvakas gone? They are hidden in us! A worldly materialist has no disguises but religious materialists are dangerous: 'Believe in God. but God's main task is to fulfil our wishes.'

In the beginning we meditate on a holy personality but later on we must feel that He is a part of the Supreme Spirit and that we are little spheres of light, parts, of that infinite light.

In the beginning of spiritual life we may think God is separate from ourselves and we all are separate from one another. Later, we find that we are His parts: we all form the different parts of a mighty organism. When we proceed further we feel that in our true spiritual nature, freed from all limited adjuncts, we are eternally one with God, and that our individuality is a myth. We become merged in the one undivided principle, the One-without-a-second.

Infinite Consciousness [1]

During japa and meditation, think i that you are a small sphere of light, part of the infinite light. In this infinite, merge I your body, mind, ego, and everybody.

To merge the personality of the Guru whom you love and depend upon, may be very difficult, but you have to do it; otherwise your progress will be hindered. Merge my body and mind. You may retain my consciousness but not the sense of personality and attachment. This attachment is to be spiritualized. Don't have the sense of physical personality. Think only of my consciousness and think that my consciousness is part of the infinite consciousness—one wave in the ocean.

You must be conscious of the ocean—the infinite Supreme Spirit. Think that this consciousness of mine is a

---

1. A short address to the monastic inmates of Sarada Math.

part of the ocean—one wave in the ocean which is Satchidananda. The ocean is more real than the wave. Behind each wave there is the ocean.

The power that brought you here (Sri Sarada Math) and has been guiding you. will protect you always. There is infinite consciousness; part of it is here, in me. Feel that (divine Consciousness) and not the personality. Depend on Thakur and Ma. You live under the protection of the banyan tree of Sri Sarada Math. I am not worried about you. Ever pray to the Eternal Guru within for light and guidance.

May Sri Guru Maharaj and the Holy Mother—the twin manifestations of the Supreme Spirit in this age—fill your heart with Their presence, purity, love and bliss. You too are a part of the Infinite Spirit like everyone else, including myself.

We have to rise above the personal plane to the domain of the Infinite Spirit which manifests itself as the disciple, the Guru and the Ishta Devata.

Do you know what I see now when I look at you? I see that you are a part of the infinite. I do not see a girl or a personality. But I see that a part of the infinite is here in you and then I talk. It is only when the Guru sees God in the disciples that he can guide, help and do real good to them.

Inner Adjustment

Get rooted in Thakur and Ma and not in a place or a person. Get rooted in the Divine and have that support. Then all problems and misery will go away. Adjustment is life. Where will you adjust? Yes, within. First adjust within and then everything becomes easy.

One day a lady came to a psychologist and complained, 'Doctor, all the people I come across are nasty. They don't behave decently.' Doctor said, 'Oh, is it? All right, I will give you some pills and you take them and report to me after a few days.'

After a few days, the lady went to the doctor who asked her, 'How do you do now?' She replied, 'Not in any way better, but people have started behaving better! They behave more decently now!' So you see, our adjustment should be first inside. Then we shall have no trouble outside.

Neither the home nor the monasteries are ideal in every respect. Wherever we stay through divine Will, we must make the best of it and improve ourselves.

When people criticise you, think over it. If you think you are at fault, then correct it. If you think you are right, then don't bother. Offer all that to the Lord. Don't bother about small matters. Some may praise you, and some may criticise you. Offer both to the Mother.

Develop *Brahmabuddhi, Atmabuddhi* as much as possible. Keep this thought either by repeating His Name (mantra) or with the help of a *stotra* or some devotional song. Life is full of adjustments. Work and worship. Although it is difficult at present, it will become easier. Go on practising it.

Work and Worship

One cannot do meditation all the time. One has to do work etc. Do the work, but maintain the spiritual mood within. Connect the work that you are doing with God. Connect your thoughts with God. Connect your thoughts about the work with God. Do all the work as a form of service to the Lord who dwells in all. 'Whatever work I do, O Lord, is your worship'—*yad yad karma karomi tat tadakhilam shambho tavaradhanam*. Develop this attitude.

Create solitude in your mind. Work and worship should go together. We do not enter into solitude by merely getting into the forest or the monastery. We must know how to annihilate the world in our mind. *Atmano mokshartham jagat hitaya cha*—work for your own salvation and for the good of the world.

At first there is a difference between work and worship. Later on, work too becomes worship, and the whole life becomes one of undivided consecration. Work and worship must go hand in hand. Both purify the mind and help us in the unfoldment of the higher consciousness in us, and they are to be looked upon as two-fold forms of spiritual practice.

We were told by Swami Brahmanandaji to do every work as a service to God. I was then studying in B.Sc. final. We took his words very seriously. One day as we were going to the college, we saw a dog with burns all over the body. We caught hold of the dog and took it to our laboratory as if we were serving God Himself. But we did not know what was to be applied. We applied carbolic acid and sulphur powder which were available in the laboratory. The dog died. What had happened? Someone told us, 'Don't you know that the dog licks its body?' When it licked the poisonous medicines applied on the body, the dog died! If you do any work, have some knowledge of the work also. Do not do harm instead of doing good!

See God in the patients and with that attitude serve them. You should be able to do worship and work for the patients with single-minded devotion. Life is full of adjustments; every minute we must adjust—no question of liking or hating the work. There are various temperaments. With every patient you have to adjust. This helps in the purification of the mind.

You should be able to give lectures. Here emotions are not enough. Intellect also is required. Make use of the little brain God has given you. You should be able to convince others and then you will understand better. Two little boys were prating about their mothers. One boy said, 'My mother can lecture on any subject!' The other boy did not lag behind; he said, 'That is nothing, my mother can lecture even when there is no subject.' See, I don't approve the second one. Always prepare well, before you go for class—never go unprepared.

Along with all that, you must be pure. Be pure like Holy Mother. I want a leader to come out of this little group. A leader is one who is the servant of all. He should also be capable and intelligent. One who can obey can lead.

Though this world is unreal, feel that the Supreme Spirit is immanent in the world. It is only a stage and feel the divine presence within. Play your part in the drama of life as well as you can. The drama is not absolutely real, but it is to be played properly for the purification of the mind. This purification will lead you to divine realization and enable you to live in your real home while you serve the Supreme Spirit in various forms.

The Theory of Karma

Each is the maker of his own destiny. If I am unhappy, it has been of my own making. Everything shows that I can be free, if I will. All powers of nature must bow down and succumb before the will of man.

Karma produces not only what we see, it also produces unseen results. Karma is never identical with fate. The law of karma is the law of self-effort and never fatalism and lethargy. If our present life is the result of our own past, it follows that we can change our future by our present efforts.

Work

Never get attached to a place; never get attached to a personality. Never think that too much work will ever kill you. Work (Mission Work) has never killed anyone so far. If anyone can die because of doing too much work, we will build a monument for him. Never seek your own comfort. I have followed this one instruction in my life and I am alive today even to the age of seventy-three years.

Belur Math authorities trunk-called me at Nagpur to come for a meeting. So I travelled by the night plane to reach in time. I don't like to travel at night, but due to work, I had to come. So it is better that we like the work and then do it. Otherwise, not liking but doing the work creates conflict. Better like it. Sometimes work comes to us as duty. It may not be very pleasant. Yet, learn to like work that comes to you as duty and do it. Thus you can avoid a lot of conflict and tension.

Divine Grace

Swami Brahmananda used to say that grace comes in the form of self-effort, yearning and striving. The sign that we have received God's grace is that we feel a tremendous urge to exercise our will-power in the right direction and we are determined to blast away all the obstacles in our spiritual path. Self-effort is mainly for the purification of the mind; one must be up and doing.

Failures are steps to success; try, try, and try again. The breeze of divine grace is constantly blowing; unfurl your sails.

Self-effort is a sign of divine grace—even self-surrender is a form of grace. There is no conflict between self-effort and self-surrender.

Grace does not necessarily mean the removal of miseries, but it always gives a devotee a wonderful poise and strength to pass through all trials and difficulties, makes him purer and purer in mind, and enables him to feel the divine presence which brings him inner peace even in the midst of the greatest suffering.

Surrender does not mean idleness or passive dependence. Surrender comes only after the utmost effort has been done. You know the story of a bird sitting on the mast of a ship. It did not know that the ship had started moving. When it suddenly realised it, it flew towards the East, West, North and South, but found only limitless ocean everywhere. Finally, when its wings were dead tired, it came back and sat on the mast resigned to the will of the Lord.

Grace of Mind

Swami Brahmanandaji used to tell us, 'My boys, you have the grace of God, the desire for spiritual knowledge. Besides these, you have the company of the holy. Now you must strive to win the grace of your mind by the practice of self-control and self-effort.'

Human birth, desire for salvation and the company of holy men are rare indeed. But even these three advantages are not enough. We must have the grace of our minds which should be eager to strive hard to attain the Supreme Goal of life.

Even if you repeatedly, fail in your attempts, the only thing I can say to you is, try and try again. Struggle! That is the moment when the divine grace descends. God helps those who help themselves. When we reach the limit of our exertion, then God helps those who cannot help themselves!

Divine grace comes in the form of self-effort which purifies the mind. Finally comes that divine grace which brings about the union between the Individual Soul and God or Brahman. This is the culmination of divine grace.

Surrender

Surrender means offering one's soul, mind and body to the Supreme Spirit, praying to be an instrument in His hands, for serving the ideal by trying to promote the welfare of all, along with that of one's own self. The central idea should be to love and serve God in man and thus realize the highest goal of human existence. Service may be physical, intellectual, moral or spiritual, according to the needs of those who come in touch with us.

Along with work, one must also think of the Lord and offer all activities to Him. There can be no surrender unless the goal of self-realization is kept constantly in view and the little ego is sacrificed. As one succeeds in practising the real dedication, the ego is not killed but transformed. The individual consciousness and the individual will become one with the divine Consciousness and divine Will. One then leads a cosmocentric life instead of an egocentric one.

And, again, unless proper precautions are taken, one runs the risk of building up an illusory egoism. Consciously or unconsciously one may develop a severely critical attitude judging oneself by easy standards and others by severe standards.

A perverse ego makes us see only other's faults. We think more of rights than of duties, thinking how much we can get and not how much we can give. See good points in others and encourage them. That is the only way to improve others.

Try to see good points in your friends and have only those in your mind. When you deal with negative ideas, they cloud your mind. Be careful and keep praying to Sri Guru Maharaj and Holy Mother, 'Protect me, protect me.'

Be Cosmocentric

The temper and irritation you speak of are just passing phases in evolution. When you are in a bad mood, your consciousness has become very limited, contracted, egocentric. Through japa and meditation on the Ishta-Devata whose consciousness is infinite, you can expand your consciousness as much as you like. You become cosmocentric.

Remember the illustration: when an elephant enters a small pool of water, the pool overflows. But nothing happens when an elephant or even several elephants enter a mighty lake.

Similarly, when you are egocentric, a small pool, little troubles will disturb your mind greatly. But when you are cosmocentric and feel that you are like a small sphere of light, a part of the Infinite Consciousness, of which everybody is also a part, many big problems and difficulties also will not disturb your mind. So we all have to expand and remain in a higher mood.

We should see our face when we get angry. Then only we will learn control over ourselves. When we get angry, we express it and burst over others and get relief. But, by that, first we hurt ourselves and then we hurt others. Better we control anger and try to reflect upon it ourselves.

Self-analysis is always for our good. It will correct, round off and smoothen our angularities. When stones rub against one another, they become rounded. Sometimes clashes are good. They round off our angularities. Maharaj (Swami Brahmananda) used to say, 'When I get angry, you fellows should not talk. When you get angry, I should not talk.'

It is better to keep quiet sometimes. We must learn when to speak, when not to speak, with whom to speak, with whom not to speak, what to speak and what not to speak.

We must see the psychological hour and then speak. When we speak at the proper time, it works. We must hiss but not bite. However, it is not good to keep quiet always. If you become a door-mat, then everybody will walk over you. Let not others take advantage of our keeping quiet. They should know that we can talk also.

Depend upon God

Human beings give a drop of love, a drop of happiness. God gives an ocean of love, an ocean of happiness and bliss. Better go to Him. Do not go to a personality for pleasure. No bargain or barter: 'I give you love, you give me love etc.' Go to the source of all love and take it by right. Be kind without becoming personal...no personal claim on anybody or anybody's love. Never allow anybody to have any personal claim on you or your affection.

All outside dependence is misery. Self-dependence is happiness. Clinging to personalities is a great bondage.

Therefore turn to the inner principle, the eternal Guru in you. Don't depend on any personality. A bubble wants to depend on other bubbles. Impossible position. Dependence on outside agencies is bondage and a source of misery. Dependence on the indwelling Atman, the Paramatman, is freedom and a source of joy. Don't cling to a personality...merge me completely in Sri Ramakrishna. Then only you will feel that the infinite supreme power is working through me. You will then get more help from me.

Instead of depending too much on any outside help, including mine, pray fervently to the Guru within for light and guidance. Whatever help I can render you, will always be at your disposal, but know for certain that you alone are the architect of your fate. So strive your utmost. Feel that Holy Mother's presence and Sri Ramakrishna's power are protecting you. It is within you all the time.

In 1933, I was deputed to Wiesbaden in Germany. On the ship, I was all alone in the second class and felt very nervous. Suddenly I felt a great presence around me and this penetrated my body and mind. I was very much overpowered. In that presence Sri Ramakrishna told me, 'Infinite Consciousness has manifested here (in Sri Ramakrishna). Don't worry. It will protect you.' I saw that presence all the time around me. It took me from place to place. Similarly feel that there is Holy Mother's presence around you protecting you all the time.

Always remember that Sri Ramakrishna and the Holy Mother are the twofold manifestations of the same Spirit and power, working for your own good and for the good of mankind. Ever remain devoted to them. They are the common source of all inspiration. Repeat the song, 'Thou art my all in all' as many times as possible.

A man said to me, 'Swamiji, I leave everything good or bad to God.' Is it so easy? For self-surrender, complete detachment is required. When the time for sleep comes, who cares for whom? Something of that mood is required.

At first one has too much faith in oneself and feels he can do everything. Then comes the time when one feels that he cannot do anything. Wave and ocean—which is more real? Wave or ocean? Behind each wave is the ocean.

Happiness

The higher forms of happiness are always born of perfect control over the body and the senses. Happiness is never born of sense enjoyment. Sense enjoyments never bring us happiness, never the feeling of perfect bliss, perfect poise and calmness which sense control always brings in its wake.

Illiteracy does not mean lack of culture. There have been people who did not know how to write but they were highly cultured.

In Nagpur, I told devotees before initiation that I will have personal interviews with each one of them. They thought that the interview would be like an officer's interview and they have to prepare for it by reading books for questions. So all of them started reading books on Swamiji, philosophy etc. I came to know about it and told them, 'No, you don't have to prepare yourselves with books. You just come and I shall have a personal talk with you.'

Love and Sympathy

Love and sympathy are the signs of spiritual life. If spiritual life does not make devotees considerate and kind to others, then what is the use of such devotion?

A perverse ego asserts itself too much. We think more of rights than duties—thinking how much we can get and not how much we can give. You will get more, if you give more. Do not approach anybody as a beggar; but approach as a giver. Look around for a place where you can sow a few seeds of happiness even for a day.

The disciples of Sri Ramakrishna were so different from the ordinary type of religious men. They lived much fuller and richer lives than ordinary spiritual men. One moment they were lost in the deepest meditation, the next moment they were actively engaged in the service of all, helping everybody.

The great disciples of Sri Ramakrishna were a class by themselves. They had intense love for God and man. Their love for man was an expression of their love for God, for, they saw the Divine in all men and women. Sitting at the feet of these great disciples of Sri Ramakrishna, the religion we learnt was not egocentric.

One should give more than what one receives. But people never think of giving. Once a man came to me and asked, 'Swamiji, what can I have here!' Of course I was very kind to him. I told him that he could attend daily prayers, lectures and attend library, etc.

We must work in such a way that others must feel like working in the same manner. We must teach them the way.

A man used to come to Swami Brahmanandaji. He came from a good family but was very miserly and would sometimes bring half a pumpkin or a few plantains. We used to watch this but Swami Brahmananda Maharaj used to be very kind to him.

Again there are devotees whose only theme is to give. They never think of receiving. Once a family had come to Bangalore for a few days. I had stayed in their house while touring the South. I gave Prasad to the lady but as she was leaving after bowing down to me, she forgot to take the Prasad. I called her back and reminded her of the prasad. Her one central theme was to give and not to take; that is why she had forgotten.

Sri Krishna

Take any aspect of Sri Krishna. He is an ideal for men, women and children. Even the animals are charmed by Him. Sri Ramakrishna used to go into samadhi while hearing the name of Sri Krishna. See how the infinite limits itself when it incarnates! Sri Krishna in his childhood showed His infinite nature to His parents. Behind His divine Personality stands the impersonal, indivisible Sat-Chid-Ananda. When the soul is tired of worldly things, it yearns to be one with the Paramatman.

The gopis in their ecstatic state realised His infinite nature. Again they loved Him in His personal aspect as well. No spiritual experience is complete unless one realises both these aspects, personal and impersonal. That means we are parts of Him. So instead of meditating on the Lord, if we meditate on ourselves, which we always do, what happens? We will be meditating on a limited personality, full of anger, lust, desires etc. and we shall imbibe some of these qualities.

Swami Brahmananda

It was most surprising how Swami Brahmananda's brother monks used to regard him so much superior to themselves. They looked upon him as the representative of Sri Ramakrishna. Swami Vivekananda was only nine days older to Swami Brahmananda. Each one of them was a spiritual giant and a personification of infinite power, knowledge, love, and along with it immense humility.

What a personality Swami Brahmananda had! He hailed from a rich family and had a majestic and princely look which charmed everyone. In the Gospel of Sri Ramakrishna you read about different categories of men. First, the bound souls immersed in worldliness. They have no idea of the glory of spiritual life. Second, those who want to become free. They struggle. Third, those who after intense struggle, succeed in becoming free, the liberated souls. Finally, there are a few who are ever free—*nityasiddhas*. They are born only for the good of the world. Swami Brahmananda was one such *nityasiddha*.

A day or two before Swami Brahmananda passed away, he called us and said, 'After the body falls off, I will sometimes come from my heavenly abode to see how my children are getting on.'

Maharaj was not the type who would give sermons day and night. Early in the morning he would meditate and be in a deep spiritual mood and after that all of us—sadhus and brahmacharis—would sit in the verandah around him. There was no need of words. The spiritual vibrations radiating from him were so strong and intense that one could tangibly feel and experience them. His mere presence was enough to uplift and elevate the mind. He showered immense love on all.

But never think it was all milk and honey. When it came to spiritual disciplining, he was indeed a very stern task master. He could see through all of us, our past and future. Sometimes we used to get such scolding's! We were like lumps of clay in his hands being given beating after beating, his loving anxiety being that the spiritual lessons learnt at his feet be digested and assimilated into our systems so that they have a transforming effect on us. But then there was a lighter side of him too. His sense of humour was such that when he cut jokes we would roll on the ground with laughter.

Sometimes we find men of realisation getting angry or attached. Even *jivanmuktas* have anger and attachment, but you can understand them and their implications only when you live with them. Love need not always take on a calm and peaceful form.

True love can often be as hard as steel; it can use harsh words. The knife of a surgeon cuts, but it cuts in order to heal. These great ones may appear cruel and heartless in some of their advice, but through the kindness of their cruelty they heal and bring new life.

Death

Death—the very word generates fear in the minds of all. In fact, fear of death is the fear of all fears. No matter how hard we may try to avoid our fate, death stands waiting for us at the end of our life.

One day a young man, a servant of the sultan, rushed breathlessly into the sultan's palace in Damascus and said, 'Please, Your Majesty, I need your swiftest horse!' 'What is the matter?' asked the sultan. The young man replied, 'As I passed through the royal garden, I saw Death. He stretched his arms towards me and frightened me. I must flee to Baghdad. The sultan readily agreed to the servant's request. Then the sultan went out in his garden looking for Death. He saw Death crouching near a patch of day-lilies and angrily asked, 'What are you doing? Why are you scaring my servant?' 'I did not mean to scare the young man', apologised Death. 'When I saw him here, I simply threw up my hands in surprise. You see,' explained Death, 'he was not supposed to be here at the palace. I am to meet him tonight at Baghdad!' The young man died at Baghdad that night.

Death is inevitable. The future is a closed book to all of us, but one thing common to all is that we have to meet death. No one can escape it. But having come into this world, why not achieve something, why not live the divine life and be a blessing to ourselves and to others?

Spiritual life is not meant for the weak-minded and cowards; for the runaways and drop-outs in life. Spiritual life is meant for the highly intelligent and cultured, for the daring and adventurous, for those who are ready to put in all their self-effort to strive and reach the state of perfection. Spiritual life is meant for those who are brilliant intellectually, beautiful emotionally and dynamic physically.

In a monastic order, we do not want weaklings, but only those who are strong physically, morally, intellectually and spiritually. It is not a dust-bin in which one can throw anything. Some people try to escape from the problems of the worldly life by taking shelter in a monastery. They make themselves and others miserable. We want only those who can stand a little of asceticism and self-control and become hardy and tough in a good sense. Such are likely to succeed.

This is a period of preparation. Merely lamenting over not having seen the Lord will not do, neither will passive prayer be enough. A spiritual seeker must be able to break the old habits and make new good ones.

There are some aspirants who, without striving hard for improving themselves in every way, go on lamenting and cursing themselves and find a morbid joy in self-condemnation, which is another form of self-love but turned upside down.

You should see that you do not condemn yourself too much and thus weaken your moral fabric.

Visiting Holy Places

Visiting holy places is an easy thing. It is difficult to make progress in the realm of spirit. Yet pilgrimages have great significance. They serve a great purpose.

The holy places in India are in all directions: Ayodhya, Mathura, Hardwar, Kanchi, Kashi, Rameswaram, Puri, Dwarka, Badri, Sringeri, etc.—East, West, North and South. The holy rivers, Ganga, Yamuna, Godavari, Narmada, Kaveri, etc. are also in all directions. Pilgrimages to these places have greatly helped to preserve the fundamental unity of India.

In different states of India, people speak different languages, and have different customs and traditions. Yet they have got the same spiritual ideas.

Nowadays pilgrims fly from place to place by train, by car, etc. In olden days they used to walk the whole distance and come in contact with people and would find that the ideas are common.

Disciplines for a Member of a Religious Institution

Have great regard for others. Intensify your sadhana. The quality of japa and meditation should be improved.

Practice japa with artha bhavanam. Each one must follow the method told by her Guru.

Perform your duties perfectly.

You must see how much you are able to give to the sangha and not how much you get. Practise relaxation. In the midst of work we must learn to practise relaxation. When we relax, the mind comes in tune with the infinite. Have a little thought of God in the mind throughout the day.

The Different Yogic Centers

There are seven centers in connection with the spiritual progress of the individual. The first and the lowest is at the level of the organ of evacuation. The second is at the sexual organ. The third centre is at the navel. The mind of worldly persons is usually on one of these centres. They think only of eating, sleeping and sexual satisfaction. The fourth centre is at the heart. As the spiritual aspirant rises to this level and his mind approaches this plane, he feels there is a lotus at the level of the heart, the petals of which are directed downwards. When this centre is reached, the bud of the lotus opens and the petals get directed upwards—the lotus blooms. But suddenly the mind falls to the lower centers again. The task in spiritual life is to make the petals of the lotus direct upwards and keep it full blown. At this stage one is able to meditate well—the mind is tranquil; breathing is rhythmic.

The fifth centre is at the throat; the sixth is at a place between the two eye-brows. When this centre opens one may have a vision of the Ishta-Devata. The seventh centre is in the head. This is the highest centre. Reaching here, one goes into samadhi. Here one sees the lotus which is in full bloom and the shining form of the Ishta-Devata seated on the lotus with a smiling face.

This reminds me of an incident about the heart. There were two doctors, one German and the other American. The German doctor said that the heart is on the right side, but the American doctor said that the physiologists say that the heart is on the left. They were thus quarrelling, when a wise man came and he asked, 'What is the matter? Why are you fighting?'

The German doctor said that the heart is on the right side but the American doctor said that it is on the left side.

The wise man said, 'What does it matter? Whether it is on the right or left side, let it be in the right place!'

One should not go deep into psychology. In western countries there was a psychologist. He used to say, 'Girls who are hysterical should get married and then they will be all right.' One day someone asked him, 'How many of your patients are hysterical?' The psychologist replied, 'Half of my patients who are hysterical are unmarried and the other half has become hysterical after marriage!'

One should not practise sadhana, breathing exercises, postures etc. without the guidance of one's Guru. The Guru is none other than Brahman Himself. He comes from time to time to teach people.

Swami Brahmanandaji used to forbid spiritual seekers from using occult powers. People then know how to know the mind of others, but they do not know how to read their own minds.

Harmony in Our Personality

Body, mind, senses and ego, all combine to form our personality.

Body: Body must be kept fit and efficient. It is necessary for us to have a new attitude towards the body. It is neither an instrument for sense gratification nor a mass of filth to be hated and neglected. The body is primarily a temple of the divine Spirit and must be nourished with pure food which brings energy, strength, health and cheerfulness.

One's health must be good to do spiritual practices. If we have headache or the stomach is not all right or the liver is not functioning well, can we meditate? No! Someone told me, 'Swamiji, I want to forget the body and meditate.' I told him, 'What! Even if you forget the body, the body will not forget you!'

No spiritual seeker can afford to neglect the body or bodily health. What can one do with a weak or a diseased body? Have a different outlook towards the body. It is not a means for sense-enjoyment nor a house of filth. It is a temple of God in which resides the Atman—*deha devalaya*—

Develop this attitude towards the body.

Mind: Mind has three faculties or functions:

(1)   Thinking or reasoning

(2)   Feeling or emotions

(3)   Willing or actions

Many times our thoughts, feelings and actions work in entirely different directions or one of them becomes too strong. We may become over-intellectual without tender feelings and without any practical actions; or we may become a whirlpool of impulses and emotions; or we may become restlessly active without caring for reason and without higher aspirations to lead a proper spiritual life. Let all these three develop fully and work together in harmony for our spiritual evolution.

Senses: Senses are always eager to run after sense-objects. With the help of discrimination, control the senses. We should break away from the hold of impulses. The very moment the impulses rise in us, we should try to expand our consciousness, for, then, these impulses at once disappear, just as the waves disappear in the ocean.

Ego: The ego becomes perverse. It thinks too much of itself, forgetting everything else. We become extremely selfish and mean. To give an illustration, a bubble on the surface of the sea thinks too much of itself. It forgets the other bubbles. It forgets even the ocean and wants to grow. What happens? The bubble bursts. This actually happens with many human beings.

In a properly integrated or harmonised personality, the ego or the individual will is brought into harmony with universal consciousness. How? Through japa, meditation, prayer and worship. Then let this ripe ego direct and guide the mind, the senses and the body.

One of the greatest lessons I learned sitting at the feet of my Master, Swami Brahmanandaji and other direct disciples of Sri Ramakrishna, was the ideal of harmonised growth—physical, intellectual, moral and spiritual.

The *mantra* has tremendous power of reviving us physically and spiritually, bringing a new strength and confidence. Such is a power of the divine name that, along with meditation, it produces harmony in the body and the mind and also quickens the right understanding.

Three Types of Reasoning

There are three types of reasoning. One is child-like reasoning. The other is logical reasoning and third, materialistic reasoning.

Supposing two buckets, one of water and the other of beer are kept in front of an ass. The ass drinks water but not the beer, because animals do not take things which harm them. This is logical reasoning. But materialistic reasoning says that the ass does not drink beer because it is an ass!

No doubt one should intellectually understand the spiritual path, but too much reasoning is not good. We are drunk with the wine of ignorance, so do not see our True Self. By leading a spiritual life we realize what we actually are.

In a place there was a king. One day he found out that many people were dying in his city. So he went to Yama

and said, 'Yama, why do so many people die in my city?
What will happen? What are you doing?'

Yama said, 'King, I take only a fixed number of people.'
Then the king returned. After some time he found out that
more people were dying than before in his city. So worried,
he thought, 'What! Even Yama—Dharmaraj—does not keep
his word?' So he came back to Yama and said, 'What is the
matter? More people are dying!' Yama said, 'What can I do?
I take my fixed number, but people die out of fear!'

Mental Blankness

There are three types of mental blankness: one is tamasic
that is, non-activity. One experiences this just before
sleep. The other is rajasic. Swamiji gives an example of two
monkeys, jumping from one branch of a tree to another. At
last they get tired and remain silent for a while only to start
their mischief again. The third and highest type is sattvik
blankness—spiritual blankness. In this state the spiritual
aspirant feels pure and at a high level.

I do not understand why so many feel mental blankness.
That shows that the spiritual ideal has not yet been fully
fixed; otherwise all the blank moments should be filled by
the Lord's Name and thoughts. So be careful. Take all the
necessary food for the mind and body. Remember, empty
stomach gives stomachache and empty head gives headache.

One day a small boy played the whole day without
taking any food. In the evening, he got pain in the stomach.
The doctor was called. He examined the child and said that
there was nothing wrong with the child except that his
stomach needed some food. After eating something, the child
became all right.

Now it so happened that in the same evening, the child's
father got severe headache. The child said, 'Oh! I know the
reason. When my stomach was empty I got stomach-ache.
Father's head is empty. That is why he has headache. If he
puts something in the head, he will be all right.'

The main cause of restlessness is that the soul is not getting enough food. Make such a strong habit of study everyday that you will feel uncomfortable if you have not read something during the day. The mind cannot always remain on the spiritual plane. Always think of the ideas that expand and elevate the mind. When the mind is expanded and elevated, all the petty and dirty ideas in the mind are swept away.

When the mind is expanded and elevated, it is easier to control the lower thoughts and to have the mind at a higher level for a long time. The mind should be in tune with the Cosmic Spirit. Then one feels expanded. A contracted mind blocks the inflow of divine grace.

There should never be any haziness in the Vedantic aspirant. We must have definite and right thoughts, definite and right emotions and feelings, definite and right actions; then alone can we proceed to the divine goal and realize it.

When I was in Holland, I saw a man who used to attend our lectures, and had read all the scriptures, etc. But he never spoke to anybody and always remained absorbed in himself. One day I asked him to come and see me. He agreed. I asked him, 'What is the matter with you? Why are you so distracted?' He had a wife, children, money and all worldly comforts. He replied, 'Swamiji, it pains me every morning and I feel, "Am I to begin the day as before?" ' Of course I gave him some spiritual instructions and this was the turning point in his spiritual life. It is really a great fortune for one to turn to spiritual life.

Spiritual Ideal

Our ideal is so high that the more we advance, the more we find that there is still so much further ground to be covered to reach the highest goal. This naturally makes us feel dejected at times. But let this very depressed mood encourage us to struggle harder and harder and move closer and closer to that blissful state which transcends all relative elation and dejection and is the Infinite Existence-Knowledge-Bliss itself. We reject the Infinite and busy ourselves with the finite which gives us a drop of joy, but brings also a mass of misery. Always remember that the real Ananda is attained only in the realization of the Infinite.

The ideal is very high and we cannot reach it simply by wishing. And yet we should hold it before us, and try to move towards it slowly and steadily, naturally passing through many ups and downs.

Our ideal is so high that the more we proceed towards it, the more we find that there is yet so much to achieve. This is good because it keeps us going and enables us to have a little taste of the divine joy as we continue to do our prayers and meditation.

Divine Love

By trying to see Sri Ramakrishna in all men and the Holy Mother in all women, the spiritual seekers can transmute all animal impulses and passions into divine love. It is this divine love that, mixed up with human and animal elements, becomes human love and animal love. Dedication is an efficient means for purifying the personality and transmuting personal love into divine love. Our love is mixed up with selfishness. Do you know the story of fifty-fifty? In Germany, there was a hotel, famous for sausages of rabbit-meat. Once a customer found the taste had changed. On enquiry, he was told by the hotel manager, 'Sir, what can I do? Rabbit-flesh has become rare. So, I added a little of horse-meat.' 'In what proportion?' enquired the customer? The manager replied, 'Fifty-fifty'. He meant one rabbit to one horse!

Our so-called love for others is of the weight of a rabbit and our self-love is of the weight of a horse; fifty-fifty indeed!

A drop of the Divine Mother's love comes through the father, mother, guru, children, students and others. Having cut themselves off from the cosmic source, human beings turn to a personality; get a drop of love and along with it a mass of misery also. If one person fails to satisfy them, then they try another person, get another drop of love and again a mass of misery as before. This goes on time and again.

In spiritual life we want to turn to the Infinite Spirit who is all love, worship Him, pray to Him, meditate on Him, have our hearts filled with a little of divine love and share this love with our fellow beings without expecting any returns.

In spiritual life, although we cut off personal relations with others to a great extent, we come to have a wider love and sympathy for all. It is through the medium of the Divine.

Value a personality because of the principle and not for its own sake. This is the only way to real peace and happiness.

Dependence on the outside agencies is a bondage and a source of misery. Dependence on the indwelling Atman, the Paramatman, is freedom and a source of joy.

On Japa and Meditation

Are you doing japa regularly? How is the japa mala?. Is it complete? Or is it broken? (Laughing) Some people do japa so vigorously that they break the mala. Then they come and ask for a new one. Without stressing the number, stress the quality of japa and meditation. It is this that will help you in your spiritual progress.

You know the parable of Sri Ramakrishna, about a parrot repeating 'Rama, Rama.' But when a cat catches it, the cry is quite different, because the name did not go deep enough. During the Mutiny some sepoys shot a sadhu. Even to the last breath the sadhu repeated 'Shivoham, Shivoham.'

A lady in Holland asked me, 'Why should I repeat the Lord's Name so many times?' I asked her, how many times she remembered her body? She replied, 'Oh, almost the whole day.' Then I asked her, 'Then how many times should you forget the body to counteract that?'

We have to repeat the name with great devotion. Without any harmony of body and mind, no proper japa or meditation can be done—head is aching, heart is palpitating. There is a girl in Delhi; she said to me, 'Swamiji, I have no time to do japa so I practice sahasranama, repeat the name for a thousand times and so on.' I said to her, 'If I ask God how many times did you listen to her, He will say, "Not even once!" If you do not listen to what you repeat, why should God listen?'

Whatever form one takes up, one must have clear conception of that deity and think of the good qualities. Ultimately it should take you from form to formlessness, from speech to speechlessness.

When I was in Madras I was very much taken up by the sea shore. I spoke about this to Swami Shivanandaji Maharaj. He said, 'My boy, *akasa* is a better symbol. It is unlimited. You can get it everywhere; even the sea is limited.' When I actually did so, I found it (sky) was not as we generally see, but it was full of light—wide and unlimited. When one gets absorbed in that, one thinks we are rays of that intense light. When one meditates on such a formless entity, then one thinks that his soul is part of the Infinite Soul and he is not the body. When that consciousness of light comes one sees divine light everywhere.

Surrender to God

Grow in vairagya, grow in wisdom, only then Mother will accept you. Pray to Mother, 'Mother! Wherever you send me, come with me.' Surrender hundred percent to Mother. If you try to handle any situation, it becomes narrow and may slip down, but if you leave it to the Mother, it expands and you find tremendous good results. Learn to leave the things to the Lord. He will do them in the right way and let them occur at the right time. Only then are the results the best. Bow down to Her will; you will feel better. Wherever you go, think that you live in Mother and Mother lives in you. Life is full of adjustments; every minute we must adjust—no question of liking or hating the work. There are various temperaments. With every patient you have to adjust. This helps in the purification of the mind.

One cannot have a blue print of life. There is always the possibility of rise and fall. Ideal is work and worship—karma and upasana. Play the drama of life as well as you can. Never expect a thing to happen and don't feel dejected either when you don't get it. Always remember—*asha hi paramam duhkham, nairashyam paramam sukham.* (Hope is the greatest misery. Greatest happiness lies in giving up all hope). Learn to depend on the Lord and not on any human being. Surrender comes only after the utmost effort is put in. Then there is no cheating God nor the self. Only when you have tried your best can you surrender as you have done.

Miscellaneous

Without calculating how much one gets, one should ascertain how much one can give to the Lord in the form of service, prayer and meditation.

You live in a unique institution. Try to render as much service as you can. Think how much you can give and act accordingly. This is the way to get more. Each one of you should develop your potentialities without trying to imitate anyone else.

Learn to think for yourself, deeply and clearly, so that your mind may be enriched in every way. Always pray to Sri Guru Maharaj and Holy Mother to make you more and more humble and better fitted to do their service.

Control your emotions a little, be they spiritual or otherwise. Don't show off your spiritual moods. Control spiritual emotions. Do not express; otherwise everything gets exhausted.

One moonlit night, some drunken men took it into their heads to go on a boat ride. They went to the ghat, hired a boat, sat at the oars and started rowing. They rowed and rowed the whole night. Early in the morning, when the effect of drink had gone, they found to their surprise that they had not moved an inch. 'What was the matter?' they asked one another. They had forgotten to raise the anchor!

So, as the anchored boat did not move, the mind that is attached to the worldly desires cannot proceed in the spiritual path...One should have single-minded devotion towards God.

People tell me to go to Bombay for collection of funds, but I tell them, 'I want human materials and not building materials.'

Your suggestion about bargaining (that I take the responsibility of your spiritual disciplines and you take the responsibility of collecting all the funds needed for the temple construction) reminds me of a story. Once a new clergyman came to a little town. A doctor went to see him and made this proposal to him, 'Sir, you please keep me out of hell and I will keep you out of heaven!' What the doctor meant was that being a sinner, he would naturally go to hell, so he wanted to be saved by the clergyman. The latter being a pious man would naturally go to heaven after his death, so the doctor proposed to keep him in good health and prolong his life on earth! ...Don't worry, you collect as much as you can; I don't want you to be a money making machine.

The line of my service is purely spiritual. I am incompetent to advise people on their family affairs, which is really outside my scope. I know only one way of finding peace and that is through spiritual practice, prayer and meditation, and that is what I can suggest to every one of you.

Questions & Answers
on Spiritual Practice

These *Questions and Answers* had taken place at different places and with different people. Most of them were asked by, and recorded by Pravrajika Saradaprana of the Sarada Math, Dakshineswar, Calcutta, in her *Memoirs of Swami Yatiswarananda*, from where they have been culled together. The last question and answer is taken from *The Vedanta Kesari* January 1999 edition. —**Editor.**

Swamiji, should we plan for the future?

Yes, just as we plan a building. But don't be too rigid after planning. It may or may not materialize. Don't make a blueprint of your life. That does not mean you should not make a general plan. But afterwards leave everything to Sri Ramakrishna and Holy Mother. Let them make you do what they like.

What is *tapas* ?

Self-discipline, sense-control and thinking of all men as Sri Ramakrishna and all women, including yourself, as Holy Mother. Merge all men and women in Them (Sri Ramakrishna and Holy Mother) and then, both of them in one Absolute Satchidananda.

Think of yourself as Atman and others also as Atman. Have a number of weapons with you. Use a knife. If it does not work, then use stronger cutting instruments and cut all the desires.

How to cut all the desires?

With the sword of discrimination and sense-control (*tapas*). By sense-control, keep the objects of enjoyment at

302

a distance. The taste for enjoyment remains and that goes only after seeing the Supreme.

Desires and the senses are our constant enemies. Hence the absolute necessity of leading a disciplined and controlled life. So long as desire is permitted to hold sway over us, we shall not be able to follow any of the spiritual teachings given to us by the great ones. It is not possible to take up each individual hankering and rid ourselves of it. No, a general pitiless massacre is necessary. Turn to the Divine and allow Him to light the divine light in you. Then all darkness will vanish. Then He Himself appears on the battlefield and fights for us.

Our heart should consciously be made a cremation ground of all our attachments, impurities, desires and our petty personality, our ego. This eternal struggle is the only true worship of the Lord.

If old desires rise again in the mind, what should we do?

Don't worry. There is a story of a man with a pet dog. The dog had been so much fondled in the beginning that it made a habit of jumping onto its master's body. Later at one time, the master felt detachment toward the dog, but the dog continued to come to the master, though it was not wanted. It did not know it was not wanted! Our mind is like that dog. It has been pampered so long that it is difficult to control it. But here, a part of the mind still wants desires. The other part doesn't want. That is the thing. It is not that desires are not wanted at all.

Swamiji, will I ever be able to meditate?

Yes, you will be. My considered opinion about your question on meditation is this: Just now you need not bother about real medita-tion. Do japa and dwell on your *Ishta Devata*. In due course, japa will develop into *dhyana* which means unbroken thought on the theme of meditation, like the unbroken current or flow of oil from one cup into another.

Through japa, the divine Spirit will become more real than the world. And then real dhyana will become possible. Do the first thing first and the next step will come of itself.

How to get concentration during japa?

When the spiritual ideal becomes strong, there will be no disturbances. Your mind wanders because you still have interest in external objects. If you have no interest in worldly affairs, if the spiritual ideal is strong, the mind won't wander.

How to make the image of the *Ishta Devata* steady in the mind during japa?

Once when Sri Ramakrishna was taken to a studio for his photograph, he asked the photographer how the image got fixed on the film. He was told that there was a solution. When the film was coated with it, the image got fixed. After that, Sri Ramakrishna used to say, 'If we have the coating of devotion on our mind, the image of the deity would be steady.' To the extent we love God, to that extent the image of the deity becomes steady in the mind. The mantra should be repeated with devotion. Because there is a lack of spiritual yearning, even after long practice, we do not get anything. Mantra repeated with devotion is very efficacious. We come to feel the divine presence, physical ailments are reduced and the diseases of the mind are removed. What are the diseases of the mind? Doubts, dullness, restlessness, attachments, desires, etc. On a day when you do japa well, you feel refreshed in body and expanded in mind.

During meditation there are more disturbances and distractions than at other times. Why?

Because at other times, your interest in your activities (like teaching, reading etc.) push away all other thoughts.

There are three interests:

1) Your interest in regular activities like teaching, reading, etc.

2) Your interest in ordinary worldly affairs.

3) Your interest in the spiritual ideal.

The first i.e. your interest in activities like teaching and reading etc. is strongest. Therefore when you do that, the mind is concentrated and other thoughts don't arise.

The second i.e. your interest in ordinary worldly affairs, though not strong, is yet stronger than the third i.e. your interest in the spiritual ideal. It is because of this that during japa and meditation, worldly thoughts disturb and distract the mind. The spiritual ideal is not strong, hence thoughts arise. Worldly things are so important to us—more real than God. That is why meditation is difficult. *Nishtha* is important.

Shall I think of my chosen deity as He is seen in the picture or as an image?

Let the picture or an image be merely an aid in bringing to your mind the living, conscious and shining form of your chosen ideal.

What is really meant by meditating on the meaning of mantras?

What is the meaning of the mantra? It is the name of God. You have a name. If I call you by name, your form also comes to my mind. Repeat the mantra and at the same time meditate on the chosen ideal—japa with *artha bhavanam*.

Some people look awful when they meditate. They look better when they get up! So have *bhavana* and meditate. If you are sincere you are sure to progress. The mantra is charged with spiritual power. The truth of this will be directly revealed to you as you practice.

Is a permanent impression produced on the minds of those college students for whom you hold classes?

On a few of them.

In that case much of your effort is wasted!

It is only when much is wasted that you can do a little good. Much of the effort is bound to be a waste in order to improve a few. Each one takes what he can. Some can absorb only a little and they will take that. Some can absorb more. What can I do?

You expect much improvement, but the result is very little. Under such circumstances disappointments are bound to be there. Here also we must not think of the results but must go on giving.

There is great suffering in the path of service. Tagore has said, 'O Lord! Give strength to those who are serving, so that they can stand the suffering in the path of service.' You put forth your best efforts, but the person can absorb only a little. You work much and there is very little result. That might disappoint you. All you can do is to improve a few out of the lot.

I have an incubator. I keep eggs in it and give them proper conditions and nourishment for growth. Some come out to be crows; some come out to be cuckoos. What can I do? We can't change crows into cuckoos. We have to see their tendencies.

Can't tendencies be overcome?

They can be overcome gradually. By good karma, bad tendencies can be overcome. In spite of the best efforts, of all those who come to the teacher for light and guidance, it is only a few who profit. This is due to *samskaras* and tendencies.

You ask us to pray to the Lord when the mind is at a lower level. But at that time we don't feel like praying.

Force yourself to repeat His Name again and again and the mind will rise. Pray—pray to Thakur.

I pray but prayer has no effect.

A (Very disapprovingly): Don't talk like that.

Then why don't we have spiritual experiences?

You don't get them because you cannot stand them. It is difficult to stand spiritual experiences for a long time. Wait, wait; in due course you will get them.

See, a one year old child wants to become *Paramahamsa* right away! Every spiritual experience requires a pushing away of maya even if it be for a while, and getting in touch with Reality. It requires hard labour. Some people want us to give them spiritual moods, ecstasies and all that. But we only prescribe the hard method. We do not know any easy route.

You say that I must see God in patients and serve them. But Thakur says that the manifestation of God is more in some and less in others.

Who denies that?

At that time I feel that instead of serving patients let me rather do japa.

This is sheer madness. Try to see the Lord even in the lesser manifestations. Those who are advanced in spiritual life will have wonderful compassion towards others. Their attitude towards others would have undergone a wonderful change. By giving, we get expanded. Expansion brings joy.

Does every spiritual aspirant feel lonely?

You have asked a very pertinent question. Does every one following the spiritual path feel lonely? This may happen at the beginning when one is following the negative practice of trying to give up one's attachment for worldly relation and things. However, renunciation not only includes this negative attitude but also positively it means love for the Supreme Spirit and all its manifestations.

What is important is the elimination of attachment, and spiritualization of all forms of love. This becomes possible as our love for the Lord becomes deep and we learn to connect all other loves with the Love Divine.

I give an illustration: Previously, the bubble loved the other bubbles forgetting the ocean. But, now with the awakening of the spiritual consciousness the bubble attains its union with the ocean and then through the ocean with all other bubbles.

After meditation, it is good to recognize the Supreme Spirit who dwells within us and also to recognize Him in all beings. To the extent we feel this unity, we also feel the urge of loving and serving the divine Spirit manifested in all beings.

For our guidance, Swami Vivekananda has left us the ideal: 'To work for one's own spiritual freedom and also for the welfare of the world;' to serve Him, the divine Spirit, in all beings. Have you read his poem *To a friend*? There you find, it concludes with the following passages:

> From highest Brahman to the yonder worm,
> And to the very minutest atom,
> Everywhere is the same God, the All-Love;
> Friend, offer mind, soul, body, at their feet.
> These are His manifold forms before thee,
> Rejecting them, where sleekest thou for God?
> Who loves all beings, without distinction,
> He indeed is worshipping best his God.

Source of the Material

Part- 1 : **Courtesy:** Sri S. V. Unnikrishnan, Senior Deputy Accountant General (Retd.), Jaipur.

Chapters: 1, 2, 3, 5, 7, 9, 10, 11, 12, 14, 15, 16

Source: Class notes taken by a devotee at Bangalore between 1954-55 and 1958-59.

Published in *Vedanta Kesari*

October/November/December	1979
January through December	1980 to 1984
January through September	1985

★ ★ ★

Part-1 : **Courtesy:** Mr. John Manetta of Athens, Greece.

Chapter: 4 Continence

Source: Readings on *Vedantasara* of Sadananda, at Wiesbaden, Germany, January 9 through February 3, 1934

Published in *Vedanta Kesari* : May 1998

Chapter: 6 Preparing for Divine Company

Source: Readings on the *Narada Bhakti Sutras*, Wiesbaden, Germany February 6 through February 9, 1934.

Published in *Prabuddha Bharata* : August 2008

Chapter: 8 How to Sublimate Our Tendencies

Source: Readings on the *Narada Bhakti Sutras*, Wiesbaden, Germany February 6 through February 9, 1934.

Published in *Vedanta Kesari* : July 2008

Chapter: 13 Unreality of the World

Source: Readings on *Vedantasara* of Sadananda, at Wiesbaden, Germany, January 9 through February 3, 1934

Published in *Vedanta Kesari* : January 1998

★ ★ ★

309

Part- 2 : **Courtesy:** Mr. John Manetta of Athens, Greece.

Chapter: 17 Drig Drishya Viveka

Source: Readings on *Drig Drishya Viveka*, Champfer, Switzerland, February 22 through March 26, 1935

Published in *Vedanta Kesari* : February, March, May to September 1999

Chapter: 18 Notes on Yoga Sutras

Source: Readings on *Uddhava Gita*, at Wiesbaden, Germany January, February 1934

Published in *Vedanta Kesari* : July to September 1998

★ ★ ★

Part- 2 : **Source:** *Reminiscences of Swami Yatiswarananda* by Late Pravrajika Saradaprana of the Sarada Math, Dakshineswar, Kolkata.

Chapter: 19 Spiritual Teachings

Published in *Vedanta Kesari* : January, March to July 2000

Chapter: 20 Questions and Answers on Spiritual Practice

Published in *Vedanta Kesari* : November 1999

★ ★ ★